Foreign Direct Investment in China

Determinants and Impact

Yingqi Wei
Lecturer in International Business
Department of Economics
Lancaster University
UK

Xiaming Liu
Senior Lecturer in Business Economics
Aston Business School
Aston University
UK

Edward Elgar
Cheltenham, UK • Northampton, MA, USA

Published by
Edward Elgar Publishing Limited
Glensanda House
Montpellier Parade
Cheltenham
Glos GL50 1UA
MK   UK

Edward Elgar Publishing, Inc.
136 West Street
Suite 202
Northampton
Massachusetts 01060
USA

A catalogue record for this book
is available from the British Library

ISBN 1 84064 494X
Printed and bound in Great Britain by MPG Books Ltd, Bodmin, Cornwall

Contents

viii   *Contents*

Tables

Figures

Preface

In 1978, when China opened its economy to the outside world, there was little inward foreign direct investment (FDI). By the end of 1999, China had approved 340,000 foreign invested firms and the contracted and realised inward FDI reached US$ 613.7 billion and US$ 307.8 billion respectively (People's Daily, Overseas Edition, 12 February, 2000). China is now among the top hosts for FDI inflows in the world. The rapid rise in inward FDI in China has been accompanied by significant achievements in international trade and economic growth. In 1978 China ranked 32nd in the world league table for foreign trade. In 1999 China's total trade reached US$ 360.6 billion and this made China the ninth largest trading power in the world. The average growth rate of GDP in China over the past two decades or so was over 8 per cent.

The fascinating developments in China's globalisation and economic growth have provided us with a tempting opportunity to identify the determinants and impact of FDI in the largest transition economy in the world. This book reports the results from a systematic and rigorous research of FDI in China.

Chapter 1 provides a preview of the book. Chapter 2 details overall trends of FDI in China, including its development stages, sources and types, regional and sectoral distributions, and impact on economic development and foreign trade.

Chapter 3 deals with the determinants of both contracted and realised FDI at the national level. The roles of relative market size, economic integration via exports and imports, relative wage rates, country risk, cultural differences and geographic distance in attracting FDI are assessed. Chapter 4 offers empirical evidence on the regional distribution of both contracted and realised FDI within China. The possible determinants investigated include the level of international trade, R&D manpower, GDP growth, infrastructure, the availability of information and investment incentives and effective wage rates.

While chapters 3 and 4 explain why FDI flows into China, the purposes of chapters 5, 6 and 7 are to examine its impacts. Chapter 5 investigates the productivity spillover effect of FDI in the Chinese electronics industry. The other explanatory variables included in the regressions are capital intensity, firm size and human capital. Using the modified convergence equations, chapter 6 looks into the role of FDI in economic growth and per capita income convergence across the Chinese regions. In addition to FDI, the convergence regressions incorporate investment in physical and human capital, domestic R&D, and international trade as the regional characteristics in the explanation of economic development. Chapter 7 discusses the linkage between the trade and FDI intensities to see whether the intensive investors in China are China's intensive trading partners. Finally, chapter 8 provides an overall summary of the findings of the book and offers policy implications and future research topics.

A panel data approach is adopted in the five empirical studies contained in this book. Given the relatively short period of China's opening up to FDI, this approach is believed to be superior and becomes a special feature of the book. Where appropriate, unit root tests under a panel data framework are conducted to avoid possible spurious regressions. Another important feature of the current research is the introduction of relatively new topics such as productivity spillovers from FDI and the interactive relationship between trade and FDI in China.

This book is written for researchers and practitioners who want to understand the determinants and impacts of FDI in China and for policy-makers in China and other developing countries or transition economies who would like to attract inward FDI and enhance the possible positive impact of FDI on economic growth. It can also serve as a supplementary textbook for students of international business.

We would like to thank Vudayagi N. Balasubramanyam and James Love for their useful comments on the book proposal. We are indebted to *Regional Studies* and *Weltwirtschaftliches Archiv* for their permission to reproduce parts of the published articles entitled 'The Regional Distribution of Foreign Direct Investment in China' and 'Country Characteristics and Foreign Direct Investment in China: A Panel Data Analysis'. Many thanks also go to David Parker, Peter Romilly, Haiyan Song and Kirit Vaidya for allowing us to include parts of the above articles which they co-authored. We are grateful to Peter Romilly and Jim Taylor for their editorial assistance and helpful comments on the book draft. Of course, we retain sole responsibility for any remaining errors.

December 2000

Yingqi Wei

Xiaming Liu

1. Introduction

The opening up of the People's Republic of China to foreign direct investment (FDI) is sometimes regarded as a fascinating development in the contemporary period of globalisation (Hayter and Han, 1998). Between 1979 and 1999, the cumulative value of contracted FDI in China reached US$ 613.7 billion and that of realised value was US$ 307.8 billion. (People's Daily, Overseas Edition, 12 February 2000). China is now the largest FDI host in the developing world.

The main purpose of this book is to provide systematic and rigorous research into FDI in the largest transition economy in the world; more specifically, to identify the determinants and impact of FDI. The current chapter aims to provide the reader with a preview of the main characteristics of FDI in China, the corresponding topics for empirical investigation and the overall structure of the book. Section 1.1 presents an overview of FDI in China, its overall development trends, sources and types, regional and sectoral distributions, and impact on economic growth and foreign trade. Sections 1.2 and 1.3 discuss research questions and the methodology issues addressed in the book. Conclusions are presented in section 1.4. Two special features of the book will be discussed in this section.

1.1 OVERVIEW OF FOREIGN DIRECT INVESTMENT IN CHINA

The development path of FDI in China has never been even. At the early stage of China's economic reforms and opening up to the outside world, FDI inflows were not significant. Its growth increased significantly in the mid-1980s and gained momentum in the early 1990s. More specifically, the past two decades of China's absorbing FDI can be divided into four periods: the experimental period (1979-83); the gradual development period (1984-91); the peak period (1992-93) and the adjustment period (1994-present). Although FDI in China comes from more than 100 countries in the world, the overwhelming source is overseas Chinese, especially those from Hong Kong (SSB, 1999). Investments from developed countries remain limited relative to their overall outward FDI stocks in the world. For instance, the

United States is the largest source of FDI in the world and China is the largest FDI recipient among developing countries, only 1 per cent of the U.S. outward FDI stock is located in China. Corresponding figures of FDI stocks from Western European countries are even smaller.

There are three main types of FDI in China: equity joint ventures (EJVs), contractual joint ventures (CJVs) and wholly foreign-owned enterprises (WFOEs). The dominant type of FDI is the EJV. CJVs were very popular at the early stage of the post-opening up period, but they have gradually become out of favour. WFOEs were not encouraged until the mid-1980s. Since 1990 WFOEs have steadily gained popularity and it is likely that they will eventually surpass EJVs to become the most popular type of FDI in China.

In terms of sectoral distribution, FDI in China has undergone significant change. Until the mid-1980s FDI was concentrated in the construction of hotels and apartments in the tourism and service industry. In 1986 China issued "the Provision of the State Council of the People's Republic of China for the Encouragement of Foreign Investment" which aimed to encourage FDI into technically advanced and/or export-oriented manufacturing enterprises as well as infrastructure and some basic industries such as new materials. The Chinese government has also encouraged FDI into agriculture and related sectors. Recently, China opened several service industries for FDI: domestic retail, banking and insurance. Following these changes approximately 60 per cent of total FDI in China is now in the manufacturing sector. The shares in agriculture and infrastructure remain very small. Within the manufacturing sector much of the investment is in labour-intensive and relatively low-tech industries such as textiles, clothing and assembly lines of mechanical and electronic products.

Geographically, FDI in China is unevenly distributed across the regions. FDI was initially allowed in the four Special Economic Zones (SEZs), before being spread along the coastal areas. This distribution pattern was partly caused by the Chinese government's then regional development strategy. In the early 1990s the Chinese government started to encourage FDI to the central and west areas. However, between 1985 and 1998 as much as 87 per cent of total inward FDI in China was located in the coastal areas. The Tenth Five-Year Plan (2001-05) calls for the development of the western areas and provides special incentives for foreign businesses to invest there. While this policy may help the absorption of FDI in the inner areas to a certain degree, the coastal areas will remain the dominant recipient of FDI for many years to come.

As a package of capital, technology and managerial skills FDI has played an important role in economic development in China. The impact of FDI in China can be felt at least in the following three important aspects:

productivity improvement, GDP or per capita income growth and international trade. In terms of productivity improvement, FDI may be involved in technology transfer and spillovers via the so-called contagion, demonstration and competition effects, and will thus help indigenous Chinese firms to enhance efficiency.

Given the significant inflows, FDI together with Chinese domestic investment and other factors of production has promoted per capita income growth across the Chinese regions. For instance, the quick economic development in the coastal areas has often been associated with the introduction of large amounts of foreign capital. During this process, FDI may affect the convergence of regional average incomes.

One important phenomenon of China's integration with the world economy is the simultaneous expansion of inward FDI and international trade. In 1980, when FDI inflows were still very limited, China ranked 26th in the world trade league table (MOFERT, 1994). In 1999, China was among the top hosts of FDI in the world and its trade ranking moved upward to ninth (People's Daily, Overseas Edition, 13 March 2000). This suggests that FDI and trade may be interrelated.

1.2 RESEARCH QUESTIONS

The preceding section has provided an overview of FDI in China, including its general development trends and impact, which will be extended in chapter 2 by providing more detailed information on each of the issues. While these descriptions are useful, research questions need to be identified from this overview and more formal and rigorous analyses are required to systematically tackle the questions.

RESEARCH QUESTION 1. THE DETERMINANTS OF FDI IN CHINA

Although FDI in China has experienced a quick though uneven development, its determinants need to be examined. An extensive empirical literature has arisen to evaluate the relative importance of various determinants of FDI. However, little systematic econometric work has been conducted for China. One of the purposes of the current research is to provide robust evidence on the main hypotheses proposed in the literature to analyse the economic, political, cultural and geographic determinants of FDI in China from a macroeconomic perspective.

RESEARCH QUESTION 2. THE REGIONAL DISTRIBUTION OF FDI IN CHINA

As indicated earlier, although FDI flowed into every province, autonomous region or central municipality, the geographical distribution of FDI in China is characterised by its concentration in the coastal areas. Since every province is promoting further inward FDI, an understanding of regional characteristics influencing locational decisions is essential for improved policies to encourage FDI. In the current research, international trade, wage rates, R&D manpower, market size, infrastructure, agglomeration and preferential policies will be used to explain the regional distribution of FDI in China.

RESEARCH QUESTION 3. FDI AND PRODUCTIVITY SPILLOVERS

FDI can bring in technology. Although technology can be diffused by various means, it is suggested that the most significant channel for the dissemination of modern technology are the external effects or "spillovers" from FDI, rather than formal technology transfer agreements (see, for example, Blomstrom, 1989). However, little empirical research has been conducted on technology or productivity spillovers from FDI in China. This book will deal with this issue.

RESEARCH QUESTION 4. FDI AND REGIONAL ECONOMIC CONVERGENCE

It is often suggested that FDI has contributed to China's rapid economic growth. How can this hypothesis be systematically tested? Given its concentration in the coastal regions, has FDI helped widen the gap or promote convergence between areas? In chapter 5 convergence regressions will be conducted to examine the impact of FDI on long-run economic growth and regional convergence in China.

RESEARCH QUESTION 5. THE INTERACTION BETWEEN FDI AND TRADE

While China's foreign trade and inward FDI have experienced rapid expansion, it is not clear whether FDI and trade are inter-related. Theory suggests that there can be a two-way linkage between FDI and trade, but empirical evidence is so far lacking. FDI and trade are the two important means of international integration and they can both have positive impacts on economic growth. An understanding of the relationship between trade and

FDI is important for economic development. This book will assess the relationship between the FDI and trade intensities to examine if an intensive trade partner is an intensive investor in China.

1.3 METHODOLOGY

Although China began to receive FDI from 1979, official data required for the assessment of research questions 1, 2, 4 and 5 at the national and regional levels are available only from the mid-1980s onwards. Given this short time period, a time series analysis of annual data is obviously inappropriate. Simple cross-section estimation using data at the regional level is also inefficient due to the very limited number of observations. Furthermore, as argued by Nigh (1985), a cross-sectional study gives little thought to a longitudinal and time-sensitive phenomenon. Since international production is a dynamic process (Dunning, 1993), the use of panel data may be the most appropriate way for a systematic and efficient analysis of the determinants, regional distribution, FDI-trade linkage and impact of FDI in this research.

In addition, a panel data set possesses several major advantages over conventional cross-sectional or time-series data (Hsiao, 1986; Baltagi, 1995). For example, it gives more informative data, more variability, less collinearity among the variables, more degrees of freedom and higher efficiency. Consequently, the reliability of the estimates of the regression parameters can be greatly increased.

There are deficiencies in data for assessing research question 4 at the regional level as separate data sets on capital stock, labour quality, firm size and productivity for the foreign and indigenous sectors are unavailable. However, a relatively complete data set is available for the electronics industry over the period 1996-98 which covers 47 sub-sectors of the electronics industry. As a result, this question is examined using the electronics industry data set. The time-series and cross-sectional data will be pooled to increase the number of observations.

In sum, one unique feature of the current research is the adoption of a panel data approach. For each research question an empirical model is established on the basis of appropriate economic theories. The estimation is conducted using a panel data set. We are interested in the long-run relationship between FDI and related variables. To avoid possible spurious regression, the order of integration of each variable is identified by conducting unit root tests within a panel framework before any regression analysis is performed.

While the panel data approach is superior to other methods for this kind of research, it does have its limitations. For example, the lemming instinct on the part of investors may be one of the reasons to explain the high volume of FDI in China, which can not be assessed by regression analysis. As a result, some case or example analyses will be provided during the discussions of the empirical results in the relevant chapters.

The results from the empirical studies of five research questions identified in section 1.2 provide important implications for policy-makers as well as business managers. While these policy implications are discussed in each empirical study of the research questions, the final chapter of this book will provide an overall summary of the empirical results and policy suggestions.

1.4 CONCLUSIONS

The sustained influx of FDI in China has become a focus of the academic as well as business sector and has provided a tempting opportunity to identify the extent to which theories might have significant power in explaining FDI in China. While the issue of FDI is certainly not new, academics have seen a renewed interest partly due to the emergence of new theories and research tools and the need to update our knowledge in light of rapid changes in the global market.

The current research aims to formulate systematic and in-depth studies of FDI in China using the existing FDI theories. There are two special features of the book: (1) the adoption of a panel data approach to the empirical investigations, and (2) the introduction of new research topics such as productivity spillovers and the trade-FDI linkage in China. All this aids a better understanding of the various important issues of FDI in China. In addition, the empirical studies in the book utilise most recent data to provide the reader with updated evidence.

The book contains eight chapters. Further to the preview in this chapter, chapter 2 will provide a detailed description of FDI in China: its development path, sources and types, sectoral and regional distributions, impacts on capital formation, industrial output values, and exports and imports. This will be used as the background information for five empirical studies presented in chapters 3 through to 7.

Chapter 3 identifies the factors entering into foreign firms' decisions to invest in China. The determinants of FDI in Chinese regions are explored in chapter 4. To study these two issues, such FDI theories as the eclectic paradigm will be applied. Chapter 5 assesses whether there are productivity spillovers from FDI in the Chinese electronics industry. The impact of FDI on economic growth and regional economic convergence will be discussed in chapter 6. A possible inter-linkage between FDI and international trade is examined in chapter 7. The studies of the third, fourth and fifth issues will be carried out in an endogenous growth framework and in line with a number of newly developed trade and FDI theories. These econometric estimations will be complemented by some case and example analyses.

Finally, chapter 8 offers overall conclusions and policy implications. Although separate conclusions and implications are drawn in each chapter, the last chapter intends to present a wider view of the themes discussed throughout the book. In addition, the limitations and future research are also discussed.

2. Foreign Direct Investment in China: Development Trends and Impact

Chapter 1 has provided a preview of foreign direct investment (FDI) in China. The current chapter extends the preview by providing a more detailed description of the development path and impact of FDI in China. It aims to offer the background information for the rigorous empirical studies to be reported in chapters 3-7. Section 2.1 reviews the overall trends in FDI inflows. Section 2.2 describes the sources and types of FDI. Section 2.3 summarises its regional and sectoral distributions. The impact of FDI on economic development and foreign trade is briefly examined in section 2.4. Finally, section 2.5 offers a conclusion.

2.1 GENERAL TRENDS IN FOREIGN DIRECT INVESTMENT IN CHINA

China can trace back its history of opening the economy to FDI to the 1950s. Because of historical, ideological and practical reasons, however, the amount of FDI in the first 30 years (1949-78) was extremely small. The new era of absorbing FDI began in 1979 when the Chinese-Foreign Joint Venture Law was promulgated. In this era, inward FDI underwent four phases of development: the experimental period (1979-83); the gradual development period (1984-91); the peak period (1992-93); and the adjustment period (1994-present).

2.1.1 Pre-reform Period: 1949-78

Long ago the Chinese Communist Party set up its well-known approach to foreign policy, 'relying mainly on our own efforts while making external assistance subsidiary'. This was regarded as the fundamental principle in foreign economic relations. The practice did not always follow the policy in the sense that external assistance was sometimes totally ignored.

Shortly after the founding of the People's Republic of China in 1949, the Korean War broke out. The United States and other major Western countries embargoed transactions with China. In order to recover and develop the national economy, the Chinese government turned to the Soviet Union, obtaining rouble loans equal to US\$ 1.427 billion for importing 156 complete plants. Meanwhile, China set up a few joint ventures with the Soviet Union and other East European countries, including the Sino-Soviet Zhongchang Railway, the Sino-Soviet Xinjiang Non-ferrous Metal Company, the Dalian Sino-Soviet Shipbuilding and Repairing Company Ltd, the Sino-Polish Joint Stock Shipping Company and the Sino-Czechoslovakian International Marine Transportation Stock Company (Liu, 1983). The establishment of these joint ventures marked the starting point of the People's Republic of China absorbing FDI. During that period, however, all the investment came from the 'socialist camp' in which China was a member.

As a result of the worsening of Sino-Soviet relations in 1960, the Soviet Union withdrew economic assistance and asked China to pay back the debt. Every Sino-Soviet joint venture was discontinued. The Chinese people had to depend on self-reliance and spent several hard years paying off all the debt by 1965. The Sino-Czechoslovakian International Marine Transportation Stock Company also ceased to trade due to the bad relations between China and the Soviet Union. However, the Sino-Polish Joint Stock Shipping Company survived.

In the 1960s, only two joint ventures were formed: the Sino-Albanian Joint Stock Shipping Company in 1962 and the Sino-Tanzanian Joint Stock Marine Transportation Company in 1967. The formation of the two joint ventures in the 1960s reflected China's policy toward external relations. As a 'bright socialist light in Europe', Albania had close relations with China. In addition, Mao Zedong put forward his third-world theory at that time, urging that all third-world countries rally to form a united front. Unfortunately, the Sino-Albanian Joint Stock Shipping Company disintegrated in 1978 as a result of the worsening relations between the two countries, but the Sino-Tanzanian Joint Stock Marine Transportation Company continued to trade. During this period, the Chinese government continued the importation of machinery, equipment and even complete plants (mainly for the oil industry, chemical fertilisers, chemical fibres, metallurgy and electronics) by means of delayed payments. This practice was halted during the Cultural Revolution.

The Chinese people gained from the use of foreign funds in the 1950s and the 1960s (see, for example, Liu, 1983). Some of the technology, equipment and complete plants imported played an important role in China's industrialisation. By creating joint ventures China learnt new technology and management skills. The Sino-Polish Joint Stock Marine Transportation Company helped to overcome difficulties in China's foreign trade at a time when Western countries were embargoing transactions with China.

Inward direct investment in China was extremely small in the first three decades of the People's Republic of China for a number of reasons. Historically, for more than 2000 years the market mechanism in China was little developed and the idea of self-sufficiency was deeply rooted. As a matter of necessity, facing the embargo from the Western countries, China relied mainly on its own painstaking efforts to realise certain achievements in economic construction, which led to the idea that the Chinese people could achieve anything they wished without foreign capital. Ideologically, during the Cultural Revolution the use of foreign capital, especially FDI, was regarded as 'contradictory to socialism', 'begging from capitalist countries', and 'losing face'. This ideology dominated China for many years until 1976 when the Cultural Revolution came to an end.

2.1.2 Post-reform Period: 1979-Present

China's decision in 1979 to accept FDI was the result of a fundamental shift in political leadership and economic policy. This shift began after the end of the Cultural Revolution and crystallised during the Third Plenary Session of the Eleventh Central Committee of the Chinese Communist Party in 1978 (UNCTC, 1988, p.54). As a very important conference in the history of the Chinese Communist Party, the Third Plenum turned the main task of the party to the 'four modernisations', i.e. the modernisation of agriculture, industry, science and technology, and national defence. The main purpose of the four modernisations was to quadruple China's 1980 gross national product of RMB 480 billion to RMB 1800 billion by the year 2000, raising the living standards of its people through economic development.

To realise this objective, China needed capital, technology and managerial expertise. The new Chinese leadership formulated the path-breaking policy of economic reform and opening the economy to the outside world. An important component of the policy was to attract FDI to China for five reasons. Firstly, it could introduce foreign capital, compensating for a shortage of capital in economic construction without increasing China's external debt burdens. Secondly, it could introduce advanced technology, equipment and management skills at the same time. Thirdly, it could help existing enterprises to improve technology and to develop more technologically advanced and export-oriented practices, thus changing the economic structure and the quality of products and increasing exports. Fourthly, it could help in training technical and management personnel and in promoting China's foreign economic co-operation. Finally, it could offer extra jobs, increasing employment and income.

The new era of absorbing FDI can be subdivided into four phases. A first is the experimental period (1979-83). During this period, a limited amount of FDI was introduced into four small special economic zones (SEZs), i.e.

Source: Han and Wong (1994), p. 163

Figure 2.1 Location of the OEZs, SEZs and OCCs

Shenzhen, Zhuhai, Shantou and Xiamen, for the purpose of experiment (see Figure 2.1). A second is the gradual development period (1984-91). Fourteen open coastal cities (OCCs) and three open economic zones (OEZs) were established in the light of China's coast-oriented regional strategy. The Chinese government adjusted the sectoral distribution of FDI. Investments in technologically advanced and export-oriented enterprises were particularly encouraged. In this period, the Income Tax Law for Enterprises with Foreign Investment and Foreign Enterprises (the Unified Income Tax Law) was passed and Hainan Special Economic Zone and Shanghai's Pudong New Area were established. A third is the peak period (1992-93), during which China's inward FDI surged after Chinese leader Deng Xiaoping launched a new wave of economic reforms early in 1992. Finally, there is the adjustment period (1994-present), during which both the number of new projects and the value of contracted FDI decreased although realised FDI continued to increase.

Experimental Period (1979-83)

In this period, China combined the Committee for Import and Export, the Ministry of Foreign Trade, the Ministry of Foreign Economic Relations and

the Administrative Committee of Foreign Investment into the Ministry of
Foreign Economic Relations and Trade (MOFERT). This was the most
senior government organisation responsible for foreign investment as well as
trade and other foreign economic affairs. China enacted and promulgated a
series of laws and regulations governing FDI, which included the Law of the
People's Republic of China on Chinese-Foreign Joint Ventures (1979) and
the Income Tax Law of the People's Republic of China Concerning Chinese-
Foreign Joint Ventures (1980). The central government also allowed
Guangdong and Fujian Provinces to adopt special policies, and established
SEZs, which marked the beginning of the new era of China's opening up to
the outside world.

Guangdong and Fujian Provinces carried out special policies and flexible
measures from 1979. According to this arrangement, both provinces were
responsible for their own fiscal revenues and expenditures, sharing with the
central government the foreign-exchange incomes augmented by increasing
exports, instead of having revenues assigned and allocated by the state. They
also gained more autonomy in foreign economic activities. The two
provinces, the original homes of many overseas Chinese, were rich in certain
resources, and adjacent to Hong Kong and Macao. They were expected to
develop their economies rapidly by exploring the above advantages, and
move ahead of the rest in economic reforms, offering the whole country their
experience.

The establishment of the SEZs was an important experiment in opening
the Chinese economy to the outside world. On 26 August 1980, the 15th
Session of the Standing Committee of the 5th National People's Congress
approved the Regulations on Special Economic Zones in Guangdong
Province, followed by the construction of the four SEZs, i.e. Shenzhen,
Zhuhai, Shantou and Xiamen. The purpose of the SEZs was to provide the
'window' and 'radiator' functions necessary to attract FDI and the transfer of
know-how (Hayter and Han, 1998). In order to attract more foreign capital
and facilitate the administration and development of the SEZs, the State
Council expanded the areas of the three SEZs in June 1983: Zhuhai increased
from 6.7 square kilometres to 15.16 square kilometres; Xiamen increased
from 2.5 square kilometres to 131 square kilometres to include the whole of
Xiamen Island; and Shantou increased from 1.67 square kilometres to 52.6
square kilometres.

The SEZs had three characteristics.

- Economic development in the SEZs depended mainly on foreign
  investment. The economy in the SEZs was mixed, dominated by Sino-
  foreign equity joint ventures (EJVs), contractual joint ventures (CJVs),
  and wholly foreign-owned enterprises (WFOEs).

- Economic activity in the SEZs was mainly market-oriented rather than controlled by the plan, as was the case in the non-SEZ areas.
- SEZs were given more autonomy in economic activities. They could, for example, approve a project of up to RMB 50 million in heavy industry and up to RMB 30 million in light industry.

Because of these features, there was a heated discussion on the basic nature of SEZs. Many thought that the SEZ economy was one of capitalism. Since the Chinese leaders had no experience in accommodating capitalist elements into China's socialist economy, they needed to experiment and therefore deliberately directed FDI into these small SEZs. If the experiment was successful, they would allow FDI in other areas. If not, the possible negative effect of the experiment would not be significant due to the small size of the SEZs.

This experiment was a response to the compromise between the Chinese leaders' aspiration and their ideology. On the one hand, they longed for foreign resources for the modernisation drive. On the other hand, they had no experience in accommodating capitalist elements into China's socialist economic system. By limiting FDI in SEZs the Western capitalist system could be used to benefit China's development goals while Chinese socialism and sovereignty would not be undermined (Breslin, 1996).

In the experimental period, the number of agreements and the cumulative values of contracted and realised FDI were only 1,392, US$ 7,742 million and US$ 1,802 million respectively[1] (see Table 2.1). Difficulties in accessing the Chinese market, the non-convertibility of the Chinese currency and the lack of precedence combined to deter foreigners from investing in China (Coughlin and Segev, 2000). As can be seen in the next section, to reduce the risk the most popular form of investment was through CJVs, though, paradoxically, there was no law governing such joint ventures in China during that period.

Gradual Development Period (1984-91)

In 1984, the Chinese leaders believed that conditions for further opening its economy were ripe. Firstly, the experiment in SEZs seemed successful because ventures with foreign investment not only absorbed foreign capital, but also adopted advanced technology and management. Indeed, they could produce much more efficiently than state-owned enterprises. Secondly, the overall economic situation at that time was also satisfactory. Rural economic reform led to continuous increases in grain output, and macroeconomic readjustment had realised a number of important achievements.

Recognising the potential benefits of FDI, Chinese policy-makers gradually loosened the restrictions (Pomfret, 1997) and began to attract more

Table 2.1 Contracted and realised FDI, 1979-98

Year	No. of Projects	Contracted FDI (US$1,000,000)	Realised FDI (US$1,000,000)
1979-83	1,392	7,742	1,802
1984	1,856	2,651	1,258
1985	3,073	5,932	1,661
1986	1,498	2,834	1,874
1987	2,233	3,709	2,314
1988	5,945	5,297	3,194
1989	5,779	5,600	3,392
1990	7,273	6,596	3,487
1991	12,978	11,977	4,366
1992	48,764	58,124	11,007
1993	83,437	111,436	27,515
1994	47,594	82,680	33,767
1995	37,001	91,282	37,521
1996	24,556	73,277	41,726
1997	21,001	51,004	45,257
1998	19,799	52,102	45,463

Year	Cumulative No. of Projects	Cumulative Contracted FDI (US$1,000,000)	Cumulative Realised FDI (US$1,000,000)
1979-83	1,392	7,742	1,802
1984	3,248	10,393	3,060
1985	6,321	16,325	4,721
1986	7,819	19,159	6,595
1987	10,052	22,868	8,909
1988	15,997	28,165	12,103
1989	21,776	33,765	15,495
1990	29,049	40,361	18,982
1991	42,027	52,338	23,348
1992	90,791	110,462	34,355
1993	174,228	221,898	61,870
1994	221,822	304,578	95,637
1995	258,823	395,860	133,158
1996	283,379	469,137	174,884
1997	304,380	520,141	220,141
1998	324,179	572,243	265,604

Source: SSB, China Statistical Yearbook, 1999

foreign investors. In April 1984, the Central Committee of the Communist Party and the State Council decided to open fourteen further coastal port cities, i.e. Dalian, Qinhuangdao, Tianjin, Yantai, Qingdao, Lianyungang, Nantong, Shanghai, Ningbo, Wenzhou, Fuzhou, Guangzhou, Zhanjiang and Beihai (see Figure 2.1). In November 1984, the State Council approved a provision that EJVs, CJVs and WFOEs in these cities should pay only 80 per cent of the current enterprise-income tax applied to local firms. If these ventures were located in the economic and technical development districts within these cities, the tax rate was only 15 per cent.

The above 14 coastal cities were the most prosperous areas in China at the time they were proclaimed. Although their population accounted for only 8 per cent of the national total, their gross industrial product came to 23 per cent and gross exports to 40 per cent. Labour productivity was 66 per cent higher than the national average (Liu, 1993). The main purpose of opening these cities was to exploit these advantages further by using foreign funds, technology and markets, updating the existing enterprises' technology and strengthening the competitive abilities of their products in world markets. These coastal cities, which were regarded as the next layer of China's opening up to the outside world after the SEZs, were expected to help other areas in economic development by transferring information, personnel resources and funds.

In January 1985, the State Council turned the Changjiang (Yangtze River) Delta, the Zhujiang (Pearl River) Delta and the South Fujian triangle area into 'Open Economic Zones' (OEZs). This marked another important step towards opening up to the outside world. The three Deltas included both cities and vast rural areas. The development strategy for the OEZs was from 'small deltas' to 'large deltas'. The more favourably placed cities such as Suzhou, Wuxi, Changzhou in Changjiang Delta, Fuzhou, Jiangmen and Quanzhou in the South Fujian triangle area and Dongguan and Xinhui in the Zhujiang Delta would develop first in order to gain experience for the development of other areas in the Deltas.

These Deltas possessed favourable natural conditions, known as 'homes for fish and rice, for silk, and for flowers and fruits'. They had relatively advanced industries and agriculture, with a long history of foreign economic relations. All of these would help the development of their foreign economic and technical exchange. The OEZs were the next layer of China's opening up to the outside world after the SEZs and the OCCs, and they were also expected to promote economic development of the interior.

Partly because of the Chinese government's initiative and the continuing improvement of the investment environment, FDI in China in 1984 and 1985 underwent a relatively healthy development in contrast to the slow

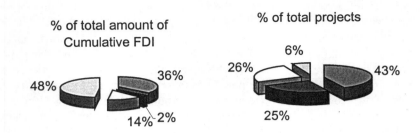

% of total amount of
Cumulative FDI

% of total projects

☒ Energy exploration, transport service, metallurgy, manufacture of machinery,
   electronics, chemicals, telecommunications equipment, construction materials

■ Agriculture, animal husbandry, fishery, forestry

☐ Light industries, textiles, foodstuffs, pharmaceuticals

☐ Tourism & service industry

Source: Chu (1987)

Figure 2.2 Sectoral distribution of cumulative FDI in China, 1979-86

investment between 1979 and 1983. Cumulative FDI in the two years was significantly higher than in the previous five years.

Although the increase in the total amount of FDI in China seemed satisfactory, structural problems were to appear. As Figure 2.2 shows, in the first seven years from 1979, investment in the construction of hotels and apartment buildings in the tourism and service industry took the lead over that in all other sectors, accounting for approximately half of the total amount of FDI brought in. The reasons for this dominance were as follows: while the policy of China's opening up to the outside world attracted in more and more foreigners for business and sightseeing, there was a serious shortage of suitable hotels and apartments to accommodate them. To address the problem, the Chinese government encouraged investment in this sector. For foreign investors, great demand, and thus promising prospects of good returns in terms of foreign exchange, lured them to invest. Consequently, too many high-level hotels and apartment buildings were built in Beijing and Shanghai, and even more so in Shenzhen and Guangzhou where the occupation rate declined sharply, especially in the low season of tourism.

While the proportion of FDI in tourism was very large, that in energy resources, raw materials and infrastructure, which were the areas the Chinese government particularly encouraged, was regarded as too small. As a result, the government began to alter the investment structure in 1986, imposing restrictions on FDI in tourist hotels in the above-mentioned cities.

In 1986 the 'Provisions of the State Council of the People's Republic of China for the Encouragement of Foreign Investment' (also known as the 22 Articles) together with other related legislation were formulated. The main purpose of the provisions and legislation was to readjust the structure of FDI in China by offering particularly favourable treatment: encouraging foreign businessmen to invest in technically advanced enterprises and export-oriented enterprises, as well as in the so-called 'basic industries' (such as new materials) and infrastructure.

Partly because of this policy and partly because of the Chinese government's austerity programme[2] which started in 1986, FDI inflows, in terms of both the number of projects approved and the contracted amount, declined sharply from 3,073 and US$ 5.9 billion in 1985 to 1,498 and US$ 2.8 billion in 1986. From 1987 to 1989, the contracted amount of FDI inflows increased gradually, but did not exceed that of 1985 (see Table 2.1).

The sectoral structure of inward FDI shifted during this period. In 1985, for example, the so-called 'manufacturing projects' approved accounted for less than 50 per cent of the total. But from 1986 to 1989, this proportion gradually increased to 60 per cent, 75 per cent, 85 per cent and 90 per cent, respectively (Wang, 1990).

During this period, China opened more areas to foreign investors: Shandong Peninsula and East Liaoning Peninsula were added to the OEZs; Hainan Province was granted full SEZ status in 1987; Shanghai's Pudong New Area was set up in 1989; and some cities and counties in the interior were opened up to the outside world.

The Pudong New Area comprised a triangular area of 350 square kilometres of Shanghai municipality's Chuansha County. This bold programme was supported by the central government. One of its purposes was to transform this old city by using foreign resources. The physical infrastructure was quickly improved and the area was to be divided into five zones: the Lujiazui Finance Zone, the Jinqiao/Qingningsi Export Processing District, the Waigaoqiao Free Trade Zone, the Zhoujiadu/Liulu Industrial Zone, and the Beicai/Zhangjiang Science and Education Zone.

Although the incentives available to foreign partners were basically similar to those in the SEZs, the Pudong New Area was not simply another SEZ because it allowed foreign investors to do things not allowed in the SEZs (see Gold, 1991). The Pudong New Area was the focus of China's propaganda on the economic reform. It was said that, if the 1980s was the age of the SEZs, the 1990s would be the age of Pudong.

Peak Period (1992-93)

Between 1992 and 1993, there was a surge in China's inward FDI. 132,201 enterprises with foreign investment were approved by the Chinese government, and contracted FDI reached US$ 169.6 billion (see Table 2.1). These two figures exceeded the corresponding figures of the previous 13 years.

The investment boom between 1992 and 1993 was closely associated with the following two events: Deng Xiaoping's tour of the southern provinces, and the opening up of new sectors and areas for FDI.

During his tour in January 1992, Deng Xiaoping urged his audience to 'emancipate the mind and pluck up the courage further and go at a faster pace'. In response to this, local governments lost no time in competing to attract foreign investment by establishing thousands of SEZs. (Unfortunately much of the confiscated land lay idle because the amount of foreign investment available fell short of the amounts that were projected.)

Since 1992 China has also allowed FDI to reach some previously forbidden sectors. These include domestic retail, finance, tourism, real estate, shipping, and resource development. Furthermore, in 1992, 28 cities and eight regions in the Yangtze River Delta Area and along the river were opened to the outside world. The opening up of these sectors and areas attracted much FDI.

Adjustment Period (1994-present)

From 1994 the investment boom in China seemed to cool down. The number of new projects approved dropped from 83,437 in 1993 to 47,594 in 1994, and the contracted value went down from US$ 111.4 billion in 1993 to US$ 82.7 billion in 1994. From 1994 to 1998, the number of new projects approved each year continued to decline, and contracted FDI was generally lower than in 1993 (see Table 2.1).

Several reasons can be identified for the above decline. First, there was increasing competition for inward FDI from other countries, including Asian, South American and Central and East European transition economies. In Asia for instance, Vietnam, Laos, Indonesia, India and Pakistan all provided many incentives to attract FDI (Jiao, 1998). Second, in 1995, the State Council divided the sectors into three categories: those in which FDI was encouraged, those in which FDI was restricted, and those in which FDI was forbidden. China tried to adjust the industrial structure of inward FDI. Third, to provide national treatment for foreign investors, the State Council announced on 28 December 1995 that it would re-impose duties for imported machinery, equipment, parts and other materials by foreign-invested firms from 1 April 2000. However, as noted by Zhang (1998), this change in taxation policy discouraged new FDI projects and reinvestment from existing enterprises. Facing this problem, the State Council responded by the end of 1997 to announce that FDI in the encouraged sectors and the second type of the restricted sectors should be exempted from import duties from 1 January 1998.

As can be seen in Table 2.1, the value of realised FDI inflows continued to increase in the adjustment period due to the large amount of FDI contracted in previous years. In contrast, the number of new projects and the contracted value of FDI in this period showed a declining trend. But FDI inflows in China were still relatively significant if we look at the growth of realised FDI in a global context. Between 1993 and 1997, China was the second-largest host country. Only in 1998 did the United Kingdom surpass China (see Table 2.2)[3]. Corresponding to the quick increase in inflows, the stock of FDI in China also increased quickly (see Table 2.3). The stock of inward FDI undertaken in China through 1998 reached US$ 261 billion.

Table 2.2 FDI inflows to selected economies, 1988-98

US$ billion

Economy	1988	1990	1992	1994	1995	1996	1997	1998
World	**159**	**208**	**158**	**254**	**389**	**359**	**464**	**644**
Developed Economies	*131*	*176*	*102*	*146*	*208*	*211*	*273*	*460*
France	8	13	21	16	24	22	23	28
United Kingdom	21	32	18	9	20	26	37	63
United States	58	48	3	45	58	76	109	193
Developing Economies	*27*	*31*	*51*	*101*	*106*	*135*	*173*	*166*
China	3	3	11	34	36	40	44	45
Brazil	3	1	1	3	5	10	18	29
Mexico	3	3	5	12	10	9	13	10
Hong Kong	3	2	2	4	3	6	6	2
Malaysia	1	2	4	4	4	5	5	4
Singapore	3	5	6	9	7	8	10	7

Note: The figures for China for 1995, 1996 and 1997 are slightly different in this table from the corresponding figures in Table 2.1 because of different data sources.

Source: UNCTD, World Investment Report, 1994 and 1999

Table 2.3 Inward FDI stock to selected economies, 1985-98

US$ billion

Economy	1985	1990	1995	1997	1998
World	**745**	**1,768**	**2,800**	**3,440**	**4,088**
Developed Economies	*538*	*1,395*	*1,982*	*2,312*	*2,785*
France	33	87	144	141	179
United Kingdom	64	219	214	276	327
United States	185	395	536	682	875
Developing Economies	*207*	*371*	*769*	*1,055*	*1,219*
China	3	19	131	216	261
Brazil	26	37	99	128	157
Mexico	19	22	41	51	61
Hong Kong	4	56	71	95	96
Malaysia	9	10	27	37	41
Singapore	13	29	60	79	86

Source: UNCTD, World Investment Report, 1999

2.2 SOURCES AND TYPES OF FOREIGN DIRECT INVESTMENT IN CHINA

2.2.1 Sources of Foreign Direct Investment in China

After China adopted the policy of opening up to the outside world, enterprises from more than 100 different countries and regions invested in China (see, SSB, China Statistical Yearbook 1999). By the end of 1998, the top 15 home countries/regions in terms of realised value of FDI were as presented in Table 2.4.

Hong Kong was the leading source of investment in the mainland, and this overwhelmingly dominant position is expected to remain for years to come due to its geographical advantage, similar cultural background and close economic relations and family links with the mainland.

The most significant feature in the sources of FDI in recent years may be that Taiwan and South Korea became important investors in mainland China. Taiwanese investment in China was officially prohibited by the Taiwanese authorities before 1987. Since 1988, Taiwan's investment has grown dramatically. By the end of 1998, Taiwan made direct investment of US$ 21.3 billion in China. A tremendous influx of capital has come from South Korea since diplomatic relations between the two countries were officially

Table 2.4 Top 15 foreign investors in China, 1979-98

Economy	No. of Projects (%)	Contracted FDI (US$ million) (%)	Realised FDI (US$ million) (%)
National total	**324,620** **(100)**	**572,494** **(100)**	**267,312** **(100)**
Hong Kong	178,922 (55.12)	297,628 (51.99)	138,434 (51.79)
Japan	17,602 (5.42)	32,543 (5.68)	21,912 (8.20)
United States	26,674 (8.22)	46,594 (8.14)	21,433 (8.02)
Taiwan	41,017 (12.64)	40,400 (7.06)	21,265 (7.96)
Singapore	7,997 (2.46)	31,091 (5.43)	12,177 (4.56)
South Korea	11,179 (3.44)	14,837 (2.59)	7,562 (2.83)
Virgin Islands	1,536 (0.47)	16,917 (2.96)	6,736 (2.52)
United Kingdom	2,324 (0.72)	15,055 (2.63)	6,540 (2.45)
Germany	1,932 (0.60)	8,397 (1.47)	3,438 (1.29)
Macao	6,164 (1.90)	8,883 (1.55)	3,328 (1.24)
France	1,473 (0.45)	4,643 (0.81)	2,698 (1.01)
Malaysia	1,780 (0.55)	4,281 (0.75)	1,764 (0.66)
Canada	3,984 (1.23)	6,366 (1.11)	1,734 (0.65)
Netherlands	646 (0.20)	3,394 (0.59)	1,659 (0.62)
Thailand	2,631 (0.81)	4,555 (0.80)	1,641 (0.61)
Others	18,759 (5.78)	36,912 (6.45)	14,991 (5.61)

Source: MOFTEC (1999)

normalised in 1991. By 1998, realised FDI by South Korea amounted to US$ 7.6 billion in China. The rapid growth of FDI from Taiwan and South Korea may also be due to rising labour costs and appreciation of the local currencies.

Although the number of approved projects and the cumulative value of contracted FDI from the United States were higher than those from Japan, realised FDI from Japan was slightly higher than that from the United States. FDI from Japan and the United States was much lower than that from Hong Kong, but these two countries were respectively the second- and third-largest investors in China.

The unique feature of FDI in China is that the majority of China's inward investment has been contributed by ethnic Chinese. Hong Kong, Taiwan and Macao were not the only sources of investment by ethnic Chinese. Some FDI from other Asian, European, Australian and North American countries was actually made by people of Chinese extraction. An overseas Chinese usually has strong affection for his/her original home and a strong feeling of commitment to his/her family. For example, in the early years of mainland China opening up to the outside world, the Taiwanese mainly invested in Fujian Province because many Taiwanese were actually Fujianese.

As discussed above, the position of China as a major host country of inward FDI is mainly due to the overwhelming contribution by overseas Chinese from Hong Kong and other Asian countries or regions. As shown in Table 2.5, the total outward FDI stock of Hong Kong by the end of 1998 was US$ 155 billion, of which 44 per cent was located in mainland China. Given that China has already resumed sovereignty of Hong Kong, the investment from Hong Kong could well be regarded as domestic. Thus, the significance of 'real' FDI in China would be much smaller. The shares of FDI stock in China in total outward stocks from Thailand, Singapore and Malaysia were also reasonably high and reached 32 per cent, 11 per cent and 5 per cent respectively. However, because of the small volumes of their total outward stocks, the absolute amounts that went to China were hardly significant.

The total outward FDI stocks from many developed countries are higher than those from Hong Kong, but only very small shares of these stocks are located in China (see Table 2.5). For instance, the United States is the dominant investor in the world, but merely 1 per cent of its total outward stock is in China. For other major investors such as the United Kingdom, Germany, the Netherlands, France and Italy, the shares of their investments in China in their total outward investments were even lower than 0.6 per cent. The relative importance of investment in China in Japan's total outward investment was the highest in the developed countries, but was still as low as approximately 3.8 per cent. In the next chapter a number of the reasons for

Table 2.5 Share of FDI stock in China, in home country/region's total outward stock, 1979-98

Country/Region	FDI Stock in China (US$1,000,000)	Total Outward FDI Stock in the World (US$1,000,000)	Share in Total Outward Stock (%)
United States	10193.44	993552	1.0260
Canada	779.70	156600	0.4979
Australia	695.93	62160	1.1196
Japan	11138.47	296056	3.7623
New Zealand	73.05	5518	1.3238
Belgium	113.81	128799	0.0884
Denmark	94.48	35821	0.2638
France	1076.72	242347	0.4443
Germany	2087.29	390090	0.5351
Italy	705.44	170746	0.4132
Netherlands	739.55	262996	0.2812
Spain	77.87	68392	0.1139
Sweden	133.84	93487	0.1432
United Kingdom	2889.94	498624	0.5796
Hong Kong	67806.02	154856	43.7865
Indonesia	244.83	2117	1.5651
Malaysia	755.08	14645	5.1559
Singapore	5413.91	47630	11.3666
Thailand	666.91	2073	32.1713

Note: * FDI stock in China is based on authors' own calculation and is derived from the inflow data with the depreciation rate equalling 10 per cent.

Sources: FDI inflow is from SSB, China Statistical Yearbook, various issues; Total outward FDI stock is from UNCTD, World Investment Report, 1999.

the relatively small amounts of FDI from developed countries will be discussed.

2.2.2 Types of Foreign Direct Investment in China

The main types of FDI in China are equity joint ventures (EJVs), contractual joint ventures (CJVs) and wholly foreign-owned enterprises (WFOEs). An EJV, according to the Chinese definition, is a limited-liability company financed and run by participants who share both risk and profit. A CJV refers to the co-operation between two separate economic entities or two separate persons who 'reach agreement in a co-operative-venture contract on such matters as the investment or conditions for co-operation, the distribution of earnings or products, the sharing of risks and loss, the manner of operation and management and the ownership of the property upon termination of the co-operative venture' (the Law on Chinese-Foreign Co-operative Joint Ventures).

In an EJV in China, the foreign side is usually expected to bring in equipment, industrial property rights (including technology), and funds as its contribution, while the Chinese side contributes land, plant, equipment and the Chinese currency. Because of joint investment, operation and risk-taking, foreign businessmen would, by Chinese government standards, be interested in economic efficiency, and thus would contribute advanced technology and equipment, which would help the existing enterprises in China to improve technology and the quality of products. Secondly, by the running of an EJV, a foreign businessman's selling channels and experience could be exploited to expand exports. In an EJV contract, an export ratio of products was usually set, and the foreign partner was responsible for the export, gaining enough foreign exchange to remit the value of the investment at a profit. As a result, while foreign businessmen served their own interests in doing so, they helped China to export its products. Thirdly, the Chinese side in an EJV could learn advanced management skills by joint operation. This form of investment was particularly encouraged by the Chinese government.

There were reasons why foreign partners generally favoured EJVs. As the main sources of FDI in China, HongKongese, Taiwanese, overseas Chinese and people of Chinese origin were in a position to make good use of specific advantages when they invested in China. These included shared culture and family relations. Because of this, there was less uncertainty but more mutual trust, and both parties could act more rationally. The Chinese partners also favoured the EJV status in order to gain preferential treatment from the government.

As for a CJV in China, profit distribution, together with other co-operative conditions, is not based on the amounts invested by both sides, but rather on the terms of the contract. Because of the flexible arrangement, this form of FDI developed relatively fast during the early stages of the opening-up period. These CJVs were established in manufacturing, agriculture, aquatic farming, schools and hospitals, transportation, and especially tourist hotels and apartment buildings.

From Table 2.6 it is clear that EJVs and CJVs were very popular during the early stages of China's opening up of its economy to FDI. However, the popularity of joint ventures, especially CJVs, gradually declined while the

Table 2.6 FDI by type of investment, 1979-98

	Type	1979-84	1985	1990	1995	1997	1998
Equity JV	No. of projects	931	1,412	4,091	20,455	9,001	8,107
	% of total	**28.7**	**45.9**	**56.2**	**55.3**	**42.9**	**40.9**
	Contracted value (US$ 1,000,000)	1,380	2,030	2,704	39,741	20,726	17,286
	% of total	**15.4**	**34.2**	**41.0**	**43.5**	**40.6**	**33.2**
	Realised value (US$ 1,000,000)	430				19,495	18,348
	% of total	**14.1**				**43.1**	**40.4**
Contract JV	No. of projects	2,212	1,611	1,317	4,787	2,373	2,003
	% of total	**68.1**	**52.4**	**18.1**	**12.9**	**11.3**	**10.1**
	Contracted value (US$ 1,000,000)	4,710	3,496	1,254	17,825	12,066	11,656
	% of total	**52.4**	**58.9**	**19.0**	**19.5**	**24**	**22.4**
	Realised value (US$ 1,000,000)	1,220				8,930	9,719
	% of total	**39.9**				**19.7**	**21.4**
WFOE	No. of projects	74	46	1,860	11,761	9,602	9,673
	% of total	**2.3**	**15.0**	**25.6**	**31.8**	**45.7**	**48.9**
	Contracted value (US$ 1,000,000)	470	46	2,444	33,658	17,658	21,753
	% of total	**5.2**	**0.8**	**37.0**	**36.9**	**34.6**	**41.8**
	Realised value (US$ 1,000,000)	100				16,188	16,470
	% of total	**3.3**				**35.8**	**36.2**
Others*	No. of projects	31	4	5	8	25	16
	% of total	**0.95**	**0.13**	**0.07**	**0.02**	**0.1**	**0.08**
	Contracted value (US$ 1,000,000)	3,760	762	584	1,328	553	1,407
	% of total	**41.8**	**12.8**	**8.9**	**1.45**	**1**	**2.7**
	Realised value (US$ 1,000,000)	1,310				644	926
	% of total	**42.8**				**1.4**	**2**

Note: *Including joint oil exploration, international leasing, compensation deals, and processing and assembly.

Source: SSB, China Statistical Yearbook, various issues

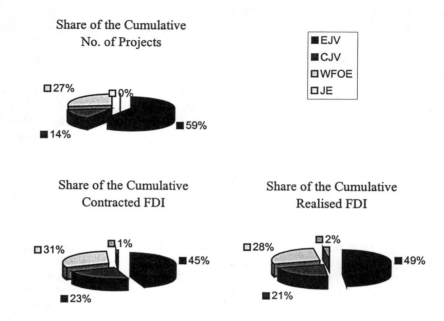

Share of the Cumulative
No. of Projects

■ EJV
■ CJV
□ WFOE
□ JE

□27%   □0%
        ■59%
■14%

Share of the Cumulative   Share of the Cumulative
Contracted FDI   Realised FDI

□31%   ■1%   □28%   ■2%
        ■45%   ■49%
    ■23%   ■21%

Source: MOFTEC (1999)

Figure 2.3 Types of cumulative FDI, 1979-98

share of WFOEs steadily increased. In 1985, WFOEs accounted for 15 per
cent of the total number of FDI projects and 0.8 per cent of total contracted
value. In 1998, the corresponding figures were 48.9 per cent and 41.8 per
cent.

The Chinese government also has its reasons for allowing WFOEs to
operate in China (see, for example, Liu, 1983). Firstly, a WFOE could bring
in advanced technology and management experience. In order to strengthen
its competitive ability, a WFOE would use advanced technology and
management skills. The efficiency of the WFOE would have a bandwagon
effect, encouraging local enterprises to improve. Secondly, the WFOE could
help China gain more foreign-exchange revenue: through income tax, land-
use fees, salary, rent, and payments for raw materials. Lastly, a WFOE could
increase employment and help in the training of local employees.

The quick development of WFOEs was prompted by several factors. The
austerity programme beginning in late 1988 caused a lack of RMB, which
made the formation of JVs more difficult for the Chinese, with the result that
the Chinese government encouraged WFOEs. For foreign businesses,

WFOEs guarantee greater management latitude and strategic consistency with their headquarters. This may also reflect the fact that foreign investors are now familiar with the local investment environment and the protection of their own property rights may be deemed to be more important than access to advantages from the formation of joint ventures.

Although WFOEs have become increasingly popular in recent years, the dominant type of FDI in terms of cumulative values between 1979 and 1998 in China remained the EJV (see Figure 2.3). CJVs ranked third although they used to be a very popular type. Based on the trend of FDI inflows, the share of WFOEs is expected to increase further in the coming years.

2.3 SECTORAL AND REGIONAL DISTRIBUTION OF FOREIGN DIRECT INVESTMENT IN CHINA

2.3.1 Sectoral Distribution of Foreign Direct Investment in China

As indicated in Figure 2.2, much of FDI between 1979 and 1986 went into tourist hotels. After the Chinese government's discouragement of investment in the tourism and real estate sectors in 1986, the average FDI inflow into manufacturing was higher than that into service sectors. The shares of cumulative FDI in different sectors are presented in Table 2.7. Although the Chinese government encouraged FDI into the agriculture and related sectors, the cumulative FDI in agriculture, forestry, animal husbandry and fishing was only less than 2 per cent. While the share of FDI in manufacturing was relatively high, it mainly entered such labour-intensive sub-sectors as textiles, clothing and assembly lines of the mechanical and electronic sub-sectors. The shares of FDI in capital and high-technology-intensive sub-sectors were very small (Cui and Kong, 1998). In the service sector, FDI was still concentrated in real estate at the expense of infrastructure such as transport, into which the Chinese government wanted to attract more FDI.

2.3.2 Regional Distribution of Foreign Direct Investment in China

The regional distribution of FDI in China is very uneven. Approximately 87 per cent of the cumulative FDI is located in the eastern regions, while the remaining 13 per cent is located in the central and western regions (see Table 2.8). The uneven geographical distribution of FDI was, as a matter of fact, part of China's regional development strategy.

China has a vast territory with a large population. For historical and geographical reasons, China underwent uneven regional development. There are three economic belts: east, west and central. The east belt is the relatively well-developed coastal area, including Liaoning, Hebei, Tianjin, Beijing, Shandong, Jiangsu, Shanghai, Zhejiang, Fujian, Guangdong, Guangxi, and Hainan; the west belt, the least developed area, refers to very dry and cold western provinces: Xinjiang, Xizhang (Tibet), Qinghai, Gansu, Ningxia, Neimenggu (Inner Mongolia), and Shaanxi. The remaining provinces belong to the central belt, consisting of Heilongjiang, Jilin, Shanxi, Henan, Anhui, Jiangxi, Hubei, Hunan, Guizhou, Sichuan, and Yunnan. A combination of both central and western belts is also known as the interior area.

Table 2.7 Sectoral distribution of contracted FDI in China

US$ billion

Sector	1979-86 FDI (%)	1987-91 FDI (%)	1992-94 FDI (%)	1979-98 No. of Projects (%)	1979-98 FDI (%)
Total	19.18 (100)	33.18 (100)	252.21 (100)	324,620 (100)	572.50 (100)
Agriculture, forestry, animal husbandry & fishing	0.57 (2.98)	0.80 (2.41)	2.84 (1.13)	8,772 (2.70)	9.355 (1.63)
Industry	7.60 (39.59)	25.66 (77.33)	127.87 (50.70)	237,054 (73.03)	338.20 (59.08)
Construction	0.31 (1.63)	0.56 (1.68)	8.11 (3.22)	8,579 (2.64)	17.76 (3.10)
Transport, warehousing, post & telecommunications	0.28 (1.48)	0.29 (0.87)	5.06 (2.01)	3,516 (1.08)	13.86 (2.42)
Wholesale & retailing, catering	1.42 (7.40)	0.44 (1.33)	9.97 (3.95)	16,733 (5.15)	20.76 (3.63)
Real estate	5.99 (31.21)	4.48 (13.51)	85.71 (33.98)	31,731 (9.77)	142.75 (24.93)
Health care, sports & social welfare	0.07 (0.34)	0.15 (0.46)	2.85 (1.13)	971 (0.30)	4.55 (0.79)
Education, culture, arts, broadcasting, film & TV	0.08 (0.42)	0.13 (0.39)	1.16 (0.46)	1,288 (0.40)	1.97 (0.34)
Scientific research & technical services	0.01 (0.05)	0.06 (0.18)	0.92 (0.37)	2,348 (0.72)	1.74 (0.30)
Others	2.86 (14.89)	0.61 (1.85)	7.72 (2.86)	13,628 (4.2)	21.56 (3.77)

Sources: Data for 1979-94 from Lee (1997); Data for 1979-98 from MOFTEC (1999)

Table 2.8 Realised FDI inflows by region*, 1985-98

US$ million

Year	1985-89	1990	1995	1997	1998	1985-98
Eastern Regions	**10,418**	**3,194**	**32,641**	**38,559**	**39,490**	**217,840**
Beijing	1,168	279	1,080	1,593	2,168	10,474
Tianjin	424	37	1,521	2,511	2,114	10,629
Hebei	180	45	547	1,101	1,429	5,221
Liaoning	422	257	1,425	2,205	2,191	11,834
Shanghai	1,127	174	2,893	4,225	3,602	22,234
Jiangsu	436	134	5,191	5,435	6,632	31,327
Zhejiang	186	42	1,258	1,504	1,318	8,342
Fujian	820	320	4,044	4,197	4,212	26,159
Shandong	419	186	2,689	2,493	2,203	16,269
Guangdong	4,825	1,582	10,260	11,711	12,020	64,237
Hainan	212	103	1,062	706	717	5,844
Guangxi	199	36	673	880	886	5,271
Central Regions	**823**	**138**	**3,429**	**4,788**	**4,420**	**23,574**
Shanxi	22	3	64	266	245	913
Inner Mongolia	26	11	58	73	91	463
Jilin	146	18	408	402	409	2,459
Heilongjiang	169	28	517	735	526	3,216
Anhui	78	14	483	434	277	2,485
Jiangxi	43	8	289	478	465	2,173
Henan	143	11	479	692	617	3,248
Hubei	97	32	625	790	973	4,590
Hunan	99	14	508	917	818	4,028
Western Regions	**608**	**97**	**1,145**	**1,554**	**1,374**	**8,608**
Sichuan	138	24	542	635	804	4,270
Guizhou	50	11	57	50	45	387
Yunnan	28	7	98	166	146	704
Shaanxi	335	47	324	628	300	2,511
Gansu	5	1	64	41	39	345
Qinghai	3		2	2		14
Ningxia	2	0	4	7	19	57
Xinjiang	49	5	55	25	22	321
Tibet						
Total	**11,849**	**3,430**	**37,216**	**44,901**	**45,284**	**250,022**

Note: *This regional classification is based on MOFTEC (1999).

Sources: Data for 1985-95 from Henley et al. (1999); Data for 1997-98 from SSB, China Statistical Yearbook, 1999

Compared with the interior area, the east has many advantages, such as better industrial and agricultural bases, with advanced science, technology and equipment, and relatively plentiful capital, and technical and managerial personnel, and convenient transportation. It also has a long history of foreign economic relations. All of this shows that the east should move ahead of the rest in international economic exchange, by means of which it could improve its science, technology and management skills, catching up with advanced world levels. On the other hand, the eastern area should help the other two areas to develop.

The western belt is rich in natural resources, with a large territory and small population. It is to be developed. The central belt has a large population and its gross industrial product accounts for approximately 30 per cent of the national total. The economic features of the belt are between those of the east and the west, like its geographical location: not too backward, with certain traditional industries and resources.

In recent Chinese history, there was a particular regional tendency in economic growth: gradual development from the coast to the interior, or from the east to the west. An emphasis given to the east in the opening up to the outside world was based on this tendency. The main purpose of the strategy was to promote the coastal economy, and then to transfer information, technology, funds and qualified personnel from this belt to the hinterland, helping along the development of the interior.

Following the strategy, China formed the 'SEZ-Pudong-OCC-OEZ-Interior' opening structure with emphasis on the coast. The SEZs, OCCs and OEZs link all the coastal areas to form a long belt, covering one entire province and 300 other cities and counties. The vast interior is the hinterland of these coastal areas. By doing this China tried to combine coastal growth with interior development, gradually solving the imbalance between the east and the west, and advancing the entire economy.

Following this strategy, the eastern coastal areas, with their higher level of economic activity and living standards, attracted more funds, technology and high-quality human resources from the interior. Some leaders in the interior were worried about the situation, warning that the deepening economic conflict might cause a worsening of political and national problems.

As a result, some economists suggested a policy of 'caring for both the east and the west and opening to the outside world in all directions' (see Hu, 1989). From their point of the view, in addition to the resource advantages, the western area, especially the southwest, also had many key enterprises and research institutes which were built during the so-called 'third-front' construction period (1960s and 1970s) with an investment of approximately RMB 200 billion. While the east and the west co-operated and supported each other, each with its own comparative advantages, the west had a certain ability to take part in international exchange directly. It could open its economy to the neighbouring countries, absorbing foreign funds to explore natural resources and to develop raw-material and manufacturing industries. It could also expand cross-border trade with neighbouring countries.

Maybe partly as a response to this, the Chinese government recently opened interior areas to the outside world. From 1992, ten central cities along the Yangtze River carried out policies similar to those applied in the coastal cities. These ten cities were Nanjing and Zhenjiang in Jiangsu Province; Maanshan, Tonglin, Wuhu and Anqin in Anhui Province; Jiujiang in Jiangxi Province; Yueyang in Hunan Province; Wuhan in Hubei Province; and Chongqing in Sichuan Province. Very recently, the Tenth Five-Year Plan (2001-05) for Economic and Social Development formally announced its national strategy to develop the western areas and encouraged more FDI into these regions (People's Daily, Overseas Edition, 19 October 2000).

At the provincial level Guangdong was still the most popular investment site with cumulative FDI of US$ 64 billion between 1985 and 1998. This accounted for 26 per cent of total FDI inflows in all regions in China (see Table 2.8). The following advantages explain Guangdong's leading position in attracting FDI. It is located next to Hong Kong and is one of the first provinces allowed to implement special policies and to establish SEZs. Guangzhou is also a traditional commercial and industrial city with a long history of foreign economic activities and is the place of origin of many overseas Chinese.

The second favourite investment site used to be Fujian province, which has similar advantages to those of Guangdong. Many Taiwanese are of Fujianese origin and much of their investment was located in Fujian. As can be seen from Table 2.8, Fujian was the third most popular location for inward FDI in China.

By 1998 Jiangsu surpassed Fujian and became the second most favourite site. Shanghai and Shandong ranked fourth and fifth respectively. All three regions have established infrastructure and industrial bases with relatively advanced technology, high-quality human resources and wide experience of foreign economic activities.

2.4 IMPACT OF FOREIGN DIRECT INVESTMENT ON ECONOMIC DEVELOPMENT AND INTERNATIONAL TRADE IN CHINA

Figure 2.4 shows that realised FDI as a percentage of China's total investment in fixed assets increased very quickly, from less than 1 per cent in 1982 to 17 per cent in 1994. Although gradually declining from 1995, this

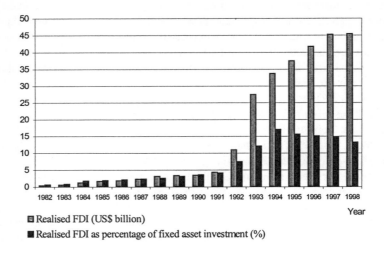

☐ Realised FDI (US$ billion)

■ Realised FDI as percentage of fixed asset investment (%)

Sources: Data for 1982-90 from Chen (1997); Data for 1991-98 from MOFTEC (1999)

Figure 2.4 Realised FDI as percentage of fixed asset investment, 1982-98

percentage was still as high as over 13 per cent in 1998. However, it should be noted that the contribution of FDI to capital formation in China may be distorted. Kueh (1992) argues that the share figures may be understated in the 1980s and exaggerated in the 1990s, due to the overvaluation of RMB in the 1980s and the major RMB depreciation against the US dollar in December 1989. Moreover, as note 3 of this chapter suggests, there is pseudo-FDI contained in China's statistics.

The contribution of FDI to economic development can be seen from Table 2.9. In 1990, the share of industrial output value (IOV) of foreign-invested enterprises (FIEs) in the national total was 2 per cent. This figure increased steadily to reach 27 per cent in 1998. The impact of FDI on China's foreign trade seemed to be mixed. In terms of total trade (imports plus exports), the share of FIEs increased dramatically from merely 0.1 per cent in 1980 to 48.7 per cent in 1998 (see Table 2.10). Put another way, almost half of China's total foreign trade was recently conducted by FIEs. This made a significant contribution to China's trade.

However, if one simply compares the imports and exports of FIEs, the net trade effect of FIEs is ambiguous. As shown in Table 2.10, the net trade effect was persistently and substantially negative until 1997. Henley et al. (1999) argue that China did not report the dividends and profit remittances overseas until 1995. If these figures were added, the net trade effect would be more negative. On the other hand, Chen (1999) and Sun (1999) note that the equipment and machinery imported by FIEs as part of their investment equities are also recorded in China's official statistics as FIE's imports. If this is deducted from FIEs' total imports then a trade surplus rather than a deficit would appear for the 1990s.

Table 2.9 Share of FIEs in total industrial output value

Year	Total IOV (RMB 100 million)	FIEs' IOV (RMB 100 million)	FIEs as % of total
1990	19701.04	448.95	2.28
1991	23135.56	1223.32	5.29
1992	29149.25	2065.59	7.09
1993	40513.68	3704.35	9.15
1994	76867.25	8649.39	11.26
1995	91963.28	13154.16	14.31
1996	99595.55	15077.53	15.14
1997	56149.70	10427.00	18.57
1998	58195.23	15532.00	27.00

Source: as Figure 2.4

Table 2.10 Share of FIEs in China's foreign trade

US$ billion

Year	Total trade	FIEs (%)	Imports	FIEs (%)	Exports	FIEs (%)
1980	38.140	0.043 (0.11)	20.020	0.034 (0.17)	18.120	0.008 (0.05)
1981	44.020	0.143 (0.33)	22.010	0.111 (0.50)	22.010	0.032 (0.15)
1982	41.600	0.329 (0.79)	19.280	0.276 (1.43)	22.320	0.053 (0.24)
1983	43.610	0.618 (1.42)	21.390	0.288 (1.35)	22.220	0.330 (1.49)
1984	53.550	0.468 (0.87)	27.410	0.399 (1.46)	26.140	0.069 (0.26)
1985	69.600	2.361 (3.39)	42.250	2.064 (4.89)	27.350	0.297 (1.09)
1986	73.886	2.985 (4.04)	42.911	2.403 (5.60)	30.940	0.582 (1.88)

Table 2.10 Continued

Year	Total trade	FIEs (%)	Imports	FIEs (%)	Exports	FIEs (%)
1987	82.595	4.584 (5.55)	43.201	3.374 (7.81)	39.414	1.210 (3.07)
1988	102.746	8.343 (8.12)	55.282	5.882 (10.64)	47.510	2.461 (5.18)
1989	111.645	13.710 (12.28)	59.153	8.796 (14.87)	52.556	4.914 (9.35)
1990	115.404	20.115 (17.43)	53.348	12.302 (23.06)	62.107	7.813 (12.58)
1991	135.684	28.955 (21.34)	63.780	16.908 (26.51)	71.922	12.047 (16.75)
1992	165.520	43.747 (26.43)	80.596	26.387 (32.74)	84.932	17.360 (20.44)
1993	195.711	67.070 (34.27)	103.959	41.833 (40.24)	91.738	25.237 (27.51)
1994	236.628	87.647 (37.04)	115.627	52.934 (45.78)	120.993	34.713 (28.69)
1995	280.867	109.819 (39.10)	132.067	62.943 (47.66)	148.765	46.876 (31.51)
1996	289.934	137.110 (47.29)	138.850	75.604 (54.45)	151.083	61.506 (40.71)
1997	325.069	152.620 (46.95)	142.370	77.720 (54.59)	182.683	74.900 (41.00)
1998	323.909	157.679 (48.68)	140.174	76.717 (54.73)	183.754	80.962 (44.06)

Sources: Data for 1980-85 from SSB, China Foreign Economic Statistical Yearbook, 1994; Data for 1986-98 from Customs Statistics, various issues.

2.5 CONCLUSIONS

The People's Republic of China started its absorption of FDI as early as the 1950s. However, there were only a few FDI projects during the first three decades, and the sources of FDI were limited to several socialist countries. The decision to open its economy to the outside world in 1979 marked a very important turning point in China's history of economic development. Since then China has experienced large inflows of foreign capital and is now one of the major hosts of FDI in the world.

The dominant source of inward FDI in China is Hong Kong, followed by Japan, the United States and Taiwan. Compared with their total outward FDI stocks in the world, however, inward investments from developed countries are still limited. The most popular type of FDI in China is the EJV, although it is likely that WFOEs will soon surpass EJVs to become the major type.

Approximately 59 per cent of FDI has gone to the manufacturing sector, much of which is in such labour-intensive industries as textiles, clothing and some assembly lines of mechanical and electronic products. FDI is still concentrated in the coastal areas. The Chinese government began to encourage such investment to the central and western regions in the 1990s.

The share of FIEs in China's total investment in fixed assets has been over 10 per cent in recent years, and that in China's total industrial output value has increased dramatically. The net trade effect of FIEs is ambiguous.

This chapter has extended the description of the development and impact of FDI offered in chapter 1. Both chapters aim to provide the background information for the empirical studies of chapters 3-7.

NOTES

1. Here we should note that the Chinese definition of FDI used to be 'broader than the ordinarily accepted usage of the term' (UNCTC, 1988). Firstly, foreign investors referred not only to foreign enterprises, individuals and other economic organisations, including overseas Chinese and compatriots from Hong Kong and Macao, but also to China's enterprises registered outside its borders, which signed the agreements (contracts) on using foreign capital with the companies and other economic organisations within the borders of the People's Republic of China (MOFERT, 1984). Secondly, FDI included the use of foreign funds for co-operative ventures, co-operative development of oil resources, compensation trade, and sometimes processing and assembly arrangements for foreign firms, as well as investment in EJVs, CJVs and WFOEs. Since 1986, however, compensation trade and processing and assembly arrangements for foreign firms have no longer been included in the Chinese official statistics for FDI.
2. The austerity programme meant the adoption of tight fiscal and monetary policies to control inflation. This reduced the availability of funds for potential Chinese partners to form joint ventures.
3. Caution must be exercised when interpreting the significance of China as a major host of FDI. As noted by Liu (1993), Harrold and Lall (1993), UNCTD (1995), and Liu et al. (1997), there was some so-called pseudo-FDI contained in China's statistics. Indigenous Chinese firms teamed up with Chinese residents abroad to invest in China, thereby receiving the privileges and protection accorded to foreign investors. A World Bank report byHarrold and Lall (1993) guessed that the 'round-tripping' funds could account for as much as 25 per cent of gross foreign investment in China in 1992 (Lardy, 1995, p. 1067and Sicular, 1998). In recent years, the Chinese government has implemented a number of measures intended to reduce this problem, for example, the national treatment for foreign affiliates.

3. Country Characteristics and Foreign Direct Investment in China

3.1 INTRODUCTION

Following the description of the general development trends of inward FDI in China in chapter 2, the current chapter offers a systematic empirical study of its political, economic, cultural and geographic determinants at the national level. Although China has already become a major host of FDI inflows in recent years, empirical research on the relationship between country characteristics and FDI is still relatively limited. Among a few examples, Wang and Swain (1995) provide an econometric analysis of factors influencing foreign capital inflows into Hungary and China during the period 1978-92. However, their study suffers problems of inconsistencies in some numerical results and a lack of degrees of freedom as noted by Matyas and Korosi (1996).

Wei (1995), Liu et al. (1997) and Dees (1998) use panel data to analyse the determinants of FDI in China. Wei's work considers outward FDI from five source countries only, i.e. Japan, the United Kingdom, the United States, France and Germany, during the period 1987-90 in spite of the fact that the largest share of FDI in China is from Asian newly industrialised countries (NICs). Dees (1998) estimates a fixed-effects model for annually cumulative FDI outflows from 11 countries/regions over the period 1983-95 and implicitly assumes that all variables in the study are stationary.

This chapter is a revised and updated version of Liu et al. (1997). A panel data set is used which covers 22 home countries/regions over the period 1983-98 for contracted FDI and 19 home countries/regions over the period 1984-98 for realised FDI. Although foreign firms which invested in China are from more than 100 different countries and regions, FDI from the countries/regions included in our sample accounted for approximately 87 per cent of total contracted FDI and more than 88 per cent of total realised FDI in China.

This chapter extends existing studies in four ways. First, the most recent data are used to cover a longer time period. Second, the determinants of both contracted FDI and realised FDI are investigated. Third, unit root tests are carried out. Panel data analysis can suffer from a spurious regression problem when time-series data on variables trend consistently upwards over the sample period. The characteristics of the data are examined in this study via unit root tests in a panel data framework to avoid possible spurious regression. As mentioned in chapter 1, this is an important improvement over previous studies. Finally, more appropriate definitions of explanatory variables are adopted. Instead of using absolute figures such as GDP growth and wage rates for China, ratios of the Chinese figures to those of the home countries/regions are used. This is based on the belief that the FDI decision is often made after a comparison of political, economic, cultural and geographic conditions of both home and host countries.

The remainder of the chapter is organised as follows. Section 3.2 reviews the literature and outlines the hypotheses to be tested. The econometric model is discussed in section 3.3. Sections 3.4 and 3.5 describe data and methodology respectively. A newly proposed method by Im, Pesaran and Shin (1997) for a unit root test for panel data is discussed in section 3.5. Section 3.6 presents the empirical results. Finally, section 3.7 offers a conclusion.

3.2 LITERATURE REVIEW AND HYPOTHESES FORMATION

Corresponding to the rapid expansion of FDI in the world economy, a number of theories/paradigms have been developed to explain its existence and growth. Agarwal (1980), Dunning (1981, 1988), Cantwell (1991) and de Mello (1997) have provided general literature surveys. In Cantwell (1991) for instance, the market power approach, internalisation theory, eclectic paradigm, competitive international industry and macroeconomic development approaches are evaluated. New approaches have been emerging in more recent literature.

The evolutionary theory of Kogut and Zander (1993) contends that the firm does not arise out of market failure. Rather, it can be viewed as a social community whose productive knowledge defines a comparative advantage. Pitelis (1996) argues that demand-side deficiencies can provide an inducement for outward investments by transnational corporations. Nachum et al. (2000) suggest that the location decisions of multinational enterprises can be influenced by the comparative advantages and disadvantages of their home countries, and that the ownership advantages of the investing firms can reflect these advantages and disadvantages.

Many of the determinants identified by the above theories/paradigms have been tested in various empirical studies. For the purposes of this study, the literature review and hypothesis formation will focus on market size, costs of borrowing, wage rates, trade, exchange rates, political risk, geographic distance and cultural differences. These are also the most commonly tested variables in the literature.

3.2.1   Market Size

The market size hypothesis argues that inward FDI is a function of the market size of the host country. Davidson (1980), Moore (1993) and Braunerhjelm and Svensson (1996) suggest that the size of the host country's market can be supposed to capture demand and scale effects. For intermediate or final goods to be produced in a host country there must be significant demand for them. In other words, sufficient potential demand warrants production.

Alternatively, a larger market size is necessary to allow for the attainment of economies of scale. Since foreign investors are economically and strategically sensible, FDI occurs only when they anticipate that sales or output volumes can possibly exceed, at least, the various costs of operating in a relatively unfamiliar environment. Buckley and Casson (1981) argue that as the absolute value of a firm's share of the foreign market rises, so the total cost of local production (i.e. FDI) falls relative to that of exporting, due largely to the avoidance of rising international transport costs.

Bajo-Rubio and Sosvilla-Rivero (1994) and Loree and Guisinger (1995) argue that different types of FDI will be influenced to different degrees by the host market. Market-oriented FDI may be more concerned with the market size than export-oriented FDI. The market size is usually measured by GDP or GNP. Two types of variables are often used either separately or together in empirical studies: the change in GDP(GNP) in absolute terms and the growth rate of GDP(GNP).

The hypothesis that inward FDI is a function of the market size of the host country has received considerable support in many empirical analyses. Ajami and BarNiv (1984) and Grosse and Trevino (1996) conclude that the size of the home country market is positively related to the amount of FDI in the host country. In their studies, market size is used as a proxy for the number of home firms that could pursue international expansion. Clegg and Scott-Green (1999) find that the impact of market size on inward FDI varies considerably between groups of the European Community (EC) member countries. Driffield and Munday (2000) detect a positive and significant relationship between inward FDI and sales in the UK industry level. Other studies such as Lee and Mansfield (1996), Pain (1997) and Pain and Lansbury (1997) also provide support for the hypothesis.

On the other hand, Pitelis (1996) regards domestic demand deficiencies as an important reason for home country firms to invest abroad. Since market size can be used as a proxy for aggregate demand, then the size of the home country market may be negatively related to the amount of FDI in the host country.

One plausible way for firms to consider FDI is, as Pain (1993) and Barrell and Pain (1996) suggest, to take the total demand, i.e. the overall level of demand in both the home and the host countries, into account. An alternative way is to compare the relative change in size of the home and host country markets. If the host country market expands more rapidly than the home country market, the host country market becomes more attractive and home country firms become more willing to enter the host country. Gaining access to the rapidly growing host country market is one of many potential advantages in launching foreign as opposed to domestic investment. Because this study focuses on a comparison between home and host countries' characteristics, the following hypothesis is to be tested, i.e. *if the ratio of host country market size to the home country market size is higher, the higher is inward FDI in the host country*.

3.2.2   Costs of Borrowing

Aliber (1970) discusses the economic relationship between FDI and the cost of borrowing in the following way: if the cost of borrowing in the home country is lower than in the host country, home country firms can have a cost advantage over host country rivals, and are in better position to enter the host country market via FDI. This economic relationship is confirmed by Pain (1993, 1997), Barrell and Pain (1996), Grosse and Trevino (1996) and Pain and Lansbury (1997), among others. Barrell and Pain (1999) also conclude that the domestic availability of low-cost funding was a particularly important influence on the scale of Japanese FDI in the 1980s. Thus, *the higher the ratio of the host country borrowing cost to the home country cost, the higher will be inward FDI in the host country*.

However, the empirical results of Belderbos and Sleuwaegen (1996) find that borrowing cost contributes to the explanation of investment decisions of Japanese electronics firms in Western industrialised countries, but not in Asia. The empirical results in Culem (1988) also fail to support this hypothesis for US FDI in the EC.

Although it seems to be a conventional wisdom, the belief that the lower home country borrowing cost would lead to higher FDI in the host country is based on the following implicit assumption: foreign investors will raise all the funds they need in their overseas operations from their home countries. This may be of some use in explaining wholly owned subsidiaries, but may be less so in explaining joint ventures where indigenous partners also contribute.

3.2.3   Wage Rates

Dunning (1993) suggests that wage rates should have an impact on the location of production. Wages are an important part of total costs, especially in labour-intensive manufacturing. As one way of obtaining potential advantages over their rivals, firms may launch FDI to make use of the abundant supply of skilled and unskilled low-cost labour to lower their manufacturing costs. Incorporating this viewpoint, Frobel et al. (1980) use international division of labour to explain why firms relocate certain types of manufacturing operations away from their home bases, especially into developing countries. The standardisation of production processes allows operations to be fragmented with minimal skills according to the most desirable combinations of inputs. This gives firms the opportunity to manage production units across countries to exploit international differences in factor prices, especially wage rates (Kumar, 1994). Thus, the argument is that the lower the labour cost in the host country, the more attractive the host country is.

FDI is associated with the labour cost not only in the host country, but also in the home country. Braunerhjelm and Svensson (1996) argue that the average wage rates in a home country should be correlated with its human capital and can capture ownership advantages. In accordance with this argument, wage rates in the home country are likely to exert a positive impact on the propensity to invest in a host country. Culem (1988) claims that the labour cost differential between home and host countries is crucial in capturing the fact that domestic investment is the opportunity cost of foreign investment. Consequently, the lower the labour cost in the host country related to the home country of investors, the more attractive the host country is.

This relationship is confirmed by, for example, Woodward and Rolfe (1993), Pain (1993) and Kumar (1994). Moore (1993) only finds weak evidence on the presence of a relatively low wage rate as an important factor in explaining German manufacturing FDI from 1980 to 1988. However, in the study by Meyer (1995), the evidence from both survey data and regression analysis shows that FDI in Central and Eastern Europe is not mainly motivated by low labour costs in that area. The studies of Swedenborg (1979), Dunning (1980) and Veugelers (1991) yield a positive relationship between the host country's wage rates and FDI flows. Clegg and Scott-Green (1999) find that the wage variable is negatively associated with US FDI, but is positively associated with Japanese FDI in the EC. They argue that wage rates may reflect manpower qualification, specialisation and skill intensity (or labour quality) or productivity, which acts as a locational advantage and would be positively related to FDI flows.

Therefore, after all wages are productivity-adjusted, the economic logic behind the negative relationship between wage rates and FDI should stand. For the given productivity levels, *the lower the ratio of the host country's wage rates to the home country's wage rates, the higher will be the inward FDI in the host country*. This is in line with the results obtained by Pain (1997) and Pain and Lansbury (1997).

3.2.4 Bilateral Trade

For an individual firm, exports and FDI are the two alternative entry modes into a host country. Barrell and Pain (1997a, b) argue that the ownership advantages of firms allow a gradual substitution of local production (i.e. FDI) for exports. With the firm-specific, knowledge-based assets which serve as the ownership advantages *vis-à-vis* the host country's competitors, the firm can exploit economies of scale arising from the 'public goods' nature of such assets and have a cost advantage to dominate the higher fixed costs of local production in a host country. In other words, firms may set up a number of different plants to undertake horizontal direct investment, with little increase in the associated costs of adapting knowledge-based assets for local needs.

Moore (1993) indicates that, if the production cost disadvantages do not overwhelm the marketing savings, the firm may be willing to undertake FDI. It will set up production facilities in the host country to replace exports so as to obtain marketing cost savings. Savings obtained through FDI might include avoiding various tariff barriers and transportation costs. If other things remain the same, then the higher the international transportation costs and tariff/non-tariff trade barriers, the more the firm will undertake FDI in the host country. FDI caused by the host country's tariff/non-tariff trade barriers is consistent with the 'tariff jumping' hypothesis. If tariff/non-tariff trade barriers are low or absent, and if there are no other cost advantages in the host country, the home country firm may export its product. This export represents an equal amount of imports to the host country. Thus, for an individual firm, trade and FDI are substitutes.

However, trade and FDI can also be expected to be complements from a microeconomic perspective. As Pain (1993) and Barrell and Pain (1997a, b) stress, FDI may be undertaken in order to help promote market access and export sales by offering improved customer support. In other words, there is sales-related FDI, which is especially true for the services sector. Once the level of exports reaches a certain point, firms producing tradable goods may at that time invest abroad in consumer-orientated service facilities.

Exports may represent parent companies' supplies of intermediate goods such as machinery or product lines for their subsidiaries in the host country.

Similarly, imports from the home to host country may represent supplies of inputs or final products by the subsidiaries for the home country's market. This argument applies in particular for vertical and export-orientation FDI (Kumar, 1994).

Kogut and Chang (1996) posit a platform entry argument. Exports can serve as platforms for future expansion including direct investment in a host country. This is because firms with strong exports to the host country have invested in distribution channels and established brand labels. They have motivation to seek to preserve the value of these assets by shifting manufacturing investment into the host country when exports are more expensive than local production under some circumstances such as an overvalued home currency.

In addition, firms which have experienced international business exposure through exports can overcome their initial inhibition against expanding into a foreign market. They are more willing to move into newer markets. Thus, a steady rise in the volume of bilateral trade will generate additional FDI for an individual firm (Banerji and Sambharya, 1996).

At an aggregate level, the impact of bilateral trade on FDI is not clear-cut. Studies by Horst (1972) and Jeon (1992) indicate a negative relationship between imports and inward FDI in the host country because growing imports imply lower tariff/non-tariff trade barriers and therefore lead to a temporary fall in FDI. Wakasugi (1994) shows that Japan's export of passenger cars to the United States was replaced by FDI, and a major reason for this was a market distortion caused by voluntary export restraint (VER) imposed by the Japanese government. Blomstrom and Lipsey (1989) illustrate that, on average, FDI will substitute for and may ultimately eliminate trade flows in the case of US and Swedish cross-border invested firms.

On the other hand, Ajami and BarNiv (1984), Ray (1989) and Grosse and Trevino (1996) argue that bilateral trade and FDI may be viewed as complementary. More bilateral trade implies a higher level of integration between the home and host countries. This may enable home country firms as a whole to obtain more information on investment opportunities in the host market. Greater exports may encourage greater FDI into the host country. In addition, given an incentive to internalise the ownership advantage, firms have a greater incentive to invest where internalisation provides greater access to specific sources of comparative advantage in the host country (Maskus and Webster, 1995; Milner and Pentecost, 1996). Since, to a certain extent, comparative advantage can be revealed by trade performance, FDI could be expected to be positively related to bilateral trade. If we follow this line of reasoning, then *the higher the bilateral trade (exports and imports), the higher will be inward FDI in the host country*.

3.2.5　Exchange Rates

In the currency area approach, chiefly reflected in the writings of Aliber (1970), the pattern of FDI can be explained in terms of the existence of different currency areas. There are several channels through which FDI can be affected by exchange rates. Froot and Stein (1991) have discussed the relative *wealth* effect of exchange rates. A rise in the exchange rate in terms of the host country currency over the home country currency implies a depreciation of the host country currency. An exchange rate change will alter both real rates of return and the value of savings in terms of the host country's currency, and will lead to capital gains or losses on existing asset holdings and shifts in portfolio shares. A real depreciation of the host country currency favours home country purchasers of host country assets and therefore leads to an increase in inward FDI in the host country.

Cushman (1985, 1987) and Culem (1988) emphasise the effect of exchange rate changes on relative *labour costs*. A real depreciation of the host country currency allows home country investors to hire more labour for a given amount of the home country currency, and is therefore associated with an increase in inward FDI in the host country. In general, *the higher the ratio of the host country currency/US$ exchange rate to the home country currency/US$ exchange rate, the higher will be inward FDI in the host country*.

The study by Klein and Rosengren (1994) supports the significance of the relative wealth effect and fails to support the relative labour cost effect. Other studies hardly distinguish these two effects. Instead, a majority of investigations on the correlation between FDI and the exchange rate have come out in favour of the negative relationship between the two. These include Dewenter (1995), Grosse and Trevino (1996), Kogut and Chang (1996), Aristotelous and Fountas (1996), and Bayoumi and Lipworth (1997).

3.2.6　Country Risk

Firms tend to avoid any uncertainty or country risks. It may be obvious that internal political, economic, and social instability in the host country and the unfriendly attitude of the host country's government increases the uncertainty for potential investors, and will thereby have a negative impact on FDI inflows. In relative terms, *the higher the degree of home country risk in relation to the host country, the higher will be inward FDI in the host country*.

However, the empirical evidence can only be judged as mixed. Loree and Guisinger (1995) demonstrate a statistically significant relationship between the flow of FDI from the United States and the composite risk variable in 1982, but not in 1977. In the study by Tu and Schive (1995) political stability is no longer considered as a significant determinant of FDI in Taiwan in the regression analysis, although it is ranked at the top of the list by foreign affiliates managers. Therefore, Tu and Schive (1995) argue that political stability might be only a precondition for FDI, and is far less important in determining the amount invested. Nigh (1985) finds that the effect of political events on US manufacturing FDI depends on whether the host country is developed or less developed. FDI in developed countries appears to be influenced only by inter-nation conflict and co-operation. For the less developed countries, however, both inter-nation conflict and co-operation have an effect on FDI. Kobrin (1979) and Tallman (1988) have failed to confirm the significance of, and Grosse and Trevino (1996) have only found weak evidence for, the negative effect of country risk on inward FDI in the host country. Jun and Singh (1996) employ two proxies to capture different aspects of country risk: political risk indices developed by Business Environment Risk Intelligence (BERI) and work days lost in production. The significance of the former is greater for developing countries with high average FDI flows including China. In contrast, the latter is more significant for developing countries with low average FDI flows.

3.2.7   Geographic Distance

In the recent literature on economic geography, proximity to market or geographic distance is considered to be an important determinant of the choice of location of the production activity since market accessibility is one of the principle motivations for firms to invest abroad. In other words, geographic distance is negatively related to FDI inflows in the host country. Solocha and Soskin (1990, 1994) and Davidson (1980) argue that geographic proximity reduces informational and managerial uncertainty, lowers monitoring costs and allows the firm to become less exposed to risk. Solocha and Soskin (1994) also stress that the importance of geographic proximity is due to the fact that some raw materials and intermediate products are often supplied from home countries' sources. In terms of transportation costs, firms should prefer to invest in nearby countries. Therefore, *the greater the geographic distance between the home and host country, the higher will be the cost of obtaining information and managing an affiliate in the host market, and the smaller will be inward FDI in the host country*. Nevertheless, given the trend towards a more global business environment and the technological progress in communications and transport sectors, this effect is expected to diminish over time.

3.2.8   Cultural Differences

Davidson (1980) and Loree and Guisinger (1995) offer a detailed explanation about how cultural similarity encourages FDI. For instance, firms invested in a host country need to hire and train more local personnel to serve the new market. With cultural similarity, the time and investment required to bring these people to full efficiency may be less. In turn, their ability to seek more profits and to save more costs might possibly be increased. Based on the internationalisation process approach, which is rooted in the behavioural theory of the firm, Benito and Gripsrud (1992) also highlight the importance of cultural differences on the location decisions of FDI. They suppose that FDI undertaken by a firm typically takes place in a country that is culturally close to the home market. In sum, as in the case of geographic distance, *the greater the cultural differences between the home and host countries, the more difficult will be the acquisition of information and the management and monitoring of an affiliate in the host market, and therefore the smaller will be inward FDI in the host country*.

Previous findings by Grosse and Trevino (1996) have supported this relationship between cultural differences and FDI. The study by Lin (1996) indicates that relatively large cultural differences did disadvantage new Japanese FDI in 11 types of US manufacturing industries for the period 1976-90. Loree and Guisinger (1995) confirm that cultural difference had a significant effect on new US FDI in 1977, but not in 1982.

3.3 EMPIRICAL MODEL OF FOREIGN DIRECT INVESTMENT DETERMINANTS FOR CHINA

The discussion of hypotheses in section 3.2 points to the following relationship,

$$FDI = f(REWA, RGDP, RER, REX, RIM, RBC, RCR, TCD, GEOD) \quad (3.1)$$

where

FDI   =   the annual inflow of real foreign direct investment in China
REWA   =   the ratio of real Chinese wage rates to real home country wage rates
RGDP   =   the ratio of real Chinese GDP to real home country GDP
RER   =   the ratio of the real RMB/US$ exchange rate to real home country currency/US$ exchange rate
REX   =   real Chinese exports to the home country
RIM   =   real Chinese imports from the home country

RBC   =   the ratio of China's real lending interest rates to the home
           country's real lending interest rates
RCR   =   the ratio of country risk ratings for China to country risk
           ratings for the home country
TCD   =   total cultural difference between China and the home country
GEOD   =   geographic distance between China and the home country

Instead of assuming a simple linear relationship between the dependent
and independent variables, our model is of the log-linear form,

$$LFDI_{it} = \beta_1 LRW_{it} + \beta_2 LRGDP_{it} + \beta_3 LRER_{it} + \beta_4 LREX_{it} + \beta_5 LRIM_{it}$$
$$+ \beta_6 LRBC_{it} + \beta_7 LRCR_{it} + \beta_8 LTCD_{it} + \beta_9 LGEOD_{it} + v_{it}$$
$$i = 1, 2, \ldots N; t = 1, 2, \ldots T \qquad (3.2)$$

where L indicates logged values, i and t denote country/region and time
respectively, N is the total number of countries/regions in the sample, T is the
overall time period, and v represents a composite term including both
intercept and the error term, the assumptions for which will be discussed in
detail later. As the impacts of all independent variables in the model on FDI
are expected to occur either simultaneously with FDI or with a lag of less
than a year, no lag is considered. All factors could be seen as (weakly)
exogenous, allowing standard panel estimation techniques to be applied.

There are several advantages of adopting a log-linear functional form.
First, in the case of FDI in China, there are extreme values arising from
surges of inflows in some years and from Hong Kong as the dominant
investor. The use of logarithms may counteract this problem statistically.
Second, it can transform a likely non-linear relationship between inward FDI
in China and the explanatory variables into a linear one. Finally, the β_is in
the log-linear model (3.2) directly measure FDI elasticities with respect to the
explanatory variables. Alternatively, these coefficients may be interpreted as
the partial derivatives of the growth rate of FDI with respect to the growth
rate of the explanatory variables.

In this study two specifications of (3.2) are estimated. In Specification (I),
contracted FDI is employed as the dependent variable and is denoted by
FDIP. In Specification (II), actual or realised FDI is used as the dependent
variable and is denoted by FDIR. Contracted FDI inflows represent foreign
firms' planned direct investment in China. They normally differ from actual
FDI flows for any particular year, not only because part of contracted FDI
never materialises, but also because in many cases contracted FDI is to be
realised over a period of several years. Therefore, the political, economic,
cultural and geographic conditions in both home and host countries which

make a firm commit itself to contracted FDI can differ from those when FDI is actually realised. This creates a time lag between the signing of a contract and the subsequent realisations of planned amounts.

3.4 DATA

The analysis in this chapter is based on a panel of data for 22 home countries/regions over the period 1983-98 for contracted FDI and for 19 home countries/regions over the period 1984-98 for realised FDI. A list of these home countries/regions is presented in Appendix 3A. A few missing values for some observations (mainly from developing countries) are extrapolated. To remove the influence of inflation, all variables except cultural differences, country risk and geographic distance are adjusted by the relevant price indexes. Detailed information on the measurement of variables and sources of the data can also be found in the Appendix to this chapter.

It has been argued that official data on the nationality breakdown of FDI in China can be somewhat biased, partly because of the multinationality of overseas Chinese investors, and partly because of pseudo-FDI by indigenous Chinese firms which team up with Chinese residents abroad to invest in China, thereby receiving the privileges and protection accorded to foreign investors (see, for example, Liu 1993; Harrold and Lall, 1993; UNCTD, 1995, 1996). This latter process is sometimes termed 'round-tripping' investment. Consequently, one must use a degree of caution when interpreting the empirical results.

Before proceeding further, it would be of interest to note the general trends of FDI in China by country of origin, since it provides a direct indicator. A detailed description of the changing pattern of FDI stocks has been reported in section 2.2.1 of chapter 2. While Table 2.4 of chapter 2 lists the top 15 foreign investors in China in terms of the cumulative total FDI projects, and contracted and realised FDI for the period 1979-98, Table 3.1 here presents the flows of contracted and realised FDI by ten leading countries/areas for selected years between 1985 and 1998.

3.5 METHODOLOGY

We are interested in the long-run relationship between FDI and all its explanatory variables. To avoid possible spurious regression, it is essential to identify the order of integration of each variable before any sensible regression analysis can be performed. There are two common situations in which long-run relationships can be identified. First, all variables are

Table 3.1 FDI in China, the major source countries, 1984-98

US$ million

	Contracted FDI in China				
	1985	1989	1993	1995	1998
Total	5932	5600	111436	91282	52102
HK/Macao	4134	3160	73939	40996	17613
U.S.	1152	641	6813	7471	6484
Japan	471	439	2960	7592	2749
Singapore	76	111	2954	8666	3002
U. K.	44	32	1988	3577	1682
Thailand	15	57	1074	638	280
Germany	20	149	249	1660	2375
Australia	14	83.6	638	1257	699
Canada	9	42	1184	982	947
France	50	10	236	642	489

	Realised FDI in China				
	1985	1989	1993	1995	1998
Total	1661	3392	27515	37521	45463
HK/Macao	956	2077	17861	20060	18508
U.S.	357	284	2063	3083	3898
Japan	315	356	1324	3108	3400
Singapore	10	84	490	1851	3404
U. K.	71	29	221	914	1175
Thailand	9	13	83	288	205
Germany	24	81	56	386	737
Australia	14	44	110	233	272
Canada	9	17	137	257	317
France	33	5	141	287	715

Sources: MOFERT, Almanac of China's Foreign Economic Relations and Trade, various issues

cointegrated. In general, a set of variables is cointegrated if the following two conditions are satisfied simultaneously: (1) each variable is integrated of order unity; and (2) there exists some linear combination of the variables that is integrated of order zero (i.e. stationary). Second, there is no reason why a long-run relationship would not exist between I(0) variables. In this case, the question of cointegration would not then arise. In neither case would there be a problem of spurious regression.

Therefore, before proceeding to the estimation of equations, all variables are tested for a unit root. By so doing, we are able to identify the possible long-run relationships between FDI and all its explanatory variables and therefore avoid possible spurious regression. In this chapter and chapters 4, 6 and 7, the unit root test for panel data proposed by Im, Pesaran and Shin (1997) (hereafter denoted as the IPS test) is employed. Compared with conventional time-series tests, the IPS test has substantially higher power (Coakley and Kulasi, 1997; Lee et al. 1997). Given the relatively short sample periods employed, conventional time-series tests are unlikely to be powerful enough to distinguish between unit root and near unit root behaviour.

The IPS test statistic referred to as the t-bar statistic is based on the average value of the Augmented Dickey-Fuller (ADF) test statistics. Im, Pesaran and Shin (1997) argue that the IPS test procedure is superior to two existing panel data unit root test approaches advanced by Quah (1992, 1994) and Levin and Lin (1992, 1993) and is simple compared with the other test approaches. This method has been used in a number of studies, for example, Lee et al. (1997) and McCoskey and Selden (1998). Because almost all the time series exhibit clear trends, we use the ADF with trend regression of order p_i which can be determined by the Akaike Information Criterion (AIC) criterion. This is because the AIC criterion is more suitable than other criteria for a short time span.

The ADF test is based on the following equation with trend

$$\Delta y_{it} = c_i + \gamma_i trend + \alpha_i y_{i,t-1} + \sum_{j=1}^{p_i} \rho_{ij} \Delta y_{i,t-j} + \upsilon_{it}$$
$$i = 1, ..., N; t = 1, ..., T \tag{3.3}$$

where y_{it} is the variable under consideration, Δ is the first order difference operator, $j = 1, 2, ..., p_i$ is the lag length of Δy_{it}, υ_{it} is the error term and is independent and identically distributed, and ρ_{ij} is the estimated vector of coefficients on the augmented lagged changes. The null hypothesis of unit roots then becomes $\alpha_i = 0$ for all i.

The standardised t-bar statistic takes the form:

$$\bar{\Psi}_{\bar{t}} = \frac{\frac{1}{N}\sum_{i=1}^{N} t_{iT}(p_i, \rho_i) - \frac{1}{N}\sum_{i=1}^{N} E[t_{iT}(p_i, 0) \mid \beta_i = 0]}{\sqrt{\frac{1}{N^2}\sum_{i-1}^{N} V[t_{iT}(p_i, 0) \mid \beta_i = 0]}} \tag{3.4}$$

where $t_{iT}(p_i, \rho_i)$ is the individual ADF statistic. The values of $E[t_T(p_i,0) \mid \alpha_i = 0]$ and $V[t_T(p_i,0) \mid \alpha_i = 0]$ are tabulated in IPS. Under the null hypothesis of a unit root, both LM-bar and t-bar statistics have a standard normal distribution. Under the alternative hypothesis of stationarity, the statistics diverge to negative infinity.

As argued in chapter 1, the use of panel data is appropriate to analyse the determinants of China's FDI inflows. This is because it takes into consideration the diversity and the specificity of unobservable behaviour of different investors, which have not been included in the regression. Generally, a panel data set can be estimated in any of three ways, depending on whether the individual cross-sectional effects are considered to be constant, fixed or random. The corresponding statistical models are the ordinary least squares (OLS) model, error components (EC) or random effects (RE) model, and least squared dummy variable (LSDV) or fixed effects (FE) model. Unobservable heterogeneity is accommodated by both the RE and FE models.

These three models have their own advantages and disadvantages. The OLS model is simple to estimate, but the assumption that the unobservable individual-specific effects do not differ is very strong and unlikely to hold in most cases. The FE model allows variation in these effects, but including dummy variables as extra regressors makes it less efficient than the RE model because of the loss of degrees of freedom. Finally, the RE model relegates the unobservable individual-specific effects into the error term and assumes that they are uncorrelated with the regressors. Violation of this assumption may cause the RE model to produce biased and inconsistent estimates.

Three tests are usually applied to identify the best statistical model. They are the likelihood ratio (LR) test for the FE model against the OLS model, the Lagrange multiplier (LM) test for the RE model against the OLS model, and the Hausman specification (HS) test for the FE model against the RE model. The procedure for restriction tests and model selection is discussed in Judge et al. (1985), Hsiao (1986), Baltagi (1995) and Greene (2000).

It must be noted that (3.2) contains two time-invariant variables of total cultural differences (TCD) and geographic distance (GEOD). The application of the FE model will lead to a problem of perfect multicollinearity. Therefore, only the RE and the OLS models are estimated and compared with each other. The basic idea behind the statistical test is as follows: if individual effects do not exist, OLS estimators are the best linear unbiased estimators and GLS estimators are inefficient and vice versa.

The main difference between the OLS and RE model lies in the assumption about v_{it}. v_{it} can be decomposed into two terms:

$$v_{it} = u_i + \varepsilon_{it} \tag{3.5}$$

The OLS model assumes that $u_i = u$, which is a constant. In the RE model, u_i denotes the ith individual, year-invariant unobserved heterogeneity, which is assumed to be random, independent and identically distributed, i.e. $u_i \sim IID(0, \sigma_u^2)$. Both models assume that ε_{it} is the remainder disturbance and varies with individuals and time. It can be thought of as the usual disturbance in the regression and is assumed to be normally distributed with a mean of zero and constant variance.

To choose between the OLS and RE models, Breusch and Pagan (1980) have derived the following Lagrange multiplier test (LM1) to identify the existence of heterogeneity with the null hypothesis $\sigma_u^2 = 0$:

$$\lambda_{LM1} = \frac{NT}{2(T-1)} [1 - \frac{\varepsilon'(I_N \otimes J_T)\varepsilon}{\varepsilon' \varepsilon}]^2 \tag{3.6}$$

where the statistic λ_{LM1} is asymptotically distributed as $\chi^2(1)$, I_N is an identity matrix of dimension N, J_T is a matrix of ones of dimension T, and $\otimes$ is Kronecker product. Under the null hypothesis of no heterogeneity, a large value of the test statistic favours the RE model against the OLS model.

3.6 EMPIRICAL RESULTS

To test for unit roots for individual variables, we first apply the ADF tests on each time series and find that few time series are stationary. However, as is well known, unless the number of observations is quite large, ADF tests tend to fail to reject the null unit root hypothesis. With only 16 annual observations in the time series, the IPS test is applied to re-examine the properties of the data in a panel framework.

The descriptive statistics and panel data unit root test results for each variable (in log form) are presented in Table 3.2. Except for LRER, the coefficients on all variables are statistically significant at the 10% level. This suggests that all variables except LRER are stationary and there exists a possible long-run relationship among these variables. Given that LRER is an I(1) variable, statistically it would be more appropriate to test the variable in

Table 3.2 Descriptive statistics and unit root test results

Variable	Maximum	Minimum	Mean	Std. Dev.	t-bar Test
LFDIP	11.1213	-5.2769	4.1079	2.6510	-2.3232**
LFDIR	10.0561	-4.2469	3.6163	2.5401	-6.1971***
LREWA	-1.0084	-5.2342	-3.4369	0.9091	-4.5699***
LRGDP	2.6705	-3.1720	0.2657	1.3490	-4.8278***
LRER	2.2672	-6.7788	-0.6501	2.2148	2.9707
LREX	10.3917	3.0798	6.4702	1.5740	-4.6549***
LRIM	10.3368	4.1786	6.8562	1.2588	-3.4246***
LRBC	0.7630	-1.2967	-0.1741	0.4054	-1.8767*
LRCR	0.5618	-0.6129	-0.2555	0.1924	-1.6877*
LTCD	5.1475	3.2189	4.6212	0.4054	
LGEOD	6.0591	3.9890	5.3611	0.5004	

Notes:
1. L indicates logged values. LFDIP = the annual inflow of real contracted FDI in China; LFDIR = the annual inflow of real realised FDI in China; LREWA = the ratio of real effective Chinese wage rates to the real effective home country's wage rates; LRGDP = the ratio of real Chinese GDP to real home country's GDP; LRER = the ratio of the real RMB/US$ exchange rate to real home country's currency/US$ exchange rate; LREX = real Chinese exports to the home country; LRIM = real Chinese imports from the home country; LRBC = the ratio of China's real lending interest rates to the home country's real lending interest rates; LRCR = the ratio of country risk ratings for China to country risk ratings for the home country; LTCD = total cultural difference between China and the home country; LGEOD = geographic distance between China and the home country.
2. There are 352 observations for all variables expect LFDIR for which only 285 observations are included.
3. Std. Dev. represents the standard deviation.
4. ***, **, * denote significance at the level of 1%, 5% and 10%, respectively. The critical values are -2.57, -1.96, and -1.65 at the confidence level of 1%, 5% and 10%, respectively.

its first difference form. If it is stationary, the first difference of LRER can then be included in the equations to be estimated. However, LRER is defined as the ratio of the real RMB/US$ exchange rate to the real home country's currency/US$ exchange rate. The first difference of this ratio does not make much economic sense. Given our interest in the long-run relationships between FDI and its explanatory variables, we pay special attention to the

Table 3.3 Parameter estimates of elasticities for contracted FDI in China

Variable	(I)		(II)	
	OLS	RE	OLS	RE
Constant	-3.0915	-2.4845	-4.6128**	-3.7437
	(2.1339)	(3.0161)	(1.8970)	(2.6374)
LREWA	-0.7847***	-0.9253***	-0.7903***	-0.9342***
	(0.1303)	(0.1910)	(0.1296)	(0.1930)
LRGDP	0.6037***	0.6949***	0.6768***	0.7541***
	(0.0482)	(0.1421)	(0.0939)	(0.1283)
LRERR	0.0693	0.0674	--	--
	(0.0482)	(0.0783)		
LREX	0.9191***	0.8321***	0.9396***	0.8414***
	(0.1306)	(0.1434)	(0.1310)	(0.1433)
LRIM	0.6294***	0.7034***	0.6582***	0.7285***
	(0.1901)	(0.1892)	(0.1865)	(0.1885)
LRBCR	-0.6416**	-0.4528	-0.5101**	-0.3465
	(0.2683)	(0.3042)	(0.2586)	(0.2836)
LRCR	-2.4076***	-2.6754***	-2.7023***	-2.9216***
	(0.6826)	(0.8391)	(0.6421)	(0.7978)
LTCD	-1.4074***	-1.6610***	-1.3911***	-1.6445***
	(0.2933)	(0.4222)	(0.2992)	(0.4284)
LGEOD	-0.0182	-0.0041	0.1646	0.1481
	(0.2701)	(0.3791)	(0.2288)	(0.3398)
R^2	0.6436	0.6403	0.6421	0.6387
Test: λ_{LM1}	2.10		3.00*	

Notes:
1. Standard errors are in parentheses.
2. ***, ** and * indicate that the coefficient is significantly different from zero at the 1%, 5% and 10% levels, respectively.

regressions when the LRER variable is excluded. For the purpose of comparison, however, the regression results with LRER included are also provided in Tables 3.3 and 3.4.

Table 3.3 contains the estimation results for contracted FDI. The estimates from the OLS and RE models are provided in pairs. In the first pair, the ratio of the real RMB/US$ exchange rate to the real home country's currency/US$ exchange rate (LRER) is included. The insignificant λ_{LM1} of 2.10 suggests that the OLS is statistically a better model than the RE. In the second pair,

LRER is excluded. The statistically significant λ_{LM1} statistics of 3.00 indicates that the RE rather than OLS model is preferred. This suggests that there is heterogeneity among investors from different countries. A simple ordinary least squares regression of a straightforward pooling of all observations without considering heterogeneity will lead to an unacceptable degree of aggregation bias or even meaningless results.

Most results in Table 3.3 are consistent with expectations. In any regression, the coefficient on relative wage rates has the expected negative sign and is highly significant. Relative GDP, real exports and imports (LREX and LRIM) also have the expected positive sign and are highly significant. All this suggests that China's relatively cheaper labour force, its more rapidly expanding market size and its trading links with the home countries are among the strong determinants of contracted FDI.

Being non-stationary in level, the relative exchange rate variable should not enter the long-run regression model. However, if we do include it in regressions merely for the purpose of comparison, the variable has the expected positive sign but is statistically insignificant. This in turn suggests that there is no long-run relationship between the exchange rate and China's FDI inflows. If there is an impact, it must be contained in the short run.

The borrowing cost variable has a negative sign in all regressions. This seems to be contrary to the conventional wisdom. The result implies that the higher the borrowing costs in China, the lower will be inward FDI in China. One possible explanation is that the dominant form of FDI in China is joint venture. Given the relative high borrowing cost in China, potential foreign partners can have a borrowing cost advantage if they borrow from the home country, but Chinese partners may have trouble in raising funds. Thus, it would be difficult to form joint ventures. Put another way, there can be a negative relationship between the relatively higher borrowing cost and inward FDI in China.

The country risk variable has the expected negative sign and is highly significant. This is slightly different from the result of Liu et al (1997) where the variable has the same sign but is statistically insignificant. This may suggest that, with more observations the Institutional Investor's ratings, which are a good indicator for credit risk assessment in the banking sector, can also be a satisfactory proxy for country risk evaluation in relation to FDI.

The coefficient on the cultural differences variable has the right sign and is highly significant. This indicates the importance of cultural influences on inward FDI in China. As mentioned in chapters 1 and 2, the bulk of China's inward investment has been made by ethnic Chinese. This is the unique feature of FDI in China. Liu (1993, p.142) also notes that overseas Chinese businessmen are mainly motivated by family and local links when they make direct investments in China. There is great affection for the motherland and especially for the home of origin and the commitment to the family have driven these overseas Chinese to visit and invest in China since the Chinese government adopted the policy of opening up to the outside world. If this sentiment motivates the FDI from overseas Chinese, then the mutual trust originating from the family and local connections and language similarity provides a solid ground for business deals between them and local Chinese. Put another way, culture similarities are the main reason for FDI from overseas Chinese.

The coefficient on the geographic distance variable is statistically insignificant. This is different from the result obtained by Wei (1995) where a negative and significant coefficient is found. One tentative explanation is that the progress in communications and transport technologies allows better co-ordination of cross-border activities so that geographic distance has become less important in international business. Thus, this variable does not enter into the explanation of the level of FDI inflows in China.

However, as discussed in section 3.2, geographic distance is positively associated with the cost of obtaining information and managing an affiliate in the host market, and therefore can be a rough measure of international transaction costs. Technical advance may to some extent reduce international transaction costs but geographic distance should be at least negatively related to FDI inflows. In our results the coefficient on this variable is sometimes positive, and this is not consistent with the expectation. While it apparently does not play a role in influencing the level of FDI flows, geographic distance is found to be a significant determinant of FDI intensities as will be shown in chapter 6.

Table 3.4 provides the estimation results for realised FDI. Compared with Table 3.3, the determinants of realised FDI seem to be very consistent with those of contracted FDI. The coefficients on wage rates, country risk, cultural differences have the expected negative sign, and are all highly significant at the 1% level. Similarly, the GDP, export and import variables are all positively signed and highly significant. As in the case of contracted FDI, geographic distance dose not enter into the explanation of the level of realised FDI.

One noticeable difference in the determinants for contracted and realised FDI is that the coefficient on relative borrowing costs is persistently negative and statistically significant. This may reinforce the argument raised when contracted FDI is explained. The joint venture is the main type of FDI in China. When a joint venture project is contracted, it may not be necessary for the partners to commit funds. However, if the relative borrowing cost is high in China, the Chinese partner may face problems in fundraising to form the joint venture. If this is the case, there will be a fall in realised FDI. Thus, the

Table 3.4 Parameter estimates of elasticities for realised FDI in China

Variable	(I) OLS	(I) RE	(II) OLS	(II) RE
Constant	-6.3874***	-2.8646	-7.0064***	-3.7847
	(2.0917)	(3.6729)	(1.6726)	(3.2455)
LREWA	-0.6626***	-1.4551***	-0.6668***	-1.4240***
	(0.1358)	(0.2267)	(0.1355)	(0.2238)
LRGDP	0.4719***	0.5952***	0.5028***	0.6184***
	(0.0969)	(0.1525)	(0.0817)	(0.1412)
LRERR	0.0283	0.0424	--	--
	(0.0447)	(0.0926)		
LREX	1.0355***	0.7132***	1.0429***	0.7344***
	(0.1403)	(0.1663)	(0.1381)	(0.1640)
LRIM	0.5313***	0.7267***	0.5433***	0.7296***
	(0.1826)	(0.1858)	(0.1818)	(0.1843)
LRBCR	-0.8406***	-0.6423**	-0.7828***	-0.6079**
	(0.2529)	(0.2857)	(0.2472)	(0.2729)
LRCR	-2.4366***	-1.8969***	-2.5591***	-2.0201***
	(0.6931)	(0.7734)	(0.6447)	(0.7339)
LTCD	-0.7443***	-1.6207***	-0.7393***	-1.5558***
	(0.2811)	(0.5421)	(0.2825)	(0.5235)
LGEOD	-0.0590	-0.2812	0.0164	-0.1869
	(0.2154)	(0.4670)	(0.1736)	(0.4234)
R^2	0.7284	0.6925	0.7281	0.6966
Test: λ_{LM1}	33.63***		34.80***	

Notes:
1. Standard errors are in parentheses.
2. ***, ** and * indicate that the coefficient is significantly different from zero at the 1%, 5% and 10% levels, respectively.

relative borrowing cost would have a significantly negative impact on realised FDI.

As in the case of Dees (1998), we include a dummy variable which equals 1 in 1990 and zero otherwise to capture the Tiananmen Square incident. We find similar results: the coefficient on this dummy is negative and significant at the 1% level in the estimation results for both contracted and realised FDI. This reinforces the argument for country risk, i.e. the political situation in the host country has an important influence on the planning and materialisation of FDI projects. The inclusion of this dummy does not have considerable impact on the magnitude and significance level of other variables and therefore detailed results are not presented here.

In summary, the empirical results from this study indicate that, relative wage rates, relative market size, exports and imports, country risk and cultural differences are the highly significant determinants of both contracted and realised FDI inflows in China. The relative exchange rate does not have a long-run relationship with all other variables, and therefore does not enter into the explanation of FDI in China. Geographical distance is not a significant explanatory variable for the level of either contracted or realised FDI. Given that the main type of inward FDI in China is the joint venture, the borrowing cost would act as a negative determinant.

Liu et al. (1997) find that relative wage rates, relative exchange rates, exports and imports are the common determinants of both contracted and realised FDI inflows in China, but relative GDP and total cultural differences are the specific determinants of contracted FDI. As they argue, the political, economic and cultural conditions under which FDI is planned are likely to be different from those under which FDI is realised, so that the determinants of contracted and realised FDI may not coincide. The current study suggests that contracted and realised FDI could have the same set of determinants. The more consistent results may be due to the fact that the current study employs a sample covering a longer time period during which the investment environment in China became more mature and stable.

Section 2.2.1 of chapter 2 suggests that the position of China as a major host for FDI in recent years is mainly due to the overwhelming contribution by overseas Chinese. In terms of FDI stock in China, contributions from developed countries are very limited. The econometric results in this study indicate the importance of cultural differences in attracting FDI from some neighbouring Asian countries or regions, especially from overseas Chinese investors. However, it may be useful to discuss why other significant determinants identified in the study could not attract more FDI from Western developed countries.

Recent FDI theory tends to suggest that multinationals are more important in total activity when countries are similar in incomes (size) than in relative factor endowments (Markusen and Venables, 1998). This relationship has been confirmed in this study and it follows that the failure to attract significant amounts of FDI from developed countries is partly caused by the still limited absolute size of the Chinese market. Imamura (1999) suggests that multinationals would only target families with annual incomes over RMB 30,000 (approximately £2,500) as their consumers. In 1995, such families were less than 1 per cent of the total families in China. This means that the Chinese market size in 1995 was only similar to that of Denmark. Even in 2000, China would have a market size only similar to that of

Germany. The uneven income distribution in China further reduced the level of total market demand. As a result, though its potential is great, the current Chinese market size should not be exaggerated.

With the continuous increase in average salaries in the coastal areas the advantage of low labour costs has been gradually weakened (Imamura, 1999). In addition, because of the lack of qualified senior managers in China highly paid expatriates are often sent to China. For instance, in one joint venture the salaries of 49 foreign technical experts and managers exceeded the salaries of nearly 4000 local Chinese employees in the venture (Wang, 1994, p.130). The annual salary of an American executive was originally US$ 200,000 when he worked in the United States, but increased to US$ 300,000 when he worked in China (Imamura, 1999). Salaries paid to foreign employees only would substantially reduce the profit a subsidiary could make. The increasing labour cost also negatively affects FDI inflows from developed countries because their investments are large and require more senior managers.

Other factors which deter FDI inflows from Western developed countries include low return rates in the short run in some industries (Imamura, 1999) and problems with the protection of intellectual property rights (Wang, X., 1998). These influences are not captured by our econometric models in this study and need to be addressed by case studies.

In addition, while our econometric models have captured heterogeneity among home countries, the events which caused the heterogeneity may need to be identified by other means. For instance, Zhang (2000) suggests that the small FDI from the United States is closely associated with troubled Sino-US relations. Wang (1999, p.95) indicates that because of poor relations with the United States in 1995, China not only cancelled the order of Boeing air planes to purchase airbuses from Europe, but also awarded a joint project on the production of buses to Daimler-Benz instead of Ford. Furthermore, some politicians in the United States often criticise US firms for transferring technologies to China. All these affect the inflows of FDI into China.

3.7 CONCLUSIONS

In this chapter the determinants of contracted and realised inward FDI in China are analysed based on a panel of data for 22 home countries/regions over the period 1983-98 for contracted FDI and for 19 home countries/regions over the period of 1984-98 for realised FDI. Investments from these countries/regions accounted for approximately 87 per cent of the total contracted FDI and more than 88 per cent of the total realised FDI in

China during the sample time period. Therefore, the conclusions generated could be viewed as relatively general.

One important feature of the current study is that, where appropriate, the explanatory variables are measured in relative terms. We assume that rational investors would compare the home and host political, economic, cultural and geographical conditions before they decide to implement any FDI projects.

The unit root test results indicate that the relative real exchange rate is not stationary in level and therefore does not enter into the long-run relationship with all other variables. The statistical tests show that the random effects models are preferable to the ordinary least square models when the relative exchange rate is excluded from the regressions. This suggests that the behaviour of investors from different origins may be different.

The empirical results show that both contracted and realised FDI could be influenced by the same set of country characteristics. FDI inflows are positively associated with China's relative market size and economic integration represented by real exports and imports, but negatively related to China's relative real wage rates, country risk and cultural differences. All these results are consistent with our expectations. Geographic distance is not a significant determinant of the level of FDI in China.

Although theory generally predicts a negative relationship between cultural differences and FDI inflows, the Chinese experience has offered an extreme example. The bulk of FDI in China has been contributed by overseas Chinese with such common cultural background as affection for the home of origin and commitment to the family.

The main type of FDI in China is the joint venture. Relatively high borrowing costs in China would cause problems in fundraising by potential Chinese partners and would eventually have a negative impact on FDI inflows. This result appears to challenge the conventional wisdom that relatively higher borrowing costs in a host country would lead home country firms to gain a cost advantage and invest more in the host.

This chapter focuses on the relative home and host country characteristics. Firm and industry-specific influences are beyond the scope of the current analysis. As suggested by Grosse and Trevino (1996), the inclusion of firm and industry-specific factors may further enhance the explanatory power of the model.

The findings from this study have important implications for the future development of FDI in China. Although the absolute size of the Chinese market is still limited as argued by Imamura (1999), China has experienced rapid economic growth. During the Ninth Five-Year Plan period (1996-2000) for instance, the average annual growth rate was over 8 per cent. The Tenth Five-Year Plan (2001-05) specifies the main tasks of China's economic and social development as to maintain a relatively high growth rate for the national economy, achieve noticeable results in strategic adjustment of the economic structure, and enhance the quality and efficiency of economic growth so that a solid basis can be established for doubling China's 2000 GDP by the year 2010. As a result, rapid economic growth is expected to continue and the potential market is extremely large. The fact that investment from the major Western countries is still very limited suggests significant potential for further growth of inward FDI in China. Zhang (2000) finds that FDI from the United States is primarily motivated by market access while that from Hong Kong is export-oriented. The Chinese economy is expected to continue its quick expansion, as will the relative size of the Chinese market.

China's foreign trade has expanded at an even higher rate than its national economy. In 1978 China ranked 32nd in the world league table for foreign trade (MOFERT, 1995/96, p.19). In 1999, China's total foreign trade reached US$ 360.6 billion and this made China the ninth-largest trading country in the world (People's Daily, Overseas Edition, 13 March 2000). In 2000, this figure is expected to exceed US$ 400 billion (Zhu, 2000). With rapid economic growth, this development trend of foreign trade is well set to be continued. As a result, FDI inflows which are found to be positively affected by trade will also expand.

While labour costs in the coastal areas have risen quickly, they are still much lower than developed and many developing countries. The cost advantage will still be an important attraction for FDI. The key problem is to raise the quality of labour. More technical and managerial education and training are needed to meet the increasing demand for qualified senior managers, scientists and technicians. By doing so, the number of foreign employees in foreign-invested enterprises in China can be reduced so that average wage rates in these firms can be substantially lowered.

China's business environment needs to be further improved. One important aspect is the protection of intellectual property rights. During the process of entry into the WTO, China needs to further improve its trade and FDI policy regimes. This will help China to attract more FDI.

APPENDIX 3A DATA SOURCES

This analysis is based on a panel of data for 22 home countries/regions over the period 1983-98 for contracted FDI and for 19 home countries/regions over the period of 1984-98 for realised FDI. The 22 home countries/regions are the United States, Canada, Australia, Japan, New Zealand, Austria, Belgium, Denmark, France, Germany, Italy, the Netherlands, Norway, Spain, Sweden, Switzerland, United Kingdom, Indonesia, Hong Kong, Malaysia, Singapore and Thailand. The 19 home countries/regions are the United States, Canada, Australia, Japan, New Zealand, Belgium, Denmark, France, Germany, Italy, the Netherlands, Spain, Sweden, United Kingdom, Indonesia, Hong Kong, Malaysia, Singapore and Thailand.

A more detailed description of the sources of data and the measurement of variables is given below.

Variable	Measurement and Sources of Data
FDIP	The real contracted annual inflow of foreign direct investment in China, derived from the nominal contracted FDI inflows deflated by the GDP index of China. Sources: *Almanac of Foreign Economic Relations and Trade of China* and *China Foreign Economic Statistical Yearbook*. A better deflator is possibly the capital goods index as used in Moore (1993), but a similar index (the price index of investment in fixed assets) is available for 1993 onwards only in China.
FDIR	The real realised annual inflow of foreign direct investment in China, derived from the nominal realised FDI inflows deflated by the GDP index of China. Sources: *Almanac of Foreign Economic Relations and Trade of China* and *China Foreign Economic Statistical Yearbook*.
REWA	The relative real effective wage rate, defined as the ratio of the change in real Chinese wage rates to real home country wage rates. All wages are productivity-adjusted. Productivity is derived by the ratio of GDP to the total labour force of the country. Sources: *Yearbook of Labour Statistics*, *World Development Indicators* and *International Financial Statistical Yearbook*.
REX and RIM	China's real exports to, and real imports from, the home country. Source: *China Statistical Yearbook* and *China Foreign Economic Statistical Yearbook*. The deflator used to convert the nominal values into real terms is the GDP deflator of China.

Variable	Measurement and Sources of Data
RGDP	The relative real GDP, defined as the ratio of real Chinese GDP to real home country GDP. Source: *World Development Indicators*.
RER	The relative real exchange rate, defined as the ratio of the real Ren-Min-Bi (RMB)/US$ exchange rate to the real home country currency/US$ exchange rate. The real exchange rate is derived from the official exchange rate deflated by the CPI deflator. Sources: *International Financial Statistical Yearbook* and *World Development Indicators*. The data on Hong Kong are obtained from *Hong Kong (Annual Review)*.
RBC	Relative real borrowing costs defined as the ratio of China's real lending interest rate to the home country's real lending interest rate. The real lending interest rate is derived from the nominal lending rate deflated by the CPI deflator. Sources: *International Financial Statistical Yearbook* and *World Development Indicators*. Hong Kong data is from the *Monthly Statistical Bulletin*.
RCR	Relative country risk defined as the ratio of annual country risk ratings for China to annual country risk ratings for the home country. The ratings are scaled from 0 to 100. The higher the rating, the lower the chance of banking default. Source: *Institutional Investor*.
GEOD	The geographic distance between China and the home country/region. It is measured by the geographic distance between the home country's capital and China's capital, Beijing. Source: *Atlas of the World*.
TCD	Total cultural differences. This is the total cultural difference between China and the home country. Hofstede (1980) developed indices to measure four dimensions of cultural difference related to management. These include power distance, uncertainty avoidance, individuality and masculinity/femininity. As constructed by Grosse and Goldberg (1991) and Grosse and Trevino (1996), the total cultural difference is the sum of the absolute values of the four-dimension differences. This measure is similar to the one developed by Kogut and Singh (1988), who divide the squares of the four-dimension differences by their variances and sum these values. Since China was not in Hofstede's sample, we follow Pan (1996) and use the ratings for Taiwan as a surrogate measure for China.

4. The Regional Distribution of Foreign Direct Investment in China

4.1 INTRODUCTION

The geographical distribution of foreign direct investment (FDI) in China is characterised by its concentration in coastal areas. Although FDI has flowed into every province, autonomous region and central municipality, the amount in the inland areas is insignificant. As indicated in chapter 2, approximately 88 per cent of the cumulative FDI over the period 1979-98 is in the eastern (coastal) regions, while the remaining 12 per cent is located in the central and western regions (see also Figure 4.1). After an examination of the determinants of inward FDI in China at the national level in chapter 3, we now assess the factors that influence the regional distribution of inward FDI within China. The Chinese government particularly encourages further inflows of FDI into the central and western regions. An understanding of the regional characteristics influencing locational decisions is essential.

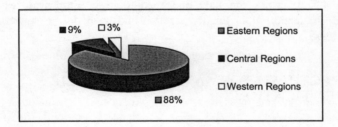

Source: As Table 2.6

Figure 4.1 Realised FDI inflows by region

Previous studies of spatial patterns of FDI in China can be divided into two groups. The first group provides detailed descriptive analysis. For instance, Kueh (1992) and Mee-kau (1993) discuss the causes of shifts in the regional distribution of FDI and their policy implications. Zhang (1994) analyses the determinants of the sub-regional distribution of foreign investment within Guangdong province. Henley et al. (1999) also mention the unevenness of the distribution of FDI inflows by province.

The second group of studies focuses on econometric estimation. Gong (1995) carries out cross-section regression analyses of the determinants of foreign investment inflows into 174 Chinese cities. Head and Ries (1996) examine the influences on locational decisions of 931 foreign investment projects in 54 Chinese cities. Broadman and Sun (1997) and Coughlin and Segev (2000) undertake a cross-section regression to examine the relationship between FDI and various independent variables. They use the sum of total yearly FDI inflows to 29 provinces and municipalities for the dependent variable. Chen (1997) and Cheng and Kwan (2000) estimate the effects of the determinants of FDI using panel data for 29 provinces and municipalities over the period 1987–94 and the period 1985–95, respectively.

This chapter is an updated version of Wei et al. (1999), and analyses the determinants of the regional distribution of FDI within China using a panel data set covering 28 provinces and municipalities over the period 1983–98 for contracted FDI and 1986–98 for realised FDI. It aims to improve on the previous panel data analyses in this area by examining the econometric properties before a statistical model is chosen and providing more robust evidence. Similar to chapter 3, this chapter extends the existing studies by covering a longer time period to make use of the most recent data, and by investigating the determinants of both contracted and realised FDI.

Section 4.2 briefly reviews the relevant literature and specifies the conceptual framework within which the determinants will be analysed. Section 4.3 describes the data and methodology. Empirical results are reported in section 4.4. Finally, section 4.5 provides a summary and conclusions.

4.2 HYPOTHESIS FORMATION AND MODEL SPECIFICATION

Various approaches have been attempted in the literature to explain regional patterns of FDI within a host country. Firm-specific advantages emphasised by Hymer (1960), Kindleberger (1969), Caves (1971) and Lall (1980) and internalisation advantages stressed by Buckley and Casson (1976) and Rugman (1981) are usually either explicitly or implicitly assumed to be given. Locational advantages are then assumed to be the main concern of multinational corporations when they consider the locational distribution of their FDI programmes. Traditional industrial location theory explains the geographical distribution of FDI in terms of transport costs, wages and infrastructure. New location theory focuses on pecuniary externalities or agglomeration associated with demand and supply linkages (Krugman, 1991a, b; Venables, 1993). Dunning's eclectic paradigm (Dunning, 1977) provides a detailed analysis of the impact of ownership, internalisation and locational advantages on the behaviour of multinational corporations.

New growth theory also emphasises agglomeration effects from knowledge spillovers among firms within and between industries (Griliches, 1979; Romer, 1986; Sala-i-Martin, 1990). One recent development is the information costs approach, which treats the conduct and hierarchical structures of multinational enterprises as the results of a rational response by economic agents to the existence of information costs (Casson, 1994a, b; Radner 1992; Mariotti and Piscitello, 1995).

A number of hypotheses have been discussed in the theoretical literature on the geographical distribution of FDI. Although different approaches focus on different influences, empirical studies tend to draw on various fields of economics and include all factors which are thought to be important in explaining the regional distribution of FDI. For the purpose of this paper, relationships between FDI inflows and such regional characteristics as the level of international trade, wages, R&D manpower, GDP growth, infrastructure, agglomeration externalities, investment incentives and links with foreign investors are examined. In this section each of these variables is discussed before our empirical model is specified and tested.

4.2.1 International Trade

The level of international trade is often used as an important indicator of a country's degree of openness. Frequent trading activities enable business partners to know more about economic, cultural, political and social situations in each other's regions, and facilitate quick flows of information on investment opportunities. Although some cross-country studies indicate that international trade and FDI are substitutes and are therefore negatively related (Horst, 1972; Jeon, 1992; Gopinath et al., 1999), many others find that they are positively correlated (Ajami and BarNiv, 1984; Ray, 1989; Grosse and Trevino, 1996; Liu et al., 1997). This chapter tests the hypothesis that there is a positive or negative relationship between FDI and international trade.

4.2.2 Wage Rates

Cheap factor inputs can be one of the host country's attractions for FDI. Thus, there would be a negative relationship between wage rates or labour costs and inward FDI. This is confirmed by Culem (1988), Yamawaki (1991), Chen (1997), Coughlin and Segev (2000) and Cheng and Kwan

(2000). However, a positive relationship between the two is found in Swedenborg (1979), Dunning (1980), and Veugelers (1991), who argue that wage rates could be treated as a proxy for labour quality. Higher wage rates imply the higher skills that foreign investors are seeking. Broadman and Sun (1997) obtain a positive but statistically insignificant coefficient on wage rates. They regard this positive sign as a 'wrong' one.

Controversy over the relationship between inward FDI and labour costs may partly be caused by different measures of wage rates. In this chapter productivity-adjusted wage rates are applied as an explanatory variable. It is reasonable to assume that qualifications, skills and experience of workers are positively related to productivity. If high money wage rates reflect high monetary labour costs, then productivity-adjusted wage rates are the effective labour costs. If levels of productivity are the same, a high money wage rate implies a high labour cost. Alternatively, if the levels of both productivity and money wage rates are higher in region A than in region B, but productivity is not sufficiently larger to compensate for the higher money wage rate in region A, then region B will have an effective labour cost advantage. Thus, if other things are equal, the higher the *effective* wage rates, the less FDI a region will attract.

4.2.3 R&D Manpower

It is widely accepted that a significant amount of R&D work by multinational corporations is carried out in their home countries. The main task of R&D in foreign subsidiaries is to adapt technologies developed in home countries to local needs (Borensztein et al., 1998). However, some studies indicate that setting up R&D activities in foreign branches is also an important motive for FDI (Pearce and Singh, 1992). Either to adapt existing technologies or to develop new technologies in subsidiaries, the local availability of R&D manpower is essential. If other things remain unchanged, the more R&D manpower a region has, the more attractive a region will be to foreign investors.

4.2.4 GDP Growth

GDP and its growth are often used in the literature as proxies for the size and growth of market demand. Many cross-country studies indicate that inward FDI is positively related to market demand in host countries (Ajami and BarNiv, 1984; Grosse and Trevino, 1996; Liu et al., 1997). This kind of relationship may well be expected at a local level within a host country (Broadman and Sun, 1997; Cheng and Kwan, 2000; Coughlin and Segev, 2000). However, it is sometimes argued that the variable may lose some of its explanatory power because of relatively easy access to neighbouring regions (Mariotti and Piscitello, 1995).

4.2.5 Infrastructure

Infrastructure is another frequently mentioned regional factor attracting FDI. Infrastructure covers many aspects, including seaports, highways, railways and telecommunications. A positive relationship between infrastructure and inward FDI is to be expected since an economy with good infrastructural investment is made more attractive. An alternative measure of infrastructure is a relative one, i.e. the ratio of infrastructure to GDP. This latter measure takes into consideration the relative economic size of each region. Empirical support for the importance of infrastructure in FDI location decisions is provided by Bartik (1985), Coughlin et al. (1991), Mariotti and Piscitello (1995), Gong (1995), Broadman and Sun (1997), Chen (1997), and Cheng and Kwan (2000). Coughlin and Segev (2000) obtain positive but insignificant coefficients on two transport infrastructure variables: air staff and highways. On the other hand, Peck (1996) argues that inward investors may be interested not only in the general modernity of the infrastructure of a region, but also in the degree to which they can exercise control over its present and future development.

4.2.6 Agglomeration

The agglomeration effect is associated with externalities. Concentration of production and urbanisation facilitate quick spillovers of knowledge and the use of joint networks of suppliers and distributors. This helps firms to enhance their levels of technology and reap economies of scale and scope. Investment in a region with substantial clustering of industrial activities is likely to involve relatively lower costs than in a region with a dispersed manufacturing sector. Thus, agglomeration will be positively correlated with inward FDI. This relationship is confirmed by a number of empirical studies including Wheeler and Mody (1992), Gong (1995) and Braunerhjelm and Svensson (1996).

4.2.7 Information Costs

Mariotti and Piscitello (1995) suggest that foreign investors suffer from a condition of adverse asymmetry in information costs compared with domestic investors. Thus, foreign investors' locational decisions on their activities within a country reflect a rational response to the existence of information costs. The measures of information costs include the distance from the country's 'core' region, age of first FDI, presence of the top 500 multinational enterprises and a 'border effect'. Basically, the smaller the distance of a region from the country's core region defined as the gravitational pole of the national economy, the older the age of the first FDI, the higher the presence of the top 500 multinational enterprises and the closer geographical and/or cultural links a region has with foreign investors, the smaller the information costs will be.

In the case of China, coastal areas can be identified as low information cost regions. First, these areas have traditionally been the industrial and commercial centres. As calculated by Kueh (1992), with a population of only 19.5 per cent of the national total, the municipalities and counties in the 11 'opened coastal provinces' of Liaoning, Hebei, Tianjin, Shandong, Jiangsu, Shanghai, Zhejiang, Fujian, Guangdong, Hainan, and Guangxi accounted for almost 40 per cent of national gross value of industrial output, 33.4 per cent of GDP and 25.9 per cent of all local budget revenue in China. Second, these areas were designated as first target regions for attracting FDI. The Shenzhen, Zhuhai, Shantou and Xiamen Special Economic Zones (SEZs) were established in 1980. Dalian, Tianjin, Qinhuangdao, Yantai, Nantong, Lianyungang, Shanghai, Ningbo, Wenzhou, Fuzhou, Guangzhou, Zhanjiang and Beihai were assigned as 14 coastal open cities (COCs) in 1984. SEZs and COCs have longer histories of hosting FDI than other regions of China. Third, the presence of the top 500 multinational enterprises in the coastal areas is much higher than in inland areas. Finally, the coastal areas have closer links with foreign investors. Liu and Song (1997) report that 66.7 per cent of the total contracted foreign investment in China for the period 1979-94 was accounted for by Asian newly industrialised countries (NICs), among which the most important grouping was overseas Chinese from Hong Kong, Macao and Taiwan. As indicated in chapter 2, approximately 61 per cent of cumulative realised FDI between 1979 and 1998 came from Hong Kong, Taiwan and Macao. Many of these overseas Chinese have close family links with residents in the coastal areas. In addition, these areas are geographically closer to the main sources of FDI.

The above discussion leads to the formation of the seventh argument: since investment in the coastal areas in China involves lower information costs, foreign investors prefer to locate their businesses there. This hypothesis may be tested by applying a dummy variable equal to 1 for all coastal areas and Beijing and 0 for other regions. A positive coefficient on the dummy is expected.

4.2.8 Investment Incentives

There is controversy over the role played by investment incentives in the attraction of FDI. While McAleese (1985) concludes that incentives offered by local governments are positively related to inward FDI in Ireland, Lim (1983) finds a negative relationship between investment incentives and the presence of FDI in 27 developing countries. According to Lim, generous fiscal incentives could be interpreted by potential foreign investors as a danger signal rather than a lure.

Since the coastal areas were specially assigned as the main regions to attract FDI, various fiscal incentives were offered there by the Chinese government. As pointed out by Gong (1995), because available incentives vary over time and by region, it is very difficult to quantify them. Instead, a dummy variable is needed to capture the effect of investment incentives (Coughlin and Segev, 2000). Because this variable takes on the same values as the information cost dummy, the two have to be combined in the following statistical analysis.

The arguments discussed under the above eight sub-headings have been tested based on the following model:

$$FDI = f(TRD, EWA, RDMP, GDPG, INFR, AGGO, CDM) \qquad (4.1)$$

This argues that foreign direct investment (FDI) in a region is influenced by the level of international trade (TRD), industrial productivity adjusted (effective) wage rates (EWA), R&D manpower (RDMP), GDP growth rates (GDPG), infrastructure (INFR), an agglomeration effect (AGGO), and a combined cross-sectional dummy (CDM) to capture the effects of low information cost and high investment incentives in the coastal regions.

4.3 DATA AND METHODOLOGY

This analysis is based on a panel of data for 28 out of 31 provinces, autonomous regions and central municipalities over the period 1983–98 for contracted FDI and 1986-98 for realised FDI in mainland China. Two provinces, Tibet and Qinghai, are omitted due to a lack of reliable data. Chongqing was part of Sichuan province until the end of 1995, in order to keep consistency, the data for Chongqing and Sichuan are combined from 1996 onwards. A more detailed description of the sources of data and the measurement of variables is given in Appendix 4A. In addition, Appendix 4B provides basic economic indicators of the Chinese regions for the period

1983-98 and consists of part of the observations used in the econometric estimations.

The methodology employed in this chapter is similar to that used in chapter 3. First of all, a log-linear functional form of (4.1) is adopted, due to similar reasons discussed in chapter 3. The model, therefore, has the following expression:

$$LFDI_{it} = \beta_1 LTRD_{it} + \beta_2 LEWA_{it} + \beta_3 LRDMP_{it} + \beta_4 LGDPG_{it}$$
$$+ \beta_5 LINFR_{it} + \beta_6 LAGGO_{it} + \beta_7 CDM + v_{it} \qquad (4.2)$$

where L indicates logged values, i and t denote individual provinces and time respectively, N and T are the total number of provinces and years in the sample, respectively, and v represents a composite term including both intercept and the error term. In addition, all the determinants of FDI are expected to occur either simultaneously with FDI or with a lag of less than a year at the regional level, just as they are at the national level. As a result, no lag is introduced in the econometric model.

Given the marked difference between the figures for contracted and realised FDI at the regional level, two specifications of (4.2) are estimated to learn whether the same set of regional characteristics influences contracted FDI (FDIP) and realised FDI (FDIR) in the same way. The results can be compared with those from the estimations at the national level.

As shown in the study carried out in chapter 3, we are interested in the long-run relationship between FDI and all its explanatory variables. To avoid possible spurious regression, the order of integration of variables is examined using the IPS test proposed by Im, Pesaran and Shin (1997). Given the unit root test results, a panel data set can then be estimated by using two statistical models: the ordinary least squares (OLS) model and random effects (RE) model. Because a dummy variable is included in our empirical model, the fixed effects (FE) model is not applicable. The choice between the OLS and the RE models is made based on the Lagrange multiplier (LM) test proposed by Breusch and Pagan (1980). Details are presented in section 3.5 in chapter 3.

4.4 EMPIRICAL RESULTS

The descriptive statistics and panel data unit root test results for each variable (in log form) are presented in Table 4.1. The results from the IPS unit root tests indicate that all variables are stationary. Therefore, we can estimate (4.2) with all variables at levels to test whether there is a long-run relationship between FDI (both contracted and realised) and its determinants.

Table 4.1 Descriptive statistics and unit root test results

Variable	Maximum	Minimum	Mean	Std. Dev.	t-bar Test
LFDIP	10.1308	-2.4724	4.7928	2.2273	-2.0072**
LFDIR	8.7206	-2.5401	4.3755	2.1605	-1.6827*
LTRD	11.1000	4.2425	7.1935	1.2761	-2.1904**
LEWA	7.8542	3.9683	5.8943	0.7450	-1.9584**
LRDMP1	-2.9337	-6.8633	-5.8152	0.7687	-3.6540***
LRDMP2	-2.6385	-5.4018	-4.5991	0.5010	-1.8420*
LGDPG	0.3378	-0.0254	0.1025	0.0429	-6.1614***
LINFR1	15.2463	7.3635	11.0308	1.5111	-2.7856***
LINFR2	9.4646	3.3873	6.3025	1.1298	-1.6967*
LAGGO	7.6532	2.1202	5.3299	1.0996	-1.7786*

Notes:
1. L indicates logged values; LFDIP = contracted FDI; LFDIR = realised FDI; LTRD = level of international trade; LEWA = industrial productivity adjusted wage rates; LRDMP = R&D manpower; LGDPG = GDP growth rate; LINFR = infrastructure; LAGGO = agglomeration effect. LRDMP1 and LRDMP2 are the two different measures of R&D manpower; and LINFR1 and LINFR2 are the two different measures of infrastructure. The different measures are used for the purpose of comparison.
2. There are 448 observations for each variable expect LFDIR for which only 364 observations are included.
3. Std. Dev. represents the standard deviation.
4. ***, **, * denote significance at the level of 1%, 5% and 10%, respectively. The critical values are -2.57, -1.96, and -1.65 at the confidence level of 1%, 5% and 10%, respectively.

As discussed in section 4.2, economic theory suggests that there are either positive or negative relationships between the dependent and explanatory variables. The results from estimating the specifications for contracted and realised FDI using this long-run regression equation are presented in Tables 4.2 and 4.3 respectively.

In Table 4.2, the results from four pairs of the OLS and RE models are presented based on the alternative combinations of the different measures of R&D manpower and infrastructure. Following the discussion of the methodology in the preceding section and in section 3.5 of chapter 3, the large values of the LM1 statistics argue in favour of the RE models against the OLS models in all four pairs. This suggests that the RE models are statistically superior to the OLS models. Thus, the economic interpretation of Table 4.2 will focus on the results from the four RE models.

Foreign Direct Investment in China

The results from all models in Table 4.2 are consistent with expectations. The coefficients of all explanatory variables are correctly signed. The estimated coefficients on international trade from all four different specifications of the RE model are statistically significant at the 1% level and indicate that, other things remaining constant, a 1 per cent increase in international trade would raise contracted FDI by about 0.6 per cent. The positive relationship between international trade and contracted FDI supports the hypothesis that high volumes of trade facilitate FDI inflows. Information on investment opportunities is one possible explanation as suggested in section 4.2.

The coefficients on the wage rate in different specifications of the RE model have different levels of significance. In the first and third cases, the significance level is 1%; in the fourth case, it is 10%; and in the second case, the coefficient is marginally insignificant with the probability of 12%. The

Table 4.2 Parameter estimates of elasticities for contracted FDI in China at regional level

	(I)		(II)	
	OLS	RE	OLS	RE
LTRD	0.7006***	0.6744***	0.6522***	0.5971***
	(0.1081)	(0.1242)	(0.1032)	(0.1208)
LEWA	-0.4812***	-0.4159***	-0.2517***	-0.1673 [a]
	(0.0905)	(0.1018)	(0.0947)	(0.1081)
LRDMP2	0.2313*	0.2769 [b]	0.2587**	0.2791*
	(0.1315)	(0.1738)	(0.1268)	(0.1714)
LGDPG	7.8282***	8.0976***	8.0732***	8.3119***
	(1.4251)	(1.4042)	(1.3903)	(1.3674)
LINFR1	--	--	0.6240***	0.6648***
			(0.0588)	(0.0627)
LINFR2	0.7905***	0.8408***	--	--
	(0.0851)	(0.0908)		
LAGGO	0.0488	0.0377	0.0544	0.0498
	(0.0732)	(0.0991)	(0.0713)	(0.0984)
CDM	0.3713*	0.3752 [c]	0.4895***	0.5414**
	(0.1972)	(0.2511)	(0.1937)	(0.2509)
Constant	-2.5511***	-2.8241***	-5.4364***	-5.9160***
	(0.8138)	(1.0786)	(0.9047)	(1.1763)
R^2	0.6893	0.6885	0.7040	0.7033
Test: λ_{LM1}	5.26**		5.79**	

Table 4.2 Continued

	(III)		(IV)	
	OLS	RE	OLS	RE
LTRD	0.6497***	0.6248***	0.6022***	0.5503***
	(0.1038)	(0.1207)	(0.1038)	(0.1181)
LEWA	-0.4962***	-0.4308***	-0.2618***	-0.1755*
	(0.0904)	(0.1021)	(0.1059)	(0.1089)
LRDMP1	0.0560	0.0711	0.0857	0.0992
	(0.0804)	(0.1098)	(0.0853)	(0.1093)
LGDPG	7.7199***	8.0455***	8.0194***	8.3063***
	(1.4363)	(1.4104)	(1.7133)	(1.3737)
LINFR1	--	--	0.6488***	0.6887***
			(0.0527)	(0.0614)
LINFR2	0.8265***	0.8766***	--	--
	(0.0824)	(0.0885)		
LAGGO	0.0779	0.0716	0.0870	0.0836
	(0.0712)	(0.0982)	(0.0669)	(0.0977)
CDM	0.4071**	0.4012 [d]	0.5173***	0.5590**
	(0.1980)	(0.2565)	(0.1886)	(0.2568)
Constant	-3.2205***	-3.6518***	-6.1611***	-6.6882***
	(0.7483)	(1.0084)	(0.9038)	(1.0792)
R^2	0.6875	0.6867	0.7020	0.7013
Test: λ_{LM1}	6.04***		7.41***	

Notes:

1. Standard errors are in parentheses.
2. ***, ** and * indicate that the coefficient is significantly different from zero at the 1%, 5% and 10% levels, respectively.
3. [a] Prob = 12.17%; [b] Prob = 11.12%; [c] Prob = 13.51%; [d] Prob = 11.78%

negative coefficient suggests that the effective wage rate is inversely related with contracted FDI inflows as expected. The result shows that a 1 per cent increase in the wage rate would lead to a 0.17-0.43 per cent decrease in contracted FDI.

The coefficients on LRDMP1 in the relevant specifications of the RE model are positive but statistically insignificant. On the other hand, those on LRDMP2 are also positive and either only marginally insignificant (first specification) or significant at the 10% level (second specification). This suggests that LRDMP2, the proportion of scientists and researchers in total employment, is a better measure of R&D manpower than the proportion of scientists and researchers in the total labour force. The positive coefficients on the R&D manpower variable indicate that FDI in different regions is also attracted by human capital. The higher the proportion of scientists and researchers in total employment, the higher the R&D capabilities, and the more productive the work force. However, similar to the case of wage rates, the absolute magnitudes of the coefficients on R&D manpower (or elasticity) are only about 0.3 per cent. That is, a 1 per cent increase in R&D manpower would result in a less than 0.3 per cent increase in contracted FDI inflows.

The FDI elasticities of both wage rates and R&D manpower reflect the comparative advantage that China offers to foreign investors. The wage rate elasticity indicates that one of the motives for foreign businesses to invest in China is to seek low unit labour costs. The bulk of FDI in China has been from Asian NICs and focused on the production and exporting of labour-intensive products. This may explain the low FDI elasticity with respect to R&D manpower. Nevertheless, the positive R&D manpower elasticity reflects the need of foreign investors for some highly skilled technical staff represented by R&D manpower.

LGDPG, the proxy for the growth rate of the provincial market demand, seems to be a much more powerful explanatory variable than international trade, effective wage rates and R&D manpower. The coefficients in all four specifications of the RE model are positive. They tend to suggest that a 1 per cent increase in the market growth rate would result in a more than 8 per cent increase in contracted FDI.

The infrastructure variable, measured either by the output of post and telecommunication services (LINFR1) or the ratio of the output of post and telecommunication services to GDP (LINFR2), also has a significant impact on FDI inflows to various regions. The FDI elasticities with respect to this variable are within the range of 0.7-0.9 per cent.

Although it has the expected positive sign, the coefficients on LAGGO in all four specifications of the RE model are statistically insignificant. This result is contradictory to that in Wei at al. (1999) where the agglomeration effect is a very powerful explanatory variable for FDI inflows to the Chinese regions. Given that the magnitude of the coefficient on GDP growth is much larger in Wei et al., the impact of LAGGO may partly be overshadowed by GDP growth.

Table 4.2 also indicates that CDM, the combined dummy variable, has the expected sign. It is significant at the 5% level in two specifications and marginally insignificant in the other two specifications of the RE model. This suggests that foreign investors would seek locations with low information costs and high investment incentives. Government policy could have a significant effect on FDI.

The evidence from Table 4.2 shows that a region with higher international trade, lower real effective wage rates, more R&D manpower, higher GDP growth, better infrastructure, and lower information costs and/or higher investment incentives attracts relatively more contracted FDI. In terms of the magnitude, however, GDP growth is the most important explanatory variable for FDI inflows to the Chinese regions.

Table 4.3 shows the results for realised FDI. All explanatory variables in both specifications of the model have the expected signs and are statistically significant. The highly significant Lagrange multiplier test statistics, however, suggest that the RE model is the preferred one. Thus, our economic interpretation should be based on the RE model.

As in the case of contracted FDI, international trade is a highly significant determinant of realised FDI even though its magnitude is relatively small. The wage rate is highly significant in two specifications but insignificant in the other two, and its magnitude is also smaller than in the case of contracted FDI. This suggests that international trade and wage rates have lost some explanatory power when used to explain realised FDI.

Table 4.3 Parameter estimates of elasticities for realised FDI in China at regional level

	(I)		(II)	
	OLS	RE	OLS	RE
LTRD	0.4955***	0.3387***	0.5443***	0.3730***
	(0.0953)	(0.1326)	(0.0891)	(0.1275)
LEWA	-0.4140***	-0.2520***	-0.2186***	-0.0495
	(0.0830)	(0.1026)	(0.0852)	(0.1064)
LRDMP2	0.3216***	0.3409*	0.3715***	0.3677*
	(0.1093)	(0.1976)	(0.1057)	(0.1965)
LGDPG	8.4657***	8.7475***	8.0252***	8.2744***
	(1.2804)	(1.1449)	(1.2544)	(1.1081)
LINFR1	--	--	0.6961***	0.7836***
			(0.0497)	(0.0525)
LINFR2	0.9276***	1.0690***	--	--
	(0.0707)	(0.0763)		
LAGGO	0.1640***	0.1503	0.1714***	0.1754
	(0.0603)	(0.1169)	(0.0589)	(0.1171)
CDM	0.6391***	0.7870***	0.6336***	0.8223***
	(0.1677)	(0.2906)	(0.1627)	(0.2900)
Constant	-3.3794***	-4.0213***	-6.5250***	-7.3928***
	(0.6881)	(1.2411)	(0.7690)	(1.3198)
R^2	0.8177	0.8142	0.8257	0.8230
Test: λ_{LM1}	97.79***		91.20***	

Table 4.3 Continued

	(III) OLS	(III) RE	(IV) OLS	(IV) RE
LTRD	0.4310***	0.2779***	0.4776***	0.3114***
	(0.0915)	(0.1310)	(0.0864)	(0.1264)
LEWA	-0.4321***	-0.2526***	-0.2334***	-0.0542
	(0.0838)	(0.1033)	(0.0862)	(0.1070)
LRDMP2	0.1454**	0.0875	0.1709***	0.1116
	(0.0670)	(0.1329)	(0.0655)	(0.1322)
LGDPG	8.5698***	8.8017	8.1395***	8.3328***
	(1.2971)	(1.1218)***	(1.2732)	(1.0902)
LINFR1	--	--	0.7263	0.8106
			(0.0488)***	(0.0505)***
LINFR2	0.9682***	1.1102***	--	--
	(0.0688)	(0.0732)		
LAGGO	0.2006***	0.1908 ^{e}	0.2152***	0.2214*
	(0.0590)	(0.1221)	(0.0576)	(0.1215)
CDM	0.6621***	0.8179***	0.6530***	0.8522***
	(0.1690)	(0.3097)	(0.1646)	(0.3077)
Constant	-3.9093***	-5.1284***	-7.2562***	-8.5210***
	(0.6414)	(1.2250)	(0.7088)	(1.2660)
R^2	0.8157	0.8117	0.8231	0.8201
Test: λ_{LM1}	103.4***		100.06***	

Notes:
1. Standard errors are in parentheses.
2. ***, ** and * indicate that the coefficient is significantly different from zero at the 1%, 5% and 10% levels, respectively.
3. ^{e} Prob = 11.81%

The coefficients on LRDMP1 are statistically insignificant but those on LRDMP2 are statistically significant at the 10% level. This shows again that the proportion of scientists and researchers in total employment is a better measure of R&D manpower than LRDMP1, the proportion of scientists and researchers in the total labour force. The magnitude of R&D manpower is slightly larger when it is used to explain realised FDI than contracted FDI.

GDP growth is statistically significant at the 1% level in any specification, and its magnitude is greater than its counterpart in the regression equations for contracted FDI. A similar pattern applies to the infrastructure variable. Regardless of whether it is measured by the output of post and telecommunication services (LINFR1) or the ratio of the output of post and telecommunication services to GDP (LINFR2), the variable is highly significant and its magnitude is greater than in the explanation of contracted FDI.

The explanatory power of agglomeration seems slightly greater in explaining realised FDI than contracted FDI. While it is not statistically significant in all specifications of the RE model for contracted FDI, the agglomeration variable is at least significant at the 10% level in one specification and marginally insignificant in another specification of the RE model for realised FDI. Finally, CDM is highly statistically significant in all specifications and its magnitude is greater than its counterpart in the regression equations for contracted FDI.

A comparison of the results from Tables 4.2 and 4.3 reveals that contracted and realised FDI seem to be determined by a very similar set of regional characteristics. International trade, wage rates, the proportion of scientists and researchers in total employment, GDP growth, infrastructure and the availability of information and incentives are all positively associated with both contracted and realised FDI inflows. The agglomeration variable is not a significant determinant of contracted FDI, but plays some role in influencing realised FDI inflows.

As discussed in chapter 3, foreign investors make their decisions and contract their investments based on a certain set of political, economic and social conditions (i.e. the investment environment). Contracted FDI is normally realised over a time period. For various reasons some contracted FDI never materialises. Thus, such regional characteristics as the political, economic and social conditions under which FDI is contracted may well be different from those under which FDI actually materialises. It is possible that the determinants of contracted FDI might not completely coincide with those of realised FDI. However, the current study reveals a smaller difference in the statistical significance and magnitude of the same set of explanatory variables for both contracted and realised FDI than that in Wei at al. (1999). This may be partly due to the fact that the data set used in the current study covers a longer time period so that the results are more stable.

The identification of nearly the same set of determinants for contracted and realised FDI at the regional level is consistent with what is obtained at the national level. Furthermore, there are a number of similar explanatory variables for inward FDI at the regional and national levels, including market size, exports and imports. This may not be surprising since the choice of a host country and that of a specific location within that country in many cases are made simultaneously.

When investigating the regional distribution of FDI within China, the current study could not differentiate the country of origin of foreign investors due to a lack of detailed data. Consequently, special features of investors from different home countries are concealed. For instance, because of the cultural, geographic and historical links some foreign investors tend to have their own preferred regional locations. As mentioned in chapter 2, FDI from Hong Kong tends to locate in Guangdong while that from Taiwan prefers to go to Fujian. Foreign companies from other countries/regions also have their preferences.

A country study by Wang (1998) indicates that FDI from Japan is highly concentrated in Shanghai, Jiangsu, Zhejiang and particularly Liaoning. Within Liaoning Province many Japanese firms are located in Dalian City because it is near Japan and its climate is very similar to that of Japan. Historically, before the Second World War, Japan had reasonable amounts of direct investment in these regions. Wang (1996) shows that by the end of 1993 Shandong accounted for as high as 41 per cent of total direct investment from Korea. Shandong was Korean firms' favourable investment location mainly because of the short distance between Shandong and Korea and the Shandong authorities' focused policy of attracting FDI from Korea. FDI from Germany, the United Kingdom and the United States does not have this kind of strong regional preferences, but tends to locate in the coastal areas (Wang 1994, 1999).

4.5 CONCLUSIONS

This chapter improves on previous studies of the regional distribution of FDI within a country by examining the econometric properties of the data set within a panel framework. An IPS test for unit roots has been employed and a long-run relationship between the spatial distribution of FDI and a number of regional characteristics in China has been found.

Efforts have also been made to expand on past knowledge and to incorporate additional considerations in an attempt to provide a more precise and comprehensive assessment of the subject. The strong evidence from this study suggests that contracted FDI is positively influenced by the level of international trade, R&D manpower, GDP growth, infrastructure, and the availability of information and investment incentives. High effective wage rates act as deterrents to FDI. Among all explanatory variables, GDP growth is a far more powerful determinant than any others in terms of the magnitude of effect on FDI.

All the significant variables for explaining contracted FDI are also the significant determinants of realised FDI. However, because FDI is contracted and materialised at different times, there are some changes in the levels of significance and magnitude when these explanatory variables are used to explain realised FDI. In addition, the agglomeration variable plays a role in attracting realised FDI into Chinese regions. As in the case of contracted FDI, the central piece of information from the regression results for realised FDI is that GDP growth is the single most important determinant.

Ideally, an econometric investigation of the regional distribution of FDI from individual host countries should be carried out so that an insight can be provided into their special features. However, the data limitation prevents us from this kind of study. The country studies cited in the current chapter show that Hong Kong, Taiwan, Korea and Japan do have their own regional preferences. Geographic distance, cultural similarities and historical links naturally influence the regional distribution of FDI.

The empirical results have important policy implications for attracting FDI into individual provinces in China. As mentioned in chapter 2, the coastal areas have attracted a dominant proportion of FDI especially due to their long commercial and industrial traditions and geographical and ethnic links with Hong Kong, Macao and Taiwan. Given the determinants identified in this study and the Chinese government's recent regional development strategy, FDI in the inner areas can be expected to increase quickly for the reasons that are now discussed.

One dominant task of the Tenth Five-Year Plan (2001-05) is to develop the western areas. Within these five years, it aims to provide the western areas with a good basis for sustainable development in the future. The construction of infrastructure including transport, water conservancy, telecommunications, electrical networks and urban utilities in the western areas is to be accelerated. In addition to the infrastructure construction, priority is given to ecological environment conservation and development, and science and technology education (People's Daily, Overseas Edition, 19 October 2000). Accordingly, the State Council's Leading Group of the Development of the Western Areas is to issue preferential policies, including a substantial increase in capital investment, transfer payments, and bank loans to the western areas. Investment projects on natural resource exploitation, transfer of firms from military to civilian use and special high-tech product development will be the first to be considered for location in the western areas (People's Daily, Overseas Edition, 23 October 2000). Thus, economic growth in the coming years will be promoted by the central government's special policies, and this helps attract FDI inflows.

The Tenth Five-Year Plan also aims to improve the investment environment and encourage inward FDI in the western areas. The Chinese government provides incentives to encourage FDI in agriculture, water conservancy, ecological environment protection, transportation, energy and natural resource development, and the establishment of technological development centres. The trade and services sectors such as commercial retail, banking, international trade, insurance and tourism are open to FDI.

More channels of attracting FDI are to be encouraged, including BOT, TOT, operating rights transfer, equity share sale and merger and reorganisation. International joint ventures in China are also encouraged to re-invest in the western areas. The expected improvement of the investment environment and the provision of incentives will stimulate FDI inflows there.

As mentioned earlier, science and technology education is part of the development strategy for the western areas. This tends to increase the number of scientists and researchers and raise R&D manpower. Given the problem that talented people are generally not very willing to work in the inner areas, the Chinese government has decided to formulate a policy to attract and retain qualified personnel, and encourage them to pioneer enterprises (People's Daily, Overseas Edition, 23 October 2000).

In addition, the Plan calls for the acceleration of economic reform and opening up to the outside world in the inner areas. Indigenous Chinese firms are to be given more autonomy for foreign trade. Preferential policies are provided for trading with the neighbouring countries. These include tax refunds for exports and imports, and preferential arrangements for import quota allocations, licence management and international travel. As a result, more trade will be expected. As the current study demonstrates, these developments will lead to more FDI inflows.

Compared with the eastern coastal areas the inner areas have their own advantages in terms of relatively lower labour costs and more natural resources. In addition, as mentioned in chapter 2, the inner areas also have many key enterprises and research institutes built during the so-called 'third-front' construction period. The strategy of developing the western areas will help reduce the seriousness of the uneven regional distribution of FDI in China.

APPENDIX 4A DATA SOURCES

This analysis is based on a panel of data for 28 out of 31 of China's provinces over the period 1983-98 for contracted FDI and 1986-98 for realised FDI. Contracted investment is the value of signed agreements and contracts. The spatial coverage is of 12 provinces in the coastal areas (Guangdong, Jiangsu, Shanghai, Fujian, Hainan, Shandong, Liaoning, Tianjin, Zhejiang, Hebei, Beijing and Guangxi) and 16 provinces in the inland areas (Henan, Shanxi, Hubei, Heilongjiang, Jilin, Shaanxi, Anhui, Hunan, Sichuan, Jiangxi, Yunnan, Inner Mongolia, Guizhou, Xinjiang, Gansu and Ningxia). Two provinces, Tibet and Qinghai, are omitted due to a lack of reliable data. Chongqing province was not separated from Sichuan until 1996 and thus been included as one combined province.

The data were compiled from the *Comprehensive Statistical Data and Materials for 50 Years of New China*; *China Regional Economy: A Profile of 17 Years of Reform and Open-up*; various volumes of *Almanac of Foreign Economic Relations and Trade of China*; *China Foreign Economic Statistical Yearbook* and *China Statistical Yearbook,* together with statistical and economic yearbooks at the provincial level. Several missing values for some observations are extrapolated. The measurement of variables used in the study is given below.

Variable	Measurement
FDIP	The contracted annual inflow of foreign direct investment in China, deflated by the corresponding provincial consumer price index (CPI) deflator.
FDIR	The realised annual inflow of foreign direct investment in China, deflated by the corresponding provincial CPI deflator.
TRD	Trade (exports + imports), deflated by the corresponding provincial CPI deflator.
EWA	The real average annual wage rate for staff and workers, adjusted by industrial productivity, which is defined as the ratio of industrial output to employees.
GDPG	The GDP growth rate.
RDMP	The R&D manpower. RDMP1 is defined as the proportion of scientists and researchers in the total labour force. RDMP2 is defined as the proportion of scientists and researchers in total employment.

Variable	Measurement
INFR	Infrastructure. INFR1 is proxied by the output of post and telecommunication services at 1990 constant prices. INFR2 is proxied by the ratio of the output of post and telecommunication services to GDP. Both the output of post and telecommunication services and GDP are at 1990 constant prices.
AGGO	The agglomeration effect, defined as the ratio of the population to the land area. The total population refers to the total number of people at the end of a year.
CDM	The combined dummy variable. It is used to capture the information costs and investment incentives. For the following provinces, the dummy is equal to one: Beijing, Tianjin, Hebei, Liaoning, Shanghai, Jiangsu, Zhejiang, Fujian, Shandong, Guangdong, Guangxi, and Hainan.

APPENDIX 4B ECONOMIC INDICATORS OF THE CHINESE REGIONS

Table 4B.1 provides basic economic indicators of the Chinese regions for 1983, 1986, 1990, 1994 and 1998. These data serve as background information for the econometric analysis in the chapter. Part (I) of the table provides a comparison of contracted and realised FDI across the regions. One important feature is that there is a marked difference between contracted and realised FDI. Although contracted FDI is generally higher than realised FDI, the reverse relationship can be true for a particular year. For instance, the contracted FDI was US$ 116.9 million but the realised FDI was US$ 277 million for Beijing in 1990. As discussed in chapter 3, the difference between contracted and realised FDI arose because some contracted FDI never materialised and because the contracting of an FDI project was a one-off action, but the realisation of FDI was completed over different time periods. From part (I) of the table it does not seem possible to establish different patterns for the relationship between contracted and realised FDI for the different regions. While it is found that there exist some common determinants of contracted and realised FDI at the national level as shown in chapter 3, it will be interesting to know whether this applies at the regional level.

Part (2) of Table 4B.1 shows the values of exports and imports by region. As in the case of FDI, trade tends to be concentrated in the eastern areas. This trend is particularly reflected by the distribution of imports. For

instance, in 1998 all provinces except Guangxi in the eastern areas had more
than US$ 1,000 million worth of imports, but in the central and western areas
only three provinces, i.e. Heilongjiang, Anhui and Sichuan, imported more
than US$ 1,000 million. The top trade performer is Guangdong province. Its
exports and imports were 31 and 58 times as high as those in 1983. Trade
volumes of Guangdong are significantly higher than any other province. This
may help to explain why Guangdong has the largest values of contracted and
realised FDI.

The volumes of post and telecommunications and GDP by regions are
presented in part (3) of Table 4B.1 as the proxies for infrastructure and
market demand for each region. As expected, the eastern areas have the
better infrastructure and higher market demands than the central and western
areas. As a result, the eastern areas should receive more inward FDI than the
central or western area. Finally, part (4) of the table shows the population
and labour force for each region. The population of a province is used as the
numerator, with its land area as the denominator to measure the
agglomeration effect. The labour force is used as the denominator with the
number of scientists and researchers as the numerator in calculating R&D
manpower. In addition, by a comparison of these two indicators one can
know the contribution of the population to the formation of the labour force
and therefore economic growth.

Table 4B.1 Economic indicators of Chinese regions, 1983-98

(I) Contracted and Realised FDI in China   US$ million

REGION	\multicolumn{5}{c}{Contracted FDI}				
	1983	1986	1990	1994	1998
Eastern Regions					
Beijing	29.3	419.5	116.9	4533.0	4096.9
Tianjin	5.6	65.8	163.7	3502.3	3076.0
Hebei	2.6	10.1	85.9	1659.6	1267.7
Liaoning	1.0	78.4	467.0	4488.5	4380.1
Shanghai	73.8	297.4	374.6	10025.7	5845.5
Jiangsu	3.4	67.0	244.2	8521.4	7577.6
Zhejiang	1.0	23.1	133.1	2893.2	1833.9
Fujian	21.2	64.6	1161.8	7179.5	5001.5
Shandong	22.0	59.3	232.8	5262.2	2201.9
Guangdong	615.5	859.0	2689.6	23824.4	9155.3
Hainan	9.3	7.1	128.8	340.6	143.2
Guangxi	16.2	84.5	125.2	1472.3	642.4

REGION	1983	1986	1990	1994	1998
Contracted FDI					
Central Regions					
Shanxi	-	4.6	12.0	214.8	409.3
Inner Mongolia	3.0	4.3	19.5	130.2	130.4
Jilin	0.8	8.2	21.7	826.1	495.4
Heilongjiang	14.6	9.0	28.7	584.0	555.0
Anhui	11.5	19.7	19.2	707.0	243.0
Jiangxi	-	20.9	28.6	391.6	419.3
Henan	0.05	27.2	21.1	791.7	530.0
Hubei	13.9	4.9	39.5	1394.3	525.0
Hunan	0.5	8.8	26.8	692.2	1094.9
Western Regions					
Sichuan	0.4	55.2	100.6	1503.4	712.2
Guizhou	-	2.2	16.3	117.7	153.1
Yunnan	7.0	1.9	2.5	284.8	330.4
Shaanxi	8.3	431.9	11.3	411.4	375.8
Gansu	-	0.9	2.9	194.1	83.6
Ningxia	-	0.1	1.0	24.2	52.0
Xinjiang	-	3.2	8.8	85.5	138.3
Realised FDI					
REGION	1983	1986	1990	1994	1998
Eastern Regions					
Beijing	-	139.9	277.0	1444.6	2064.2
Tianjin	0.4	42.9	83.2	1015.0	2518.0
Hebei	-	6.9	39.4	523.4	1638.9
Liaoning	2.8	33.0	248.3	1423.9	2204.7
Shanghai	10.7	97.5	177.2	3231.0	3637.9
Jiangsu	-	18.1	141.1	4176.7	6652.0
Zhejiang	1.8	18.5	48.4	1144.5	1318.0
Fujian	14.4	61.5	290.0	3712.0	4012.1
Shandong	-	19.4	150.8	2535.7	2222.6
Guangdong	245.2	643.9	1459.8	9397.1	12020.1
Hainan	1.9	30.4	100.6	874.4	717.2
Guangxi	-	37.0	30.3	815.1	886.1
Central Regions					
Shanxi	-	0.2	3.4	31.7	244.5
Inner Mongolia	-	1.0	10.6	40.1	56.4
Jilin	-	0.6	16.9	318.3	409.2
Heilongjiang	-	17.3	25.3	342.3	526.4
Anhui	-	7.9	9.6	370.0	322.3

Table 4B.1 Continued

REGION	Realised FDI				
	1983	1986	1990	1994	1998
Central Regions					
Jiangxi	-	4.6	6.2	261.7	464.9
Henan	-	6.1	10.5	424.9	617.9
Hubei	-	12.5	29.0	601.8	920.1
Hunan	0.3	9.5	11.2	325.1	818.2
Western Regions					
Sichuan	-	15.2	10.3	515.5	935.1
Guizhou	-	0.7	4.7	63.6	45.4
Yunnan	-	3.5	2.6	203.0	145.7
Shaanxi	-	37.2	41.9	238.1	300.1
Gansu	-	0.2	4.7	26.8	38.6
Ningxia	-	0.1	1.0	49.0	5.0
Xinjiang	-	14.6	7.1	48.3	21.7

(II) Exports and Imports   **US$ million**

REGION	Exports				
	1983	1986	1990	1994	1998
Eastern Regions					
Beijing	590	653	1122	1959	2829
Tianjin	1427	1255	1786	2400	5694
Hebei	817	1053	1737	2522	4306
Liaoning	3918	3080	5606	6865	8363
Shanghai	3648	3582	5321	9077	16328
Jiangsu	1372	1870	2944	6686	15651
Zhejiang	652	1156	2259	6319	12009
Fujian	194	686	2449	6430	9959
Shandong	1808	2135	3497	7252	13159
Guangdong	2385	4251	22221	50211	75618
Hainan	16	38	471	987	885
Guangxi	343	430	729	1602	2418
Central Regions					
Shanxi	28	302	458	803	1452
Inner Mongolia	57	171	325	596	823
Jilin	167	525	791	1348	749
Heilongjiang	273	615	1087	1838	2035
Anhui	170	367	654	1276	2015
Jiangxi	216	305	561	1066	1651
Henan	280	453	867	1022	1187

Foreign Direct Investment in China

REGION	Exports				
	1983	1986	1990	1994	1998
Central Regions					
Hubei	412	725	1072	2097	2805
Hunan	400	503	806	1947	2202
Western Regions					
Sichuan	93	338	716	1514	1675
Guizhou	42	64	154	373	443
Yunnan	119	197	562	1053	1263
Shaanxi	54	172	461	1216	1177
Guansu	46	101	186	373	425
Ningxia	30	53	77	146	282
Xinjiang	97	205	335	576	808
REGION	Imports				
	1983	1986	1990	1994	1998
Eastern Regions					
Beijing	106	1016	1029	2734	3676
Tianjin	151	409	424	913	4808
Hebei	52	78	215	389	1113
Liaoning	78	349	712	2929	4766
Shanghai	492	1622	2110	6790	9718
Jiangsu	79	542	1195	5073	10775
Zhejiang	26	134	291	2139	3689
Fujian	370	662	1890	5759	7201
Shandong	117	408	695	2020	6270
Guangdong	931	2558	19677	46452	54180
Hainan	68	139	466	1710	1025
Guangxi	58	115	169	858	566
Central Regions					
Shanxi	50	86	63	177	248
Inner Mongolia	33	68	160	466	562
Jilin	52	192	318	1199	904
Heilongjiang	53	195	406	1256	1778
Anhui	24	122	83	572	1105
Jiangxi	27	69	70	315	229
Henan	25	54	137	610	545
Hubei	31	136	118	751	687
Hunan	57	121	136	761	874

REGION	Imports				
	1983	1986	1990	1994	1998
Western Regions					
Sichuan	25	120	125	873	1184
Guizhou	11	22	64	162	266
Yunnan	29	128	189	550	772
Shaanxi	-	63	117	384	875
Guansu	11	35	16	136	110
Ningxia	8	21	8	32	51
Xinjiang	20	79	75	464	724

(III) GDP and Infrastructure   RMB 100 million

	GDP				
	1983	1986	1990	1994	1998
Eastern Regions					
Beijing	183	285	501	1084	2011
Tianjin	123	195	311	725	1336
Hebei	277	401	715	1619	2833
Liaoning	364	605	1063	2462	3882
Shanghai	1262	1667	2103	3396	5433
Jiangsu	438	745	1417	4057	7200
Zhejiang	256	500	898	2667	4987
Fujian	128	223	522	1676	3330
Shandong	460	742	1511	3872	7162
Guangdong	369	668	1559	4517	7919
Hainan	31	48	102	331	439
Guangxi	135	205	449	1198	1903
Central Regions					
Shanxi	155	235	429	854	1601
Inner Mongolia	106	182	319	682	1192
Jilin	150	227	425	969	1558
Heilongjiang	328	503	935	2224	4357
Anhui	216	383	658	1488	2805
Jiangxi	144	231	429	948	1852
Henan	263	442	824	1879	3704
Hubei	597	807	1148	1992	3209
Hunan	257	398	744	1694	3211
Western Regions					
Sichuan	311	458	891	2001	5010
Guizhou	87	140	260	521	842

Table 4B.1 Continued

	GDP				
	1983	1986	1990	1994	1998
Western Regions					
Yunnan	120	182	452	974	1794
Shaanxi	123	208	404	817	1382
Guansu	92	141	243	452	870
Ningxia	21	35	65	134	227
Xinjiang	79	129	274	674	1117
	Volume of Post and Telecommunications				
REGION	1983	1986	1990	1994	1998
Eastern Regions					
Beijing	3.85	6.21	12.22	41.88	129.10
Tianjin	0.79	1.25	3.27	13.25	47.41
Hebei	2.00	2.76	5.56	21.78	88.51
Liaoning	2.48	3.66	8.40	32.24	124.93
Shanghai	2.58	3.94	10.23	39.19	139.87
Jiangsu	2.80	4.50	9.98	51.78	167.78
Zhejiang	2.38	3.92	8.65	42.92	157.72
Fujian	1.53	2.31	7.32	36.48	131.84
Shandong	2.39	3.38	7.51	40.40	133.89
Guangdong	1.31	2.54	26.30	142.78	418.18
Hainan	0.21	0.28	0.96	8.67	18.47
Guangxi	1.09	1.40	2.71	13.30	52.66
Central Regions					
Shanxi	1.34	1.61	2.55	9.20	39.62
Inner Mongolia	0.98	1.26	2.23	6.97	24.78
Jilin	1.32	1.85	4.16	15.51	53.85
Heilongjiang	1.75	2.35	4.78	18.50	83.92
Anhui	1.18	1.72	3.40	15.54	57.33
Jiangxi	1.07	1.50	2.85	9.65	39.90
Henan	1.59	2.10	4.90	18.89	103.56
Hubei	1.69	2.34	4.80	19.91	83.52
Hunan	1.50	1.96	4.44	21.54	76.00
Western Regions					
Sichuan	2.29	3.18	6.74	23.96	71.95
Guizhou	0.56	0.76	1.36	4.21	21.21
Yunnan	0.99	1.34	2.43	9.15	44.38
Shaanxi	1.22	1.59	3.23	10.32	39.54
Guansu	0.64	0.89	1.72	5.14	20.31
Ningxia	0.16	0.23	0.47	1.48	6.66
Xinjiang	0.62	0.90	1.74	5.61	25.06

(IV) Population and Labour Force   **10,000 persons**

REGION	Population				
	1983	1986	1990	1994	1998
Eastern Regions					
Beijing	954	1032	1104	1164	1223
Tianjin	785	815	866	891	905
Hebei	5420	5627	6159	6388	6569
Liaoning	3629	3726	3917	4007	4090
Shanghai	1194	1232	1283	1299	1307
Jiangsu	6135	6270	6767	7021	7182
Zhejiang	3963	4070	4235	4341	4447
Fujian	2640	2749	3000	3127	3261
Shandong	7564	7776	8424	8653	8872
Guangdong	5494	5741	6246	6691	7116
Hainan	581	606	651	691	733
Guangxi	3733	3946	4242	4493	4675
Central Regions					
Shanxi	2588	2714	2899	3045	3172
Inner Mongolia	1970	2041	2163	2260	2345
Jilin	2270	2315	2440	2516	2603
Heilongjiang	3306	3385	3543	3672	3773
Anhui	5056	5217	5661	5938	6152
Jiangxi	3395	3576	3811	4015	4191
Henan	7632	7985	8649	9027	9315
Hubei	4866	5048	5439	5719	5907
Hunan	5509	5696	6111	6303	6502
Western Regions					
Sichuan	7337	7512	7893	8099	8316
Guizhou	2901	3026	3268	3458	3658
Yunnan	3331	3480	3731	3939	4144
Shaanxi	2931	3043	3316	3481	3596
Guansu	2000	2085	2255	2378	2519
Ningxia	399	424	466	504	537
Xinjiang	1333	1384	1529	1633	1747

Table 4B.1 Continued

REGION	\multicolumn{5}{c}{Labour Force}
	1983	1986	1990	1994	1998
Eastern Regions					
Beijing	552	590	627	664	622
Tianjin	436	467	470	513	508
Hebei	2489	2626	2955	3210	3367
Liaoning	1639	1799	1897	2009	1959
Shanghai	769	783	788	850	836
Jiangsu	3057	3350	3569	3640	3688
Zhejiang	2141	2386	2554	2641	2613
Fujian	1057	1189	1348	1554	1622
Shandong	3795	3651	4043	4382	5288
Guangdong	2570	2812	3118	3493	3784
Hainan	253	276	305	336	341
Guangxi	1713	1896	2109	2336	2499
Central Regions					
Shanxi	1080	1189	1304	1404	1398
Inner Mongolia	799	875	925	1033	1050
Jilin	848	988	1169	1250	1240
Heilongjiang	1196	1324	1436	1515	1700
Anhui	2234	2496	2808	3120	3379
Jiangxi	1498	1623	1817	2008	2094
Henan	3289	3598	4086	4448	5000
Hubei	2145	2293	2479	2562	2627
Hunan	2594	2809	3159	3400	3603
Western Regions					
Sichuan	3565	3886	4304	4580	4534
Guizhou	1234	1383	1652	1828	1844
Yunnan	1583	1731	1923	2109	2241
Shaanxi	1285	1409	1576	1720	1788
Guansu	994	1099	1292	1439	1540
Ningxia	163	183	211	233	255
Xinjiang	546	575	618	658	681

Notes:
1. The data on realised FDI are slightly different in this table from the corresponding data in Table 2.6 due to the different data sources.
2. The business volume of post and telecommunications is in 1990 constant prices.

Sources: Comprehensive Statistical Data and Materials for 50 Years of New China; China Regional Economy: A Profile of 17 Years of Reform and Open-up.

5. Productivity Spillovers from Foreign Direct Investment in the Chinese Electronics Industry

5.1 INTRODUCTION

In chapters 3 and 4 the determinants of inward foreign direct investment (FDI) were examined. The current and next two chapters aim to assess the impact of FDI on productivity, per capita income and international trade, respectively. Due to a lack of data on productivity at the regional level, this chapter examines the impact of FDI on labour productivity in the Chinese electronics industry, for which relatively complete information is provided by the authorities.

FDI is a composite bundle of capital stock, know-how and technology (Balasubramanyam et al., 1996). It affects local productivity in a number of ways. When additional capital, new technology and managerial skills are introduced by FDI, there will be a direct effect on productive efficiency. In addition, FDI promotes the use of more advanced technologies by domestic firms and provides specific productivity-increasing labour training and skill acquisition (de Mello, 1997), and therefore provides indirect effects by knowledge diffusion (Blomstrom and Kokko, 1998). Mansfield and Romeo (1980) and Blomstrom (1989), among others, suggest that the most significant channels for the dissemination of modern technology are external effects or 'spillovers' from FDI, rather than formal technology transfer agreements.

The growth of FDI in the Chinese electronics industry was very slow before the mid-1980s, during which the main forms of introducing foreign technologies were imports, licensing and compensation trade, and only a very limited number of joint ventures were established (Wang, 1997). From 1986, inward FDI in the electronics industry began to accelerate due to encouragement from the Chinese authorities. As indicated in Figure 5.1, the net value of fixed assets of foreign-invested enterprises (FIEs) accounted for as high as 26 per cent of the total in the industry in 1998. This shows the importance of FDI in the capital formation of the Chinese electronics industry. Furthermore, the industrial value added of the FIEs was higher than either state-owned or other locally owned firms in 1998, and exports by FIEs well exceeded the sum of both state-owned and other locally owned firms. FDI has made significant contributions to the output and exports in that industry.

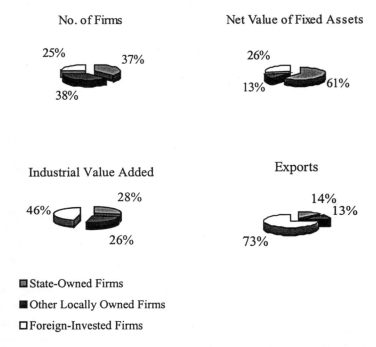

No. of Firms

25%   37%
38%

Net Value of Fixed Assets

26%
13%   61%

Industrial Value Added

28%
46%
26%

Exports

14%
13%
73%

■ State-Owned Firms
■ Other Locally Owned Firms
□ Foreign-Invested Firms

Source: Ministry of China Information Industry, Yearbook of China's Electronics Industry, 1999

Figure 5.1 Firm number, industrial output and exports by ownership, 1998

Given the importance of FDI in the Chinese electronics industry, a natural question arises: how does FDI affect productivity improvement? While there are a number of empirical investigations of the impact of FDI on local productivity in developing countries, few econometric studies have been carried out for China. The current chapter examines this issue using a panel data set for the period 1996-98. In this study productivity is assumed to be determined by capital intensity, human capital and firm size, as well as the degree of foreign presence in the industry.

In section 5.2, the literature regarding the impact of FDI on productivity is reviewed. The empirical model, data and methodology are discussed in section 5.3. Section 5.4 provides the results from the statistical estimations. The final section presents the conclusions and discusses the implications for policy-makers and company managers.

5.2 FOREIGN DIRECT INVESTMENT AND PRODUCTIVITY SPILLOVERS

The contribution of FDI to efficiency improvement has been widely documented (see, for example, Findlay, 1978; Das, 1987; Walz, 1997; Markusen and Venables, 1999; de Mello, 1999). FDI has been viewed as an important source of both direct capital inputs and technology and knowledge spillovers (Blomstrom and Kokko, 1998) and has therefore been introduced as a separate variable, in addition to labour and capital, in the traditional production function. Balasubramanyam et al. (1996) have developed the following model to assess the impact of FDI on growth in developing countries:

$$y = \alpha + \beta l + \gamma(I/Y) + \psi(FDI/Y) + \phi x \qquad (5.1)$$

where y is the growth rate of GDP, l is the growth rate of labour input, I is domestic investment, FDI is foreign direct investment, Y is domestic GDP and x is the growth rate of exports. Using a sample of 46 developing countries, their study concludes that the beneficial effect of FDI, in terms of enhanced economic growth, is stronger in those countries which pursue an outwardly oriented trade policy than it is in those countries adopting an inwardly oriented policy. This type of model introduces FDI as an additional source of investment and examines its overall impact on economic growth.

On the other hand, a number of studies investigate indirect or spillover effects of FDI. Caves (1974, p.176) suggests that productivity spillovers occur when the multinational firm 'cannot capture all quasi-rents due to its productive activities, or to the removal of distortions by the subsidiary's competitive pressure'. Multinational firms may raise productivity levels among locally owned firms in the industries which they enter by improving the allocation of resources in those industries. Where FDI occurs in industries with high entry barriers, monopolistic distortions and their associated inefficiencies are reduced. In addition, through either the multinational's competitive force or demonstration effect, locally owned firms operating in imperfect markets may be induced to achieve a higher level of technical or X-efficiency (Leibenstein, 1966). Finally, the presence of multinational subsidiaries in an industry may speed the process or lower the cost of the transfer of technology. The threat of competition may stimulate domestic firms to innovate. Imitation effects and the movement of personnel trained by multinational subsidiaries also enhance the transfer of technology to local firms. FDI is believed to be a very important source of human capital augmentation and technical change especially in developing countries (de Mello, 1997).

To assess the externalities or indirect impact of FDI on local firms in an industry the following type of model is often applied:

$$LP_l = f(CI_l, LQ_l, FS_l, FP, OV) \qquad (5.2)$$

That is, the labour productivity in local firms (LP_l) is influenced by the capital intensity (CI_l) and labour quality (LQ_l) in local firms, the size of local firms (FS_l), foreign presence (FP) in the industry, and a vector of other possible explanatory variables (OV) such as the industry concentration ratio, R&D intensity in local firms and the technology gap between local and foreign firms.

Using this type of model, Caves (1974) carries out a pioneering econometric test for productivity spillovers from FDI. Using an augmented production function, Caves finds that the very presence of foreign firms had a positive impact on labour productivity in Australian manufacturing. Subsequent studies of this type by Globerman (1979) for Canada, by Blomstrom and Persson (1983), Blomstrom (1989), Kokko (1994), and Blomstrom and Wolff (1994) for Mexico, by Kokko et al. (1996) for the Uruguayan manufacturing sector, by Chuang and Lin (1999) for Taiwanese manufacturing, and by Liu et al. (2000) for UK manufacturing, confirm positive productivity spillovers from FDI.

While FDI-related externalities can be shown to produce high capital elasticity estimates, FDI can have some offsetting negative effects to the positive effects on local productivity. As Aitken and Harrison (1999) argue, the entry of foreign firms producing for the local market can draw demand from local firms, causing them to cut production. Thus, the productivity of local firms would fall as they are forced back up their average cost curves. As a result, net local productivity can decline.

The study of Haddad and Harrison (1993) for Morocco suggests that foreign presence has no significant effect on local labour productivity. The paper concludes that large technology gaps inhibit spillovers from FDI to local firms in Moroccan manufacturing. Grether (1999) finds that FDI has a positive influence on productivity efficiency at the plant level, but not at the sector level in Mexican manufacturing. Aitken and Harrison (1999) conclude that FDI negatively affects the productivity of locally owned plants in Venezuelan industry. Using matched establishment-level data, Okamoto

(1999) finds that technology transfer from Japanese assemblers to US-owned suppliers in the US auto parts industry explains only a small part of their improvement in economic performance.

As indicated above, there have been a number of empirical investigations into the impact of FDI on local productivity in developing countries. However, few econometric studies have been carried out for China. Fleisher and Chen (1997) find that total productivity is roughly twice as high in China's coastal provinces as it is in the interior areas, and that investment in higher education and FDI help to explain the productivity gap. Dougherty (1997) attempts to assess the impact of international technology transfer on total factor productivity in a number of broadly defined industrial sectors. Given the importance of FDI in capital formation and output, the current study examines the role of FDI in the productivity improvement in the Chinese electronics industry.

5.3 MODEL, DATA AND METHODOLOGY

Based on the discussion in the preceding section, the following simple empirical model for productivity impact is adopted to assess the overall impact of FDI on the Chinese electronics industry alongside other possible explanatory variables:

$$LP = f(CI, FS, LQ, FP) \qquad (5.3)$$

LP, CI, FS, LQ and FP are as defined for (5.2) above. The basic difference between (5.2) and (5.3) is that there is no subscript in the latter. This implies that the LP, CI, FS and LQ variables in (5.3) do not distinguish between local and foreign firms. Rather, they are the integrated measures of labour productivity, capital intensity, firm size and human capital of *both* local and foreign firms. In other words, (5.3) examines both the direct and indirect impacts of foreign firms on the overall labour productivity in China's electronics industry.

The data used for estimations are from the *Yearbook of China's Electronics Industries, 1997, 1998* and *1999*. In the yearbook, the electronics industry is divided into nine categories, namely (I) radar, (II) communications equipment, (III) broadcasting and TV, (IV) computers, (V) components, (VI) measurement equipment, (VII) special equipment, (VIII) household electronic appliances, and (IX) other electronic devices. These categories are then divided into 47 sub-sectors. Due to some missing data, our sample consists of 41 sub-sectors only.

The sub-sectors are detailed in Table 5.1 along with information on firm size and the capital/labour ratio. As is evident from the table, foreign capital accounted for varying percentages of total capital in the different sub-sectors. For instance, in the complete radar manufacturing sector, foreign capital amounted to a mere 1 per cent of total capital on average over the period 1996-98, whereas it amounted to 65 per cent of total capital in the electronic heating equipment sub-sector.

Table 5.1 China's electronics industry, 1996-98

Category	K_f/K	K/L	K/Y	firm size
I. Radar				
Complete radar manufacture	1.2311	1.9147	0.3122	59177
Special equipment & parts for radar	1.7437	0.8224	1.5431	2321
II. Communications Equipment				
Wireless transmission equipment manufacture	21.8544	5.1273	2.1657	30878
Exchange equipment manufacture	30.4337	8.4946	0.8575	24173
Wire communications terminal equipment	38.1237	3.1113	1.1884	5812
Wireless communication terminal equipment	32.8871	5.9971	0.2986	54825
Others	16.2522	3.6114	1.4000	6457
III. Broadcast & TV				
Broadcast & TV equipment manufacture	2.9027	2.3128	2.5941	1705
TV set manufacture	28.4263	5.249	1.1604	30985
Radio & recorder manufacture	36.7231	2.9793	1.2106	10011
Video manufacture	47.2273	17.3272	2.6633	42123
Others	21.777	4.1677	2.5588	2030
IV. Computer				
Complete computer manufacture	15.1064	5.0432	0.9118	24025
Computer exterior equipment manufacture	46.144	5.7214	0.9432	21388
Computer necessary accessories manufacture	16.1847	5.5873	1.0484	4654
Software manufacture	15.3015	7.5641	0.7766	5254
Calculator manufacture	45.7108	2.0051	1.2017	15477
Others	69.5599	10.2727	2.1352	10099
V. Electronics Components				
Electronic micro-electrical machine	29.0590	2.8293	2.668	3635

Table 5.1 Continued

Category	K_f/K	K/L	K/Y	firm size
V. Electronics Components				
Electronic electrical wire and cable manufacture	12.0793	4.0294	0.9969	8008
Electronic storage battery	20.7358	1.6611	1.6275	5480
Electronic dry battery	78.8808	9.3314	1.5183	9131
Electronic component manufacture	29.4864	2.7553	1.3959	2821
Electron component special material	39.4012	4.0928	2.5573	1872
Others	33.3621	2.1594	1.2209	1998
VI. Electronic Measuring Equipment				
Electron measuring instrument	6.0632	2.4100	1.9358	1246
Others	23.0276	3.2736	1.4003	1848
VII. Electronics Special Equipment				
Electronic special equipment manufacture	29.7506	2.6823	1.9611	2160
Electronic industrial mould & gear manufacture	24.1003	2.1395	2.1287	470
Others	19.352	2.4677	1.0885	2232
VIII. Household Electronic Appliances				
Refrigerator manufacture	24.9129	8.2622	1.7204	42421
Electric heating equipment	64.6789	3.9024	2.0183	8964
Electronic toy manufacture	28.8084	1.3434	1.5915	1669
Other household electronic appliance	42.9226	6.3778	1.3706	12547
Others	35.7514	3.7390	1.5036	1692
IX. Electronic Device				
Bulb manufacture	42.4407	4.0576	1.5461	2215
Electrical vacuum valve device manufacture	33.0177	9.7229	1.8327	39140
Semi-conductor device manufacture	30.4874	2.3629	2.0408	1447
Integrated circuit manufacture	42.9847	11.1162	3.182	8984
Electronic device material manufacture	34.8098	5.7394	1.5287	6042
Others	50.9389	8.3568	1.9293	7197

Notes: * K_f/K = Share of Foreign Capital (%); K/L = Capital/Labour ratio; K/Y = Capital/Output ratio; Firm size is measured by the industrial sales revenue (RMB 10,000) divided by the total number of firms in each sub-sector.

It would be ideal to assess the respective effects of FDI on productivity in locally and foreign-owned sectors rather than the combined productivity of both local and foreign sectors. However, separate data on the productivity of the different types of ownership are unavailable.

The log-linear functional form of (5.3) for our panel data set is

$$lp_{it} = \beta_{0t} + \beta_{1t} ci_{it} + \beta_{2t} fs_{it} + \beta_{3t} lq_{it} + \beta_{4t} fp_{it} + \varepsilon_{it}$$
$$i = 1, ..., N \ (N = 41); \ t = 1, ...T \ (T = 3) \tag{5.4}$$

where i and t denote the cross-section and time-series observations respectively. ε_{it} is a disturbance term which varies across individuals and time and $\varepsilon_{it} \sim N(0, \Sigma)$, where Σ is a positive definite matrix. The lower case indicates the logarithm, and all variables in the sample are in real terms.

The variables in (5.4) are defined as follows:

lp, labour productivity, is measured as the ratio of value added to the number of annual employees in each sub-sector of the electronics industry.

ci, capital intensity, is the ratio of the net value of fixed capital stock to the number of annual employees in each sub-sector.

fs, firm size, is the industrial sales revenue divided by the number of firms in each sub-sector.

lq, labour quality or human capital, is the number of engineers and managers divided by the total number of annual employees in each sub-sector.

fp, foreign presence, is measured by the ratio of foreign capital to total capital in each sub-sector.

The coefficients βs in (5.4) are directly the productivity elasticities with respect to the various explanatory variables. All these coefficients are assumed to be positive. Capital intensity (*ci*) means the amount of capital commanded by each worker. The firm size variable (*fs*) represents scale economies. Labour quality (*lq*) or human capital indicates the level of knowledge or skills of the labour force. Human capital is accumulated via education and on-the-job training. As a result, human capital should be measured in this way in any empirical study. Due to the data limitation, the current study uses the ratio of managers and engineers to all employees as a crude proxy for true labour quality. This proxy can be seen as reflecting the knowledge level of engineering and management training in the electronics sector. Education and on-the-job training on the part of workers are unfortunately ignored.

As the title suggests, the focus of this chapter is on the productivity impact of foreign presence (*fp*). It is generally believed that FDI brings in a package of capital, technology and managerial skills. Thus, the hypothesis to be tested in the current empirical study is as follows: ***FDI has had a positive impact*** *on labour productivity in the electronics industry in China directly and indirectly by its contagion, demonstration and competition effects.*

The above hypothesis indicates a one-way relationship from FDI to productivity. However, FDI can be motivated in different ways. It can be market, efficiency or strategic asset seeking (Dunning, 1993). As a result, the apparent connection of foreign presence and high productivity may be caused by the fact that FDI is attracted by the high efficiency in the host country. This gives rise to a possible endogeneity problem which needs to be dealt with.

Another concern with (5.4) is the stability of the coefficients. The policy of economic reforms and opening up to the outside world has made China experience dramatic changes. Accordingly, coefficients in (5.4) are initially allowed to vary across time.

The cost of allowing coefficients to vary is a relatively small number of degrees of freedom in each cross-section equation, which may lead to an inefficient use of information. Therefore, a Wald test is conducted to examine whether it is possible to impose constant coefficient restrictions on any explanatory variables over time. Based on Wald test statistics, a restricted system is then estimated.

A system of equations can be estimated in any of six ways, depending on whether there exists endogeneity, measurement errors, groupwise heteroscedasticity and contemporaneous correlation in the errors across equations. Since standard econometrics textbooks for system analysis (see, for example, Judge et al., 1985; Greene, 2000) offer full descriptions of the estimation techniques and statistical tests, only a brief review is provided here. Ordinary least squares (OLS) is the most efficient estimation technique if none of the above problems exist. Weighted ordinary least squares (WLS) is the OLS version accounting for groupwise heteroscedasticity only. Two-stage least squares (2SLS) is a technique accounting for endogeneity and measurement errors. Weighted two-stage least squares (W2SLS) is the 2SLS version accounting for groupwise heteroscedasticity. The seemingly unrelated regression estimation (SUR) method accounts for both heteroscedasticity and contemporaneous correlation. Finally, three-stage least squares (3SLS) is the 2SLS version of the SUR method, and is thus an appropriate estimation method if all four problems exist.

Necessary statistical tests are carried out to determine an appropriate statistical model and avoid biased or misleading results. The Lagrange multiplier (LM2) statistic (λ_{LM2}), under the null hypothesis of equal variances between two cross-section equations, is used to choose between OLS and WLS and between 2SLS and W2SLS.

$$\lambda_{LM2} = \frac{N}{2}\sum_t [\frac{\hat{\sigma}_t^2}{\hat{\sigma}^2} - 1]^2 \qquad (5.5)$$

where $\hat{\sigma}_t^2$ represents the disturbance variances and $\hat{\sigma}^2$ is a simple average of the sum of $\hat{\sigma}_t^2$. The statistic λ_{LM2} is asymptotically distributed as $\chi^2(T)$.

To choose between the OLS and SUR models, we use the Lagrange multiplier test (λ_{LM3}) derived by Breusch and Pagan (1980) for the null hypothesis that Σ is a diagonal matrix.

$$\lambda_{LM3} = N\sum_{i=2}^{T}\sum_{j=1}^{i-1} r_{ij}^2 \qquad (5.6)$$

where r_{ij} is the ijth residual cross-sectional correlation coefficient. The statistic λ_{LM3} is asymptotically distributed as $\chi^2(T(T-1)/2)$.

Given the possible endogeneity of *fp* and the measurement error of *lq*, as discussed above, the Hausman (HS) test was employed. This test is based on the existence of two estimators, b_{3sls} and b_{sure}, which are estimators of the regressors in the 3SLS and SUR models, respectively,

$$HS = N[b_{3sls} - b_{sure}]'\{Var[b_{3sls} - b_{sure}]\}^{-1}[b_{3sls} - b_{sure}] \sim \chi^2(k) \qquad (5.7)$$

where *k* is the number of unknown parameters in b_{3sls} and b_{sure} and *Var* is the variance-covariance matrix.

Large values of the LM2, LM3 and HS statistics argue in favour of the WLS model against the OLS model, the W2SLS model against the 2SLS model, the SUR model against the OLS model, and the 3SLS model against the SUR model, respectively.

Another sensible way of tackling the endogeneity problem is the adoption of generalised method of moments (GMM) estimation techniques. As is well known, this method is more general. Any of the system estimators provided above can be set up as special cases of GMM.

Finally, in order to avoid model mis-specification, Ramsey's RESET test is conducted.

5.4 EMPIRICAL RESULTS

Table 5.2 presents the results from the OLS, WLS, 2SLS, W2SLS, SUR and 3SLS regressions. As discussed in the previous section, four tests have been performed to compare the six statistical models. The λ_{LM2} statistics of 8.60 and 8.59 are statistically significant at the 5% level, suggesting the existence of groupwise heteroscedasticity. Similarly, the λ_{LM3} statistics of 21.8 is statistically significant at the 1% level, indicating the existence of heteroscedasticity and contemporaneous correlation problems. Furthermore, the highly significant HS statistic of 18.45 indicates that the 3SLS model is better than the SUR model. All this suggests that the 3SLS model is the preferred statistical model. In addition, 3SLS is an instrumental variable method. This can be used to check the robustness of the results conditional on the possible presence of measurement errors for labour quality. Finally, none of the χ^2 values of Ramsey's RESET is statistically significant. As a result, the model is not mis-specified and our interpretation of the econometric estimations is based on the 3SLS model.

The estimation results are slightly different for different years. For 1996, the coefficient for the capital intensity variable (*ci*) has the expected positive sign but is marginally statistically insignificant. This indicates that capital intensity may not be a very important determinant of labour productivity in China's electronics industry. This may appear to be a surprising result. However, as indicated in Table 5.1, a number of sub-sectors are not particularly capital-intensive in nature. For instance, the capital/labour ratios for special equipment and parts for radar and the electronic toy manufacture were less than or around 1. On the other hand, the equivalent ratio in video manufacture was 17.33 on average over the period 1996-98. The statistically insignificant result for capital stock may, therefore, mask a differing importance of capital intensity across the sub-sectors. The results reported here simply show that, in aggregate, a rise in capital intensity was not strongly associated with a rise in labour productivity. A similar word of caution is appropriate when interpreting the firm size, labour quality and foreign presence explanatory variables.

The insignificance of the capital intensity variable may also be caused by the problem of a small number of degrees of freedom arising from unnecessarily allowing the coefficients to vary. As will be seen in Table 5.3, where restrictions are imposed on coefficients of variables, the capital intensity variable is indeed a significant explanatory variable, but not as highly significant as the others. The loss of degrees of freedom makes it statistically insignificant in Table 5.2.

Foreign Direct Investment in China

Table 5.2 The unrestricted results of the econometric estimations of labour productivity

Variables	OLS/WLS 1996	1997	1998
ci	0.2097	0.1262	0.0712
	$(0.1532)^a$	(0.2179)	(0.1551)
	$(0.1436)^b$	(0.2042)	(0.1454)
fs	0.3270***	0.4376***	0.4737***
	(0.0693)	(0.1029)	(0.0650)
	(0.0649)	(0.0964)	(0.0609)
lq	1.2406***	0.3301	0.6788***
	(0.2920)	(0.3596)	(0.2187)
	(0.2736)	(0.3370)	(0.2049)
fp	0.1178	0.2743**	0.2063***
	(0.0638)*	(0.1362)	(0.0835)
	(0.0598)**	(0.1276)	(0.0782)
c	8.5298***	5.7607	6.3155***
	(0.7135)	(1.0123)	(0.6212)
	(0.6685)	(0.9486)	(0.5821)
R^2	0.6697	0.5214	0.7615
Wald test 1	OLS: 10.4285		WLS: 11.8769
RESET test	OLS: 2.2806		WLS: 2.6041
Variables	2SLS/W2SLS 1996	1997	1998
ci	0.2171	0.1265	0.0694
	$(0.1558)^a$	(0.2183)	(0.1563)
	$(0.1460)^b$	(0.2046)	(0.1464)
fs	0.3266	0.4382***	0.4737***
	(0.0695)	(0.1029)	(0.0651)
	(0.0651)	0.0965)	(0.0610)
lq	1.1988***	0.3171	0.6957***
	(0.2978)	(0.3649)	(0.2218)
	(0.2790)	(0.3420)	(0.2078)
fp	0.1203*	0.2748**	0.2053
	(0.0696)	(0.1378)	(0.0853)**
	(0.0652)	(0.1292)	(0.0799)***
c	8.4549***	5.7354***	6.3460***
	(0.7181)	(1.0160)	(0.6230)
	(0.6729)	(0.9520)	(0.5838)

Table 5.2 Continued

Variables	2SLS/W2SLS		
	1996	1997	1998
R^2	0.6694	0.5214	0.7614
Wald test 1	2SLS: 9.6161		W2SLS: 10.9517
RESET test	2SLS: 2.1391		W2SLS: 2.5798
λ_{LM2}	*OLS vs. WLS*: 8.60**		*2SLS vs. W2SLS*: 8.59**

Variables	SUR		
	1996	1997	1998
ci	0.1659	0.1338	0.1799
	(0.1352)	(0.1948)	(0.1318)
fs	0.3622***	0.4622***	0.4359***
	(0.0616)	(0.0927)	(0.0563)
lq	1.1780***	0.1028	0.5495***
	(0.2624)	(0.3237)	(0.1941)
fp	0.1116**	0.1947*	0.1633**
	(0.0545)	(0.1170)	(0.0683)
c	8.2241***	5.4686***	6.4289***
	(0.6486)	(0.9227)	(0.5538)
R^2	0.6655	0.5130	0.7566
Wald test 1/2		13.9653* / 2.7863	
RESET test		7.2928	

Variables	3SLS		
	1996	1997	1998
ci	0.1613	0.1361	0.1768
	(0.1361)	(0.1945)	(0.1312)
fs	0.3659***	0.4624***	0.4344***
	(0.0613)	(0.0927)	(0.0559)
lq	1.1268***	0.0518	0.5516***
	(0.2661)	(0.3281)	(0.1961)
fp	0.1234**	0.1962*	0.1688**
	(0.0588)	(0.1174)	(0.0689)
c	8.0911***	5.3868***	6.4327***
	(0.6517)	(0.9282)	(0.5545)
R^2	0.6634	0.5111	0.7567
Wald test 1/2		13.6703* / 2.4995	
RESET test		7.5511	
	OLS vs. SUR: 21.78***		*3SLS vs. SUR*: 18.45***

Notes:

1. ^{a} Standard errors are in parentheses when groupwise heteroscedasticity is not taken into account; ^{b} Standard errors are in parentheses when groupwise heteroscedasticity is taken into account.
2.   *, ** and *** denote significance at the 10%, 5% and 1% level, respectively.
3.   Wald test 1 is used to test whether β_i s (i = 1, 2, 3 & 4) are constant over time and is asymptotically distributed as χ^2 (8); Wald test 2 is used to test whether β_i s (i = 1, 2 & 4) are constant over time and is asymptotically distributed as χ^2 (6); RESET test is asymptotically distributed as χ^2 (6).

The firm size variable (*fs*) has the expected positive sign and is statistically significant at the 1% level for 1996. The coefficient of 0.4 implies that a 1 per cent increase in the firm size will result in a 0.4 per cent increase in labour productivity. This finding supports the existence of important scale economies in electronics manufacturing in China. The labour quality variable (*lq*) also has a significant and positive sign. The labour productivity elasticity with respect to this explanatory variable was as high as 1.13 in 1996. This means that a 1 per cent rise in human capital leads to slightly more than a 1 per cent rise in labour productivity. In terms of magnitude, human capital is the most important determinant of labour productivity among the explanatory variables. This shows the potential importance of education and skill enhancement in raising economic efficiency, as supported by a number of studies including Lee and Lee (1995), Eicher (1996) and Fleisher and Chen (1997). At the same time, the result may be biased by the human capital variable used, the ratio of managers and engineers to all employees. This should be borne in mind when interpreting the result.

Finally, the coefficient on the foreign presence variable (*fp*) is statistically significant and positive. This indicates that FDI in China's electronics industry plays a positive role in enhancing labour productivity, as expected. However, compared with other explanatory variables, the magnitude of foreign presence is the smallest. A 1 per cent increase in foreign presence only raises labour productivity by 0.12 per cent.

The 3SLS regression results for 1997 have one important feature: labour quality is no longer statistically significant. A careful examination of the raw data indicates that the number of engineers in 1997 is much smaller than in 1996. We tried to find out reasons for this dramatic fall without success, but infer that this is the main cause of the insignificance of the labour quality variable.

Another important feature is that the significance level of the coefficient on foreign presence fell from 5% in 1996 to 10% in 1997. Since the extent to which local firms benefit from the very presence of foreign firms depends largely on their own technological capabilities, the fall in the significance of FDI may be a consequence of the large decline in the number of engineers who are the driving force for technical competence. The elasticity of foreign presence (0.20) is, however, greater than the elasticities for capital intensity (0.14) and human capital (0.05), in 1997. As is the case for 1996, the coefficient on firm size is highly significant.

The 3SLS results for 1998 show a similar pattern to that for 1996. The coefficient on capital intensity is still statistically insignificant. The firm size and labour quality variables are significant at the 1% level and foreign presence is statistically significant at the 5% level. Labour quality is still the most important determinant of labour productivity. However, its magnitude is much smaller than that for 1996. Foreign presence is still the least important explanatory variable in terms of the magnitude, but its difference with the labour quality and capital intensity variable is reduced.

The statistics of Wald test 1 in Table 5.2 show that the imposition of constant coefficient restrictions on all four explanatory variables (fp, fs, ci, and lq) across time is accepted by OLS, WLS, 2SLS and W2SLS, but rejected by SUR and 3SLS. However, the statistics of Wald test 2 indicate the acceptance of constant coefficients on fp, fs, and ci across time by all models. Table 5.3, therefore, presents the results of the econometric estimations with constant coefficient restrictions on these three variables.

By correctly imposing constant coefficient restrictions on all four explanatory variables (fp, fs, ci, and lq) across time for the OLS, WLS, 2SLS and W2SLS models, all explanatory variables are statistically significant at least at the 5% level in Table 5.3.

Turning to the results from the preferred 3SLS model of Table 5.3, where labour quality is allowed to vary according to the Wald test statistics, it is clear that capital intensity is statistically significant at the 10% level. This again confirms that capital intensity is an important factor influencing labour productivity, although it is not as highly significant as the other explanatory variables. The results on labour quality are generally consistent with those presented in Table 5.2: the variable is not statistically significant for 1997 because of the dramatic fall in the number of engineers in the electronics industry. Firm size and foreign presence are highly significant. In terms of magnitude, the foreign presence variable is not as important as the capital intensity and firm size variables in raising productivity. The impact of foreign presence is more important than labour quality in 1996 and 1997, but much less important in 1998.

Table 5.3 The restricted results of the econometric estimations of labour productivity

Variables	OLS	WLS	2SLS
ci	0.2057**	0.1921**	0.2026**
	(0.1014)	(0.0936)	(0.1026)
fs	0.3945***	0.4031***	0.3953***
	(0.0460)	(0.0418)	(0.0461)
lq	0.6985***	0.7418***	0.6930***
	(0.1677)	(0.1517)	(0.1705)
fp	0.1686***	0.1638***	0.1743***
	(0.0514)	(0.0468)	(0.0542)
c-1996	7.0344***	7.0570***	7.0071***
	(0.4523)	(0.4082)	(0.4546)
c-1997	6.8648***	6.8869***	6.8369***
	(0.4588)	(0.4191)	(0.4611)
c-1998	6.9557***	6.9764***	6.9279***
	(0.4690)	(0.4207)	(0.4713)
R^2-1996	0.6105	0.6155	0.6073
R^2-1997	0.4878	0.4819	0.4897
R^2-1998	0.7504	0.7511	0.7509
Variables	W2SLS	SUR	3SLS
ci	0.1883**	0.1904*	0.1832*
	(0.0948)	(0.1060)	(0.1073)
fs	0.4042***	0.4133***	0.4128***
	(0.0419)	(0.0478)	(0.0479)
lq-1996		1.1410***	1.1146***
		(0.2529)	(0.2569)
lq-1997	0.7393***	0.0745	0.0705
	(0.1542)	(0.3079)	(0.3117)
lq-1998		0.5398***	0.5652***
		(0.1892)	(0.1917)
fp	0.1690***	0.1353***	0.1485***
	(0.0494)	(0.0465)	(0.0499)
c-1996	7.0348***	7.6319***	7.5688***
	(0.4104)	(0.5268)	(0.5300)
c-1997	6.8640***	5.9533***	5.9213***
	(0.4212)	(0.6164)	(0.6202)
c-1998	6.9536***	6.6869***	6.6984***
	(0.4229)	(0.5165)	(0.5187)
R^2-1996	0.6131	0.6525	0.6505

Table 5.3 Continued

R^2-1997	0.4836	0.5044	0.5062
R^2-1998	0.7517	0.7515	0.7532

Notes:
1. Standard errors are in parentheses.
2. *, ** and *** denote significance at the 10%, 5% and 1% level, respectively.

Table 5.4 GMM results of the econometric estimations of labour productivity

Variables	1996	1997	1998
ci	0.1871***	0.1976***	0.1096*
	(0.0417)	(0.0572)	(0.0659)
fs	0.3507***	0.3765***	0.4394***
	(0.0371)	(0.0389)	(0.0252)
lq	0.9280***	0.4740***	0.7288***
	(0.1605)	(0.1284)	(0.1040)
fp	0.1596***	0.2307***	0.1807***
	(0.0356)	(0.0334)	(0.0245)
c	7.7339***	6.5562***	6.6928***
	(0.4764)	(0.4545)	(0.3299)
R^2	0.6436	0.5114	0.7580

Notes:
1. Standard errors are in parentheses.
2. *, ** and *** denote significance at the 10%, 5% and 1% level, respectively.

Finally, the empirical results for unrestricted GMM regressions are presented in Table 5.4. All explanatory variables in the GMM model are statistically significant for any of the three years. The general pattern is that labour quality is the most significant determinant of labour productivity in terms of magnitude, followed by firm size. The productivity elasticities of labour quality vary from 0.47 to 0.93 per cent and those of firm size from 0.35 to 0.44 per cent. The productivity elasticity of foreign presence is smaller than that of capital intensity for 1996, but greater for both 1997 and 1998.

A number of common results emerge from the GMM and the 3SLS. First, all the explanatory variables included are significant in explaining labour productivity in the Chinese electronics industry. Second, foreign presence is not as important as firm size and labour quality in raising labour productivity.

Several case studies published in China may be used to explain the limited role of FDI in productivity improvement. Cui and Kong (1998) indicate that market-oriented FDI by a number of well-known multinational enterprises tended to develop a monopoly position in the Chinese market and indigenous Chinese firms were disadvantaged during the competition. On the other hand, Wang (1997) suggests that 80 per cent of the FDI projects in the electronics industry were small-scale with low technology. They rushed headlong into mass production of popular products. As a result, supplies substantially exceeded demands and this led to low profits and even losses for many firms. For instance, before 1990 a number of indigenous Chinese firms had already introduced technologies to produce magnetic heads for tape recorders. After meeting domestic demand, these firms exported their products and earned more than US$ 0.1 billion each year. After 1990 however, some FIEs were established in the coastal areas to produce similar products, with the result that the indigenous Chinese firms were gradually crowded out.

Wang (1997) also shows the existence of unnecessary competition in the production of colour TV sets. In the 1990s China was already the largest colour TV producer in the world and its technology and quality of products reached international standards. However, in the mid-1990s, the so-called 'unite foreign to defeat domestic' phenomenon appeared, i.e. a number of new joint ventures were formed to compete with domestic firms. Chang Hong was a leading state-owned colour TV producer in China. The slogan of some FIEs was then 'to overtake Chang Hong in three years and to squeeze out Chang Hong in five years'. This led to a sharp increase in excess capacities of TV production in China, with the result that competition became even more fierce and complex. It was difficult for many firms to survive and economic efficiency decreased substantially.

In addition to the problem of crowding out, FIEs are found to tightly control their key technologies. According to Yin (1997), there were 70 firms in the micro-electronic circuit sub-sector. Among the top eight firms there were five joint ventures, one wholly foreign-owned enterprise and two state-owned enterprises. In these joint ventures, the average equity share of the foreign partners was 66 per cent. The technologies of these FIEs were more advanced than the state-owned enterprises. The Chinese partners were interested in obtaining advanced technologies but the terms for technology transfer were very harsh, and in some cases no technology was allowed to be transferred.

From these case studies the following reasons for the limited role of FDI in China's electronics industry can be identified. They are the increase in excess capacities caused by the replication of industrial projects, the low efficiency of many indigenous Chinese firms arising from complex and perhaps unnecessary competition and the restricted transfer of technology by foreign firms. The first two reasons are closely related. Competition exerted by FIEs is expected to force indigenous firms to improve efficiency, but in China competition is driven by the rapid expansion of new production capacities. Imamura (1999) among others suggests that the existence of excess productive capacities is a very serious problem in China. Even in the foreign-invested firms less than half of the production capacities were employed in the electricity equipment, computer, home electrical appliance, photocopier, automobile, and bicycle sectors. In Chinese statistics, computers, home electrical appliances and photocopiers belong to the electronics industry.

Although its contributions are not as important as firm size and labour quality, FDI does nevertheless positively affect productivity in China's electronics industry. However, caution must be used when one interprets the productivity impact of FDI in China. As mentioned earlier, the current study only examined the influence of FDI on the combined productivity of locally and foreign-owned sectors because of the lack of separate data on productivity, capital intensity, firm size and human capital for these two sectors. We can say that Blomstrom and Wolff (1994), Kokko et al. (1996) and Chuang and Lin (1999) find a positive impact of FDI on productivity in local firms in developing countries, but the current study could only show that FDI has a positive impact on the combined productivity of local and foreign firms.

Although it is not possible to know the specific productivity impact of FDI on indigenous Chinese firms, this study appears to suggest that China's electronics industry as a whole benefits from the presence of foreign firms in terms of labour productivity. Therefore, an increase of FDI in the industry may further improve efficiency. As will be discussed in the next section however, the role of FDI in raising productivity can be further enhanced by the implementation of appropriate industrial policies.

5.5 CONCLUSIONS

This chapter has assessed the impact of FDI on labour productivity in China's electronics industry. A panel data set from the official publications was used, which divides the industry into 47 sub-sectors and covers the period 1996-98. An empirical model was established from the literature review that incorporates both direct and indirect (spillover) effects of inward FDI on productivity in the industry. These effects were measured in terms of the degree of foreign presence in the sub-sectors of the Chinese electronics industry. The impact was assessed alongside other possible explanatory variables, namely capital intensity, labour quality and firm size for scale effects.

The OLS, WLS, 2SLS, W2SLS, SUR and 3SLS models were estimated and the results indicate that all explanatory variables have the expected, positive sign. After correctly imposing constant coefficient restrictions, all explanatory variables are statistically significant except for labour quality in the SUR and 3SLS models for 1997 due to a significant drop in the number of engineers. The diagnostic tests suggest that the 3SLS model is the most appropriate statistical model for the given data set. The alternative preferred model is the GMM, which shows a similar pattern of productivity determination in the Chinese electronics industry.

The Chinese evidence tends to suggest that FDI has a positive impact on labour productivity in the Chinese electronics industry. In terms of the relative magnitude of the impact on labour productivity, the human capital variable is the most important determinant, followed by firm size, and then capital intensity or foreign presence. The case studies cited in this study have provided three reasons for the limited role of FDI in raising productivity in China's electronics industry. Competition in the form of establishing new enterprises caused large quantities of production capacities to be idle; indigenous Chinese firms gradually lost their market shares; and FIEs restricted their transfer of technologies. The competition described in the case studies is consistent with what is discussed in Aitken and Harrison (1999), i.e. the entry of foreign firms producing for the local market draws demand from local firms and reduces net local productivity.

The empirical results from this study have implications for policy-makers and enterprise management. Firstly, the significant coefficient on capital intensity indicates the importance of embodied technology on the improvement of labour productivity. Thus, the government authorities need to encourage investment in fixed capital formation and upgrading and enterprise managers need to pay attention to the enhancement of capital intensity by introducing new machinery and equipment. On the other hand, the small values of the coefficient on capital intensity do suggest the importance of the rate of utilisation of production capacities. Higher efficiency should be sought by a fuller use of productive assets.

Secondly, the positive and significant coefficient on the firm size variable confirms the importance of scale economies at a time when many enterprises produced very similar products and at low scales of production. As indicated in the pie charts in section 5.1, the number of foreign firms was smaller than state-owned or other locally owned enterprises, but their industrial value added was the largest. The number of other locally owned enterprises was the highest, but their industrial value added was the smallest. If FIEs still need to reduce the number of factories to benefit more from economies of scale as indicated by Wang (1997), the restructuring of firm sizes in the state-owned and especially other locally owned sectors is really imminent. As Shi (1998) indicates, the decision in the Maoist period to disperse industrial production around the country to minimise the threat from military attack and, more recently, from managers and local party officials using their greater autonomy from central planning to build more factories, led to the existence of a large number of small indigenous Chinese enterprises in this industry. Further restructuring of the industry needs the co-operation of the central government and local authorities.

Thirdly, the positive and significant coefficient on labour quality from the GMM model and from the 3SLS model for 1996 and 1998 suggests that human capital is a very important determinant of labour productivity in the electronics sector. The result suggests that more investment in education and training, reflected in this study because of data limitations in terms of engineering and managerial skills, might significantly enhance labour productivity. The Tenth Five-Year Plan (2001-05) regards qualified personnel as the most important resource for economic development and intends to train and provide a large number of specialised experts in the areas of information technology, finance, accounting, foreign trade, law and modern business management (People's Daily, Overseas Edition, 19 October 2000). This would certainly improve labour quality in China. At firm level, the larger the proportion of engineers in total employees, the higher the firm's technological competence. Thus, the recruitment of more qualified engineers and the provision of more on-the-job technical training should help a firm to benefit more from the contagion and demonstration effects of foreign presence and from competition with foreign firms.

Finally, the finding that FDI played a limited positive role in productivity improvement suggests the importance of the effective use of FDI. While FDI should continue to be encouraged, appropriate industrial policies are needed to provide guidance for the direction of investment. The *Guiding Catalogue for Foreign Investment in Industry* published by the Chinese government is useful for this purpose because it classifies investment in certain industries as 'encouraged', 'restricted' or 'prohibited'. If one particular sub-industry already has sufficient production capacities, further investment in this industry should be restricted. By doing so the low efficiency caused by overdue replication of industrial projects can be avoided. Competition is essential for efficiency improvement, but competition in the form of establishing excess capacities may produce more harm than benefits and should therefore be avoided.

6. Endogenous Growth Theory and Regional Income Convergence in China

6.1 INTRODUCTION

Since China started the process of economic reform and opening up to the outside world in late 1978, its real GDP has grown on average by over 8 per cent a year. This is a remarkable achievement. As a result, it would be interesting to investigate the following issues. What are the determinants of Chinese economic growth? Do poor regions tend to converge towards rich ones in China? Put another way, have regional income gaps been widened or narrowed in the post-reform period? What is the role of foreign direct investment (FDI) in this development process? This chapter intends to answer these questions[1].

In the literature, standard or augmented convergence regressions are often used to assess whether economic growth leads to increasing income inequality. In the case of China, Jian et al. (1996) conclude that market-oriented reforms beginning in 1978 helped to equalise regional incomes. The convergence was strongly associated with the rise in rural productivity and was particularly strong in those provinces allowed to integrate with the outside world. Using cross-section and panel data, Chen and Fleisher (1996) identify conditional convergence of regional per capita income from 1978 to 1993. Mody and Wang (1997) find evidence of absolute convergence of the growth of industrial output during 1985-89, and of the log of per capita GDP in 1995, both in seven coastal regions. By using the shrinkage method for panel data, Choi and Li (2000) find that growth convergence exists in China and that the low-income provinces of the central and western regions experience higher convergence rates.

This chapter tests endogenous growth theory using a panel of annual data covering 28 provinces across China between 1986 and 1998. It differs from the existing literature on convergence in China in several ways. First, the study is explicitly based on an endogenous growth model. Second, it covers most recent data and should provide more robust empirical results. Third, as a unique feature of this book, panel data unit roots tests are applied to examine the econometric properties of the data and a long-run relationship is identified between the dependent and explanatory variables.

The rest of the chapter is organised as follows. Section 6.2 reviews the literature on economic growth and convergence. In section 6.3, a conceptual model for endogenous growth is developed and the techniques of econometric analysis used are briefly discussed. The empirical results concerning growth and convergence of per capita GDP across Chinese provinces are presented in section 6.4. Conclusions and policy implications are provided in section 6.5.

6.2 LITERATURE REVIEW

Barro and Sala-i-Martin (1992a) put forward two measures of convergence: β- and σ-convergence. β-convergence exists if there is a negative and significant relationship between the growth rate of per capita income and its level in the previous year. Convergence may be conditional if additional explanatory variables have a significant impact on the growth rate. Convergence can also be absolute if those additional variables individually and jointly have no impact on the growth rate. σ-convergence means that the dispersion of the cross-section per capita income tends to fall over time. This chapter examines β-convergence only, since one of our main concerns here is to assess the contribution of FDI to economic growth in China.

Convergence is closely associated with neo-classical theory that emphasises the existence of the steady state and diminishing returns to capital. This implies that poor regions with low capital/output ratios grow systematically faster than their rich counterparts, so there is a tendency towards regional convergence. Put another way, since the rate of return is negatively related to the stock of capital, an integrated economy will experience general convergence of regional incomes over time, provided that there are no major barriers to the operation of market processes. Regional disparities are only short-run phenomena and will automatically disappear over time. This is especially true of regions within a single country.

New or endogenous growth theory emphasises the importance of investment in physical, human capital and R&D for economic growth and increasing returns to both types of capital. Crafts (1996) distinguishes two major types of endogenous growth theory. The first uses endogenous broad capital models which emphasise externalities generated by investment in physical and human capital and relate technological characteristics to 'learning by doing' and 'technological (knowledge) spillovers'. The second uses endogenous innovation growth models which postulate that technological progress results from deliberate innovation. A standard production function for endogenous growth models is as follows (see Grossman and Helpman, 1991):

$$Y = Af(K, L, D) \tag{6.1}$$

where Y, K, and L denotes GDP, physical capital and labour force, respectively, A is a constant, and D is an index of the creation of intermediate goods which embody technological knowledge and which are augmented by R&D activities. D is also a positive function of the amount of resources allocated to R&D because of the spillover effects of increased technological knowledge. R&D (both domestic and global) is crucial for economic development. It may be divided into two types: the first leads to product innovation and the second to product imitation.

Given the different social, political and economic environments and capabilities to undertake R&D, different countries follow different innovation processes. This suggests that the rates of growth diverge across economies. The more resources allocated to R&D, the higher the incentive for firms to innovate, the greater the firms' abilities to create new technological ideas, and the higher the rate of growth a country will enjoy. In endogenous innovation growth models there can be multiple steady states and persistent divergence.

However, endogenous growth theory does not exclude the possibility of convergence. If a 'leading edge' economy innovates, and if its innovations are effectively imitated, diffused and assimilated into production in 'follower' economies at very low costs, then there can be a process of convergence between interdependent economies. As Romer (1993) emphasises, rapid growth is a positive function of both access to new technological ideas and the diffusion of these ideas through the production structure. Put another way, in the spirit of endogenous growth theory, technology creation and spillovers are the engine of economic growth. They can take place through a variety of channels that involve the transmission and diffusion of ideas and new technologies. Domestic R&D activities, investment in physical and human capital, FDI by multinational enterprises (MNEs) and trade of high-tech products, machinery and equipment are certainly important conduits to access and imitate new ideas.

Domestic R&D activities can enhance technological capabilities which are found to be positively correlated with economic growth or productivity (see, for example, Coe and Helpman, 1995; Coe et al., 1997 and Bayoumi et al., 1999). Individual domestic firms or institutes invest in R&D to acquire advanced know-how and to create valuable rent-yielding and intangible assets, which will increase output in society as a whole. If some countries have capabilities to imitate, given the lower cost of imitation compared with innovation, it is possible for them to catch up.

Investment in physical capital often reflects an increase in embodied technology. Increases in human capital affect the ability of firms to learn and absorb new technology. Barro and Sala-i-Martin (1995) explain how investment in education and human capital raises skills and efficiency in production through the adoption and development of new technology. A high level of human capital allows tangible inputs to be used effectively. Mankiw et al. (1992) contend that the quantitative implications of different saving and population growth rates are biased upward if human capital is not accounted for in the model. The role of human capital in the empirical analysis of growth has been strongly emphasised and the contribution of human capital to economic growth is by now part of received knowledge. Since innovations and their imitation are positively related to the size and quality of human capital, increased investment in education and on-the-job training will lead to rapid innovative progress and will help a country to catch up.

Balasubramanyam et al. (1996, 1999) and de Mello (1997, 1999) argue that many of the growth-promoting factors identified by endogenous growth theory can be initiated and nurtured to promote growth through FDI. In most cases, what FDI transfers are not only capital and managerial skills, but also embodied and tacit technologies. The special role that FDI plays in tacit technology transfer and diffusion can not be replaced by any other forms of international integration. In addition, numerous studies have shown that the output or productivity of local firms improves when a country hosts FDI (see, for example, Aitken et al. 1997; Liu et al. 2000). MNEs may develop new products and technologies earlier than local firms, and may exert competitive pressure on them and force them to imitate or innovate. MNEs always try to preserve their own knowledge and technology, but spillover through 'learning by doing' or 'learning by watching' to domestic firms creates economic growth. Another route for the diffusion of new ideas is the switch of labour from foreign subsidiaries to local firms. Because of the above reasons, FDI is recognised as a major source of rapid growth, especially in developing countries (de Mello, 1997; Borensztein et al., 1998).

Sachs and Warner (1995) suggest that policies towards open trade are important in promoting economic growth and convergence, as international trade (including both exports and imports) facilitates technology creation and transfer. International trade enables a country to use a large variety of technologically advanced physical capital, which enhances the productivity of its own resources. International trade promotes across-the-board learning in product design, facilitates the diffusion and imitation of foreign technologies and helps the creation of innovations.

In the traditional convergence regression population growth is also included. Population growth means that the quantity of available labour services in the aggregate production function increases over time. Assume that the law of variable proportions holds. In the absence of technical change an increase in only labour services, the other inputs remaining fixed, will lead to a less than proportionate change in output and further increases in this input will lead to diminishing increases in output. However, it is now often argued that population growth places pressure on limited resources for providing adequate health and education, and the effect of population growth on economic development *per se* has been very controversial (Amponsah et al., 1999).

Because R&D, FDI, trade and human capital are important means for the development and diffusion of technological ideas, these variables may be used to replace the index of innovation creation in the basic endogenous innovation growth model. Thus, (6.1) can be modified as follows:

$$Y = Af(DK, PG, FDI, EX, IM, RDE, HC) \tag{6.2}$$

where *DK* denotes domestic capital stock and PG population growth, *FDI, EX, IM, RDE* and *HC* represent realised FDI stock, exports, imports, R&D expenditure and human capital, respectively. These factors are expected to have a positive impact on the rate of technological progress and hence growth. Given technology transfer and adoption, conditional convergence can occur among interdependent countries. It is obvious that, although both neo-classical theory and endogenous innovation models accept the possible existence of convergence, their reasons for catch up are different.

Regional convergence has been subject to a large number of empirical studies. Barro and Sala-i-Martin (1991, 1992a, 1992b, 1995) find evidence for absolute β-convergence for the regions of the United States (48 contiguous states, 1880-1990), Canada (10 provinces, 1961-1991), Japan (47 prefectures, 1955-1990) and Europe (90 regions, 1950-1990). The speed with which regions of different countries converge to their respective national means is very similar, at approximately 2 per cent per year. Barro and Sala-i-Martin (1995) also find conditional β-convergence for a large sample of developed and developing countries. The speed of conditional convergence is identical to that of absolute convergence. Murthy and Ukpolo (1999) report that African countries exhibit conditional convergence at the rate of 1.7 per cent per year over the period of 1960-1985. Sala-i-Martin (1994, 1996), Barro and Sala-i-Martin (1995) and Miller (1996) argue that regions within a country or within Organisation for Economic Co-operation and Development (OECD) countries share similar structural characteristics and are therefore more likely to converge.

However, the speed of convergence of 2 per cent is quite slow. This implies that it will take a region 35 years to eliminate half the initial gap from its steady state. Reasons provided in the literature for the low convergence rate include the high costs of imitation and implementation of new technologies (Sala-i-Martin, 1994), inappropriate measurement of variables and application of estimation techniques (Murthy and Chien, 1997), and omission of medium-term macroeconomic variables (Andres et al., 1996). Islam (1995) and Cellini (1997) note that the speed of convergence increases when the panel data approach is used. Using panel data sets, Andres et al. (1996) find that the estimated speeds of convergence increase dramatically when such variables as public consumption, variance of M1 growth, export growth, budget surplus and inflation are included in the model.

Other convergence studies include Herz and Roger (1995) and Hofer and Worgotter (1995), which investigate regional convergence in West Germany and Austria, respectively. Mankiw et al. (1992), Miller (1996), Andres et al. (1996) and Murthy and Chien (1997) deal with economic growth in OECD countries. Persson (1997) attempts to test for convergence in per capita income across the 24 Swedish counties, adjusting for differences in spatial price levels. Nagaraj et al. (2000) examine the growth performance of Indian states during 1970-94. All these studies provide clear evidence of long-run regional convergence, especially conditional β-convergence. However, the results are by no means universal. The β- and σ-convergence tests of Tsionas (2000) show that in the period 1977-96 regional incomes in the United States did not converge.

6.3 EMPIRICAL MODELS AND METHODOLOGY

In this chapter a modified endogenous growth model is employed to investigate regional economic growth and per capita income convergence in China. Since a panel data set is used here, we follow Knight et al. (1993), Islam (1995) and Miller (1996) to specify a model with heterogeneity across economies. The heterogeneity may be due to the structural differences across regions. The panel data approach is superior to a cross-section approach since the latter implicitly assumes the same production function for different regions and may be inappropriate if heterogeneity across regions is significant.

Unobserved differences between the regions are allowed for by the specification of individual regional effects A_i. Based on the assumption that convergence to the steady state occurs at a rate equal to λ, we have the endogenous innovation growth convergence regression:

$$y_{it} = \gamma LY_{i,t-1} + \beta T + \zeta_1 LDK_{it} + \zeta_2 LPG_{it} + \zeta_3 LFDI_{it} + \zeta_4 LEX_{it}$$
$$+ \zeta_5 LIM_{it} + \zeta_6 LRDE_{it} + \zeta_7 LHC_{it} + \delta_i + \varepsilon_{it}$$
$$i = 1, ..., N \ (N = 28); \ t = 1, ..., T \ (T = 13) \qquad\qquad (6.3)$$

where $\gamma = -(1 - e^{-\lambda})$, L indicates logged values, i and t denote the cross-section and time series observations respectively, ε_{it} is a disturbance term which varies across individuals and time and possesses the usual properties, the ζs are the elasticities of output, y and Y denote the growth rate and the level of real per capita GDP, respectively, T is the time trend, capturing the unobserved or exogenous technical progress, and DK and FDI are domestic capital and FDI, respectively. Because of the problem in measuring capital stock especially in a developing country, we follow common practice in empirical studies and approximate the rate of growth of the capital stock by the share of investment in GDP (see Balasubramanyam et al. 1996, 1999). Thus, DK is the ratio of investment in fixed assets to GDP, $FDIR$ is the ratio of realised annual inflow of FDI to GDP, PG is population growth, EX and IM are exports and imports, respectively, RDE is R&D expenditure and HC is human capital. Full definitions and sources of the variables are given in Appendix 6A.

As discussed in the preceding section, endogenous growth theory suggests positive relationships between economic growth on the one hand and FDI, exports and imports, R&D expenditure, human capital and domestic investment on the other. Before a formal econometric analysis is conducted in the next section, it may be useful to visually examine these relationships in China using the scatter diagrams provided in Figures 6.1 to 6.6.

Figure 6.1 shows the connection between FDI and per capita GDP growth. In terms of the relative share of FDI in GDP, the coastal provinces or cities of Hainan, Tianjin, Guangdong, Fujian, Beijing and Jiangsu are the top regional hosts, while Xinjiang and Ningxia are the most disadvantaged inner areas. A positive relationship between the log of FDI as a percentage of GDP and the growth rate of GDP per capita can be easily identified from the figure.

From Figure 6.2 a clear pattern for exports and growth emerges. As the log of exports increases, so the growth rate of GDP per capita rises. Guangdong is the obvious top performer for exports followed by Jiangsu and Shandong, among others. Ningxia is the poorest exporter followed by Gansu and Guizhou. Figure 6.3 reveals a very similar pattern for the log of imports and the growth of GDP per capita.

The relationship between R&D and growth is presented in Figure 6.4. Different from the FDI and import and export patterns, Beijing is the top performer for R&D expenditure. This is not surprising however, given that a large number of the state research institutions are located in the capital. On the other hand, Ningxia, Hainan, Guizhou, Xinjiang and Inner Mongolia are at the bottom. A generally positive connection between the log of R&D expenditure and the growth of GDP per capita can be detected in the figure.

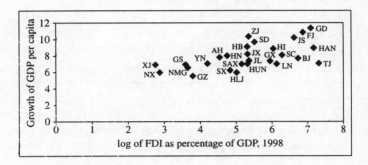

Notes:

BJ = Beijing; TJ = Tianjin; HI = Hebei; SX = Shanxi; NMG = Inner Mongolia; LN = Liaoning; JL = Jilin; HLJ = Heilongjiang; SH = Shanghai; JS = Jiangsu; ZJ = Zhejiang; AH = Anhui; FJ = Fujian; JX = Jiangxi; SD = Shandong; HN = Henan; HB = Hubei; HUN = Hunan; GD = Guangdong; GX = Guangxi; HAN = Hainan; SC = Sichuan; GZ = Guizhou; YN = Yunnan; SAX = Shaanxi; GS = Gansu; NX = Ningxia; XJ = Xinjiang

Figure 6.1 Per capita GDP growth and FDI, 1986-98

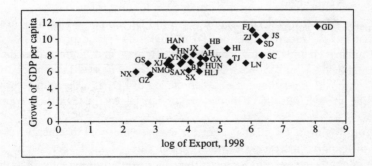

Notes: As Figure 6.1

Figure 6.2 Per capita GDP growth and export, 1986-98

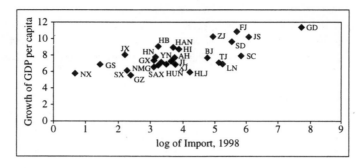

Notes: As Figure 6.1

Figure 6.3 Per capita GDP growth and import, 1986-98

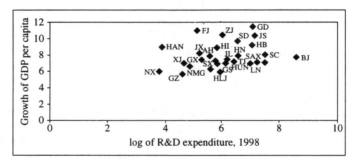

Notes: As Figure 6.1

Figure 6.4 Per capita GDP growth and R&D expenditure, 1986-98

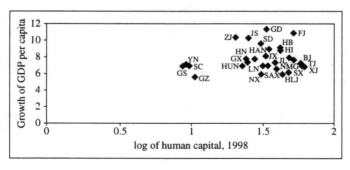

Notes: As Figure 6.1

Figure 6.5 Per capita GDP growth and human capital, 1986-98

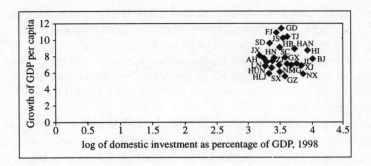

Notes: As Figure 6.1

Figure 6.6 Per capita GDP growth and domestic investment, 1986-98

It is somewhat surprising that Xinjiang ranks first in terms of human capital, as indicated by Figure 6.5. Human capital is defined in this study as the ratio of the secondary school plus higher education enrolment to the total labour force. Although Xinjiang is a remote inner area, education may be emphasised there. Tianjin and Beijing rank second and third, respectively, and Gansu, Yunnan, Sichuan and Guizhou are the obvious losers. Again a positive relationship between the log of human capital and the growth of GDP per capita can be found in the figure.

Finally, Figure 6.6 shows that the logs of domestic investment as a percentage of GDP for different provinces cluster closely together. This may indicate that although absolute values of domestic investment in fixed capital in the inner areas are smaller than the coastal areas, the shares of the investment in GDP across regions are relatively close across all Chinese regions because of the relatively smaller values of GDP in the inner areas. It may also indicate the Chinese government's efforts to balance regional economies by allocating domestic investment evenly across the regions.

Following Sala-i-Martin (1994), the explanatory variables in (6.3), excluding lagged per capita GDP, can be interpreted as the determinants of long-run economic growth. Given the research objective of this book, we are particularly interested in the role of FDI in growth.

As Miller (1996) indicates, a convergence test based on such a panel data equation as the above is superior to the conventional cross-section test because the initial level of output per capita is updated each year[2]. We first consider absolute convergence. If there is no absolute convergence, we discuss conditional convergence with FDI, exports, imports, R&D expenditure, human capital, capital and population included in the model.

To avoid possible spurious correlation[3], the IPS unit root tests are first conducted to check the data properties of the variables involved in this study. As discussed in chapter 3, a panel data set can be estimated in any of three ways, depending on whether the individual cross-section effects are considered to be constant, fixed or random. The corresponding statistical models are the ordinary least squares (OLS), fixed effects (FE) and random effects (RE) models.

More specifically, the three statistical models differ mainly in the assumptions concerning δ_i, which is time-invariant and accounts for any unobservable individual- specific effect not included in the regression. In the OLS model, the δ_i s are treated as an intercept which is held constant across the individual cross-section units. The FE model allows the δ_i s to vary between units and treats them as parameters to be estimated. In other words, dummy variables are employed to capture the unobserved heterogeneity. In the RE model, the δ_i s are assumed to be a random variable that is independent and identically distributed, i.e. $\delta_i \sim IID(0, \sigma_\delta^2)$.

As noted in chapter 3, these three models have their own advantages and disadvantages. We apply the three tests above to determine the appropriate model. To choose between the OLS and RE models, we use Breusch and Pagan (1980)'s LM test (λ_{LM1}) for the null hypothesis that the OLS estimators are best linear unbiased. For details, see section 3.5 of chapter 3.

The other two tests are the likelihood ratio (LR) test for the FE model against the OLS model and the Hausman specification (HS) test for the FE model against the RE model. The LR test statistic, under the null hypothesis of constant individual-specific effects is:

$$LR = NT * \ln(1 + \frac{RSS_r - RSS_u}{RSS_u}) \sim \chi^2(N-1) \qquad (6.4)$$

where RSS_r and RSS_u represent the residual sums of squares in the OLS and FE models respectively. The LR statistic is asymptotically distributed as $\chi^2(N-1)$.

The HS test is based on the Wald criterion:

$$HS = [b_{fe} - b_{re}]'Var[b_{fe} - b_{re}]^{-1}[b_{fe} - b_{re}] \sim \chi^2(k) \qquad (6.5)$$

where b_{fe} and b_{re} are estimators of the regressors in the FE and RE models, respectively, k is the number of regressors and *Var* is the variance-covariance matrix. The null hypothesis of the HS test is that the RE model is the correct specification. The HS statistic is asymptotically distributed as $\chi^2(k)$.

Large values of the LR, LM and HS statistics argue in favour of the FE model against the OLS model, the RE model against the OLS model and the FE model against the RE model, respectively.

Finally, the Lagrange multiplier (LM2) statistic (λ_{LM2}) is used to identify whether there is groupwise heteroscedasticity. Details regarding this test can be found in section 5.3 of chapter 5.

6.4 EMPIRICAL RESULTS

Although a visual examination of the relationships between per capita income growth and various regional characteristics is provided in the preceding section, a formal econometric analysis is needed to assess regional economic growth processes. This empirical work is based on a panel of data on 28 provinces of China over the period 1986-98. Table 6.1 presents descriptive statistics and panel data unit root test results for each variable (in log form except for the growth rate of per capita GDP) involved in the analysis. The null hypothesis of non-stationarity is rejected at the 10% level for all the variables, suggesting the possibility of the existence of a long-run relationship between the dependent and explanatory variables.

Following the discussion of the methodology in the preceding section, three tests are performed to compare the OLS, FE and RE models. The large values of the LR, LM1 and HS statistics argue in favour of the FE model against the OLS and RE models, which implies the existence of significant region-specific effects. The results from the estimation of the FE model are reported in Table 6.2. Regression of per capita GDP growth against the lagged per capita GDP is shown in column (2) for analysing absolute convergence. Columns (3) to (6) contain the regression results for conditional convergence. Columns (3) and (4) present results of the conventional Solow model, while columns (5) and (6) report the results of the endogenous growth model. The difference between columns (3) and (4) and columns (5) and (6) is that groupwise heteroscedasticity is taken into consideration in (4) and (6) but not in columns (3) and (5). While the results from columns (4) and (6) are statistically preferred according to the LM2 statistic, those in columns (3) and (5) are included for the purpose of comparison. As a matter of fact, the magnitudes of the corresponding coefficients in columns (3) and (4), and (5) and (6) are very similar. In addition, except for the population growth and FDI variables in columns (5) and (6), the levels of significance of the corresponding coefficients are the same.

Table 6.1 Descriptive statistics and unit root test results

Variable	Maximum	Minimum	Mean	Std. Dev.	t-bar Test
y	0.3229	-0.0790	0.0857	0.0454	-4.2406***
LY(-1)	5.7579	4.1733	4.8575	0.3606	-15.5405***
LDK	-0.3155	-2.4288	-1.2420	0.2987	-10.0205***
LPG	0.0503	0.0008	0.0129	0.0069	-6.4735***
LHC	-2.6575	-3.8061	-3.2826	0.2515	-2.3447**
LRDE	8.6948	3.5841	5.9757	1.0594	-2.1129**
LFDI	12.3964	3.0924	8.8205	1.9262	-1.7247*
LEX	17.2787	10.1043	13.2633	1.2808	-1.8053*
LIM	17.0309	8.2647	12.3637	1.5730	-1.8392*

Notes:
1. L indicates logged values, LY = GDP per capita; LDK = domestic capital; LPG = population growth; LHC = human capital; LRDE = R&D expenditure; LFDI = realised FDI; LEX = real exports; LIM = real imports.
2. There are 364 observations for all variables.
3. Std. Dev. represents the standard deviation.
4. ***, **, * denote significance at the level of 1%, 5% and 10%, respectively. The critical values are -2.57, -1.96, and -1.65 at the confidence level of 1%, 5% and 10%, respectively.

As indicated in column (2) of Table 6.2, although it is highly significant, the coefficient on the lagged per capita GDP variable is positive. This indicates that there is no evidence of absolute or unconditional convergence. The estimated convergence rate is negative and implies a highly significant trend of divergence in income growth: a region with a higher initial level of income would have a higher growth rate of per capita GDP.

After controlling for the determinants of growth, the regression coefficients on the lagged per capita GDP variable are still highly significant but become negative as shown in columns (3) to (6). This suggests the existence of conditional convergence of regional per capita income within China. Put another way, holding other things constant, poor regions will catch up with the richer regions in terms of per capita GDP. The conditional convergence rate λ is approximately 15 to 24 per cent for the 28 provinces included in the sample during the period of 1983-98. This value is much higher than those reported elsewhere in the literature. It implies that the time required to eliminate half of an initial gap from the steady state is between three and five years.

Table 6.2 Estimation results for absolute and conditional convergence (Dependent variable = per capita GDP growth)

	(I)	(II)		(III)	
		OLS	WLS	OLS	WLS
$LY(-1)$	0.0328***	-0.1387***	-0.1381***	-0.2193***	-0.2159***
	(0.0067)	(0.0221)	(0.0149)	(0.0263)	(0.0156)
LDK		0.0727***	0.0681***	0.0327***	0.0287***
		(0.0109)	(0.0060)	(0.0093)	(0.0049)
LPG		-1.5410***	-1.5067***	-0.6048*	-0.6645***
		(0.3934)	(0.2509)	(0.3601)	(0.1661)
LHC				0.1042***	0.0964***
				(0.0201)	(0.0112)
$LRDE$				0.0486***	0.0435***
				(0.0111)	(0.0059)
$LFDI$				0.0058**	0.0064***
				(0.0027)	(0.0015)
LEX				0.0352***	0.0280***
				(0.0094)	(0.0061)
LIM				0.0180***	0.0150***
				(0.0058)	(0.0033)
T		0.0123***	0.0120***	0.0097***	0.0109***
		(0.0020)	(0.0012)	(0.0022)	(0.0013)
R^2	0.0627	0.3842	0.6494	0.5487	0.7622
Implied λ	-0.0323	0.1493	0.1486	0.2476	0.2432
Half-life (Years)		4.64	4.66	2.80	2.85
Hypothesis Tests		LR: 109.15*** λ_{LM1}: 26.49*** HS: 40.00*** λ_{LM2}: 158.82***		LR: 152.84*** λ_{LM1}: 6.44*** HS: 102.50*** λ_{LM2}: 185.81***	

Notes:

1. White-heteroscedasticity corrected standard errors are in parentheses.
2. ***, ** and * indicate that the coefficient is significantly different from zero at the 1%, 5% and 10% levels, respectively.

Focusing on columns (3) and (4), the estimated coefficient on domestic capital is positive and significant. This confirms the importance of domestic investment in physical assets. The coefficient on population growth is negative and significant, suggesting a negative impact of population growth on per capita GDP growth in China. The time trend has a positive sign on its coefficient and is significant at the 1% level, indicating that there remains exogenous technical progress which is put at 1 per cent per annum.

Comparing column (4) with column (6), we note that the inclusion of human capital, R&D expenditure, FDI, exports and imports reduces the positive effect of domestic capital and the negative effect of population growth on per capita GDP growth, while improving the explanatory power of the equation. In addition, the estimated coefficients on the lagged per capita GDP are larger in absolute value. This indicates stronger convergence tendencies.

In column (6), the coefficients of human capital, R&D expenditure, FDI, exports and imports all have the expected positive sign and are highly significant. The elasticity of GDP per capita growth with respect to human capital is even higher than for domestic capital and foreign capital, indicating that a 1 per cent increase in the ratio of the weighted sum of the secondary and higher education enrolment to total labour force will cause a 0.09 per cent rise in per capita GDP. Thus, investment in education or human capital plays a more important role than physical investment in economic growth in China. In other words, high stocks of human capital increase the efficiency with which people exploit economic opportunities. This finding is different from the result obtained by Wei et al. (2001) where human capital is insignificant in all cases. This may be due to a better measure of human capital in the current study. We take into account enrolment at two levels: secondary and higher education.

The R&D variable has a smaller magnitude than human capital. A 1 per cent rise in total R&D expenditure of state-owned institutions will cause a 0.04 per cent increase in per capita GDP. However, the coefficient is higher than that of exports, imports and FDI, and this suggests that domestic R&D activities in each province of China is more important.

Column (6) of Table 6.2 also indicates that a 1 per cent increase in exports and imports would raise economic growth by 0.028 per cent and 0.015 per cent per year respectively. The statistical significance suggests that they are important sources of GDP growth, although the magnitudes of these coefficients are relatively small.

Finally, the coefficient on the FDI variable, in which we are most interested, takes the value of 0.64 per cent only, and is the smallest in terms of magnitude. This suggests that the impact of FDI on the growth of per capita income is limited. It is even smaller than that of domestic investment in physical assets. This may not be surprising given that FDI still accounts for a small proportion of total investment in China. However, we need to bear in mind that spillovers from FDI may take a variety of forms. For example, the effects of the transmission of knowledge on business practices, management techniques and the establishment of buyer-supplier linkages can not be completely captured by the actual amount of FDI inflows.

In the literature, alternative measurements of openness are adopted. For instance, lagged exports and imports are occasionally used. Furthermore, instead of levels, the growth in exports and imports or the shares of exports and imports in GDP are sometimes employed. In addition, FDI enters into the equation with a one year lag (see, for example, Barrell and Pain, 1997). To test the robustness of the endogenous growth model these different measures are included. According to the statistical test results, the fixed effects models allowing for groupwise heteroscedasticity are selected for all specifications. The final results are presented in Table 6.3.

It can be found that lagged FDI in the different specifications in columns (4) to (6) of Table 6.3 is still highly significant at the 1% level, although the magnitudes of the coefficients are slightly smaller than those in columns (5) and (6) of Table 6.2. The significance level of the export growth variable in column (2) is 5%, but it is still 1% in column (5). Import growth is highly significant in both cases. As expected, the magnitudes of both export and import growth variables are slightly smaller than those of levels. The export share in GDP is the only insignificant variable among all alternative measures, but the import share in GDP is still highly significant. Finally, lagged exports and imports are highly significant but the magnitudes of these two variables are noticeably lower than in columns (5) and (6) of Table 6.2. This may suggest that the impact of trade on per capita income growth is more contemporaneous than lagged.

Given that the estimation results are not very sensitive to the changes in measurement of a number of variables, it may be reasonable to argue that our empirical models are robust. We are now in a position to provide an overall summary of the study as follows. Domestic capital has a positive and significant impact, while population growth has a negative and significant impact on the growth of per capita income, as suggested by both neo-classical and endogenous growth theories. However, their estimated coefficients become smaller when all the explanatory variables facilitating knowledge creation, diffusion and imitation are taken into consideration. In addition, the inclusion of these variables increases the conditional convergence rate of GDP per capita. All these results lend strong support to the endogenous growth theory.

Table 6.3 Estimation results for conditional convergence with alternative measures of openness variables including export, import and FDI

	(I)	(II)	(III)	(IV)	(V)
$LY(-1)$	-0.1523***	-0.1731***	-0.2094***	-0.1564***	-0.1768***
	(0.0167)	0.0164)	(0.0183)	(0.0156)	(0.0161)
LDK	0.0258***	0.0213***	0.0358***	0.0333***	0.0297***
	(0.0049)	(0.0057)	(0.0053)	(0.0051)	(0.0058)
LPG	-0.6641***	-0.6720***	-0.6813***	-0.6058***	-0.6251***
	(0.1663)	(0.1748)	(0.2210)	(0.2085)	(0.2212)
LHC	0.0678***	0.0841***	0.0921***	0.0666***	0.0835***
	(0.0110)	(0.0119)	(0.0123)	(0.0109)	(0.0121)
LRDE	0.0540***	0.0517***	0.0603***	0.0694***	0.0652***
	(0.0056)	(0.0060)	(0.0062)	(0.0055)	(0.0060)
LFDI	0.0086***	0.0082***	--	--	--
	(0.0013)	(0.0015)			
$LFDI(-1)$	--	--	0.0042***	0.0048***	0.0046***
			(0.0007)	(0.0007)	(0.0007)
ΔLEX	0.0102**	--	--	0.0118***	--
	(0.0048)			(0.0048)	
ΔLIM	0.0122***	--	--	0.0115***	--
	(0.0032)			(0.0032)	
LEXGDP	--	0.0036	--	--	-0.0019
		(0.0056)			(0.0053)
LIMGDP	--	0.0091***	--	--	0.0103***
		(0.0035)			(0.0035)
$LEX(-1)$	--	--	0.0173***	--	--
			(0.0051)		
$LIM(-1)$	--	--	0.0076***	--	--
			(0.0030)		
T	0.0108***	0.0113***	0.0116***	0.0107***	0.0113***
	(0.0014)	(0.0014)	(0.0014)	(0.0013)	(0.0014)
R^2	0.7431	0.7230	0.7200	0.7378	0.7122
Implied λ	0.1652	0.1901	0.2350	0.1701	0.1946
Half-life (Years)	4.20	3.65	2.95	4.08	3.56
Hypothesis Tests					
LR:	111.68***	131.44***	144.38***	131.25***	148.10***
λ_{LM1}:	8.28***	12.65***	4.50**	7.35***	11.73***
HS:	49.40***	75.38***	107.88***	75.80***	97.75***
λ_{LM2}:	180.12***	179.75***	208.55***	195.55***	198.67***

Notes:
1. Δ indicates the first difference of the variable.
2. White-heteroscedasticity corrected standard errors are in parentheses.
3. ***, ** and * indicate that the coefficient is significantly different from zero at the 1%, 5% and 10% levels, respectively.

6.5 CONCLUSIONS

This chapter examines the issue of regional income convergence using panel data for 28 provinces in China for the period 1986-1998. There is no evidence of absolute convergence. Rather, a positive and significant relationship between the rate of growth and its initial level has been detected. This implies the possibility of persistent divergence in regional per capita income.

However, the empirical results indicate the existence of conditional convergence. The overall convergence rate is approximately 24 per cent which is much higher than previous empirical findings of approximately 2 per cent. The lower convergence rate found in previous studies may be due to the omission of some growth-promoting factors identified by the endogenous growth theory.

This study provides support for the endogenous growth theory for two reasons. First, the importance of investment in physical and human capital, domestic R&D, FDI and international trade in economic growth is confirmed. Second, given technological diffusion, transfer and imitation facilitated by investment in physical and human capital, domestic R&D, FDI and trade, regional per capita incomes do converge. In other words, both domestic and foreign R&D activities are the engine of China's economic growth.

Compared with all other explanatory variables which facilitate knowledge creation and diffusion, FDI, the explanatory variable in which we are most interested, has played a limited but important role in economic growth and per capita income convergence. Population growth has a negative impact on income growth.

The results from this study have important policy implications. Given the sensitivity of economic growth to investment in physical and human capital and domestic R&D, the Chinese government needs to encourage investment in fixed assets, education and training, and innovations and their diffusion.

The strong evidence for convergence conditional on the integration of China into the world economy suggests that China should further liberalise its international trade and investment policies. Increased trade and foreign investment opportunities will enable provinces in China to draw upon foreign technical knowledge and converge to their steady state at a faster rate. In addition, the population control policy adopted by the Chinese government should be continued and accompanied by better education and training opportunities. It is the quality rather than the size of population that matters in per capita income growth. By doing so, economic growth can be sustained and regional convergence in per capita income can be promoted.

APPENDIX 6A DATA SOURCES

The panel data set used in this chapter covers 28 provinces within China over the period 1986-1998. The data are mainly compiled from *Comprehensive Statistical Data and Materials on 50 Years of New China, China Regional Economy: a profile of 17 years of reform and open-up*, various volumes of Chinese statistical and economic yearbooks at both central and provincial levels, including *Almanac of Foreign Economic Relations and Trade of China, China Foreign Economic Statistical Yearbook* and *China Statistical Yearbook*. When figures conflict, we adopt the central and most recent available sources. Mainland China consists of 30 provinces, but because of data imperfections for realised FDI for Tibet and Qinghai provinces, these two regions are removed from the sample. In addition, Chongqing was part of Sichuan province before the end of 1996, and thus, in order to maintain consistency, the data for Chongqing and Sichuan provinces are combined from 1996 onwards.

Variable	Measurement
y	The growth rate of real GDP per capita, defined as the difference of the log of the real per capita GDP index in a given year and that in the previous year.
Y	Real GDP per capita.
DK	The ratio of investment in fixed assets to GDP.
PO	Total population.
HC	Human capital, defined as the ratio of the weighted sum of the secondary school enrolments and the high education enrolments to the total labour force.
FDIR	The ratio of realised annual inflow of foreign direct investment to GDP.
EX	Total exports, deflated by the corresponding province consumer price index (CPI) deflator.
IM	Total imports, deflated by the corresponding province CPI deflator.
RDE	Total R&D expenditure of state-owned institutions, deflated by the corresponding province CPI deflator.

NOTES

1. A different version of this study will appear as Wei et al. (2001).
2. Lichtenberg (1994) argues that the conventional cross-section test, in which growth rates are usually the average across the whole time-series sample, captures 'regression to the mean' rather than the convergence hypothesis.
3. In fact, most studies on the determinants of output growth are based on a first-difference specification, which may avoid the spurious correlation problem. However, this specification discards the information embodied in the long-run relationship between the levels of the variables.

7. Foreign Direct Investment and Trade Interactions in China

7.1 INTRODUCTION

International trade and foreign direct investment (FDI) are two important means of economic integration into the world economy. Given the rapid expansion of both trade and FDI in the post-reform period in China, it is useful to know whether they are interrelated. In chapters 3 and 4, the regression results indicate that the level of international trade is a positive determinant of FDI inflows in China. In these analyses of the determinants of FDI at the national and regional levels, trade is assumed to be exogenous and therefore single equation models are applied. This single equation approach is widely adopted in the literature.

FDI and trade can however be interrelated. The United Nations Conference on Trade and Development compares the global pattern of FDI with that of international trade and observes interlinkages between them (UNCTD, World Investment Report 1991, 1996). Petri (1994) examines the similarities and differences of global FDI and trade clusters and concludes that although investment is less strongly clustered than trade, FDI is an especially important channel for bridging regional blocs. While at the global level trade and FDI are related, little is known about whether China's intense trade partners are also intense direct investors in China. An understanding of this relationship is important for promoting trade and FDI in China. In addition, since FDI has a positive impact on productivity as shown in chapter 5, and both FDI and trade have a positive impact on per capita income growth as indicated in chapter 6, an investigation of the relationship between trade and FDI can have important policy implications for economic development in China.

This chapter investigates the possible interactive relationships between trade and FDI. In particular, it examines the linkage between trade and FDI intensities and explores their possible common determinants such as market size, general economic activities, comparative advantage and international transaction costs. The next section reviews the relevant theoretical and empirical literatures. Section 7.3 provides a description of the relationship between trade and FDI intensities in China. Section 7.4 describes our model, data and methodology. The empirical results are presented in section 7.5 and section 7.6 concludes and provides policy implications.

7.2 LITERATURE REVIEW

7.2.1 Theoretical Linkages

International production and trade are frequently seen as alternative means of delivering goods and certain services to foreign markets. This is reflected by the fact that separate theories are often used to explain the international patterns of FDI and trade. However, recent literature tends to argue that these two international economic activities are interlinked, although the development of integrated theory to explain both FDI and trade is still at a stage of infancy (UNCTD, 1996).

The discussion of the linkage between international trade and FDI normally focuses on two related issues. First, are there any common determinants of FDI and trade? Second, do FDI and trade substitute or complement each other? The interaction between the two activities has important policy implications for economic development. In this section the literature review of the common determinants is first provided followed by that of the substitution-complement relationship between trade and FDI.

With a number of assumptions such as constant returns to scale, perfect competition and zero transportation costs, the standard Heckscher-Ohlin (H-O) model suggests that a country should have a comparative advantage in those commodities that use its abundant factors intensively. A country should export those commodities that use its abundant factors intensively and import these commodities that require factors in which it is comparatively poorly endowed. Since commodities differ in their factor requirements and countries differ in their factor endowments, every country should have a comparative advantage in something and should be involved in relatively significant amounts of international trade.

However, it is often argued that the H-O theory fails to explain much of modern trade which is based on economies of scale, imperfect competition, and differences in technological changes among nations. Helpman (1984a) and Helpman and Krugman (1985) suggest that even if two countries are identical in every respect, each country can still gain from trade. If each country specialises, a larger scale of production may make possible a greater division of labour and specialisation and permit the introduction of more specialised and productive machinery, and will therefore lead to an increase in productivity. Intra-industry trade in differentiated products arises in order to take advantage of important economies of scale in production, which result when each firm or plant produces only one or a few styles or varieties of a product (Krugman, 1980; Lancaster, 1980; Helpman, 1981). It follows that while trade based on comparative advantage (inter-industry trade) is likely to be larger when the difference in factor endowments among nations is greater, intra-industry trade is likely to be larger among economies of similar size and factor proportions. However, if the definition of comparative advantage is modified, then 'comparative advantage is somewhere in the background' (Lancaster, 1980) even for intra-industry trade, because it can be argued that inter-industry trade reflects *natural* comparative advantage, while intra-industry trade reflects *acquired* comparative advantage (Salvatore, 1995).

While the basic H-O model explains *static* comparative advantage, the product cycle model (Vernon, 1966) explains *dynamic* comparative advantage for new products and new production processes and predicts FDI from the innovating nation to nations with cheaper labour. This model shows some linkage between trade and FDI.

The H-O model assumes zero transportation costs. Salvatore (1995) suggests that although it just modifies rather than rejects the H-O model, the relaxation of this assumption helps understand the patterns of both trade and international production. Transportation costs reduce the volume and gains from trade. Furthermore, transaction costs affect trade by influencing the location of production and trade. For instance, resource-oriented industries tend to locate near the source of the raw materials used by the industry because the cost of transporting the raw materials is substantially higher than that of shipping the finished product to market. This implies a negative relationship between transportation costs and trade and a positive relationship between transportation costs and foreign production.

FDI or international production is determined by three sets of factors: ownership (firm-specific) advantages, internalisation advantages and location (country-specific) advantages (Dunning, 1981; Dunning, 1988). In other words, FDI is the combination of an investor's firm-specific advantages with a host country's site-specific advantages. It occurs when a firm possessing the ownership advantage perceives it to be in its best interest to internalise its use rather than to sell the right of using the advantage, because the markets are costly and inefficient for undertaking certain types of transactions.

It is generally accepted that the explanatory power of the basic H-O model for patterns of FDI is weak given that much of FDI as well as modern trade occurs between countries similar in their resource abundance and income levels (UNCTD, 1996). However, as Dunning (1979), Porter (1990), Nachum (1999) and Nachum et al. (2000) argue, the activities of firms have been shown to be related to the characteristics of their home country and to reflect the resources abundant in these locations. As a result, there are a number of links between the comparative advantage of countries and the international activity of firms.

Nachum et al. (2000) suggest that firms invest in foreign countries in order to gain access to resources that are not available, or that are available on less favourable terms in their home countries. During this process, firms steer away from their home country activities which require immobile resources in which the country is comparatively disadvantaged, but which can be performed competitively in other countries, using their firm-specific advantages. This implies that FDI takes place in industries in which the home country of the investing firm is comparatively disadvantageous. For instance, export-seeking investment aims to move production facilities to another location as the relative costs of factors of production at home rise. Market-seeking investment is launched by firms probably because of the relatively quicker expansion of a foreign market with trade barriers and because of the need for proximity to clients. But for efficiency- or strategic asset-seeking investment factor endowments are less important in influencing their location decisions. Thus, the relationship between FDI and the comparative advantage of the home country is generally not straightforward.

Although there are clear differences in patterns of FDI and trade flows, Petri (1994) argues that both flows are sensitive to common determinants such as international transaction costs. Given the different features of these two international activities, the exact types of international transaction costs do not completely coincide. For instance, cheaper transport is needed for trade, and relative ease of operation in a foreign environment is necessary for investment. However, some of the most important costs for trade and FDI are similar: both transactions require familiarity with the foreign business environment. Petri (1994) suggests that the costs of assembling and maintaining this knowledge based on specific partners probably dominate other types of transaction costs.

The literature reviewed so far tends to regard transportation costs, comparative advantage and international transaction costs as the common determinants of trade and FDI. Transportation costs are negatively related to trade but may be positively related to FDI. Comparative advantage may be negatively related to outward FDI but positively related to inward FDI. International transaction costs are the deterrent of both trade and FDI. The relationship between trade and FDI is also reflected by their direct connections, i.e. they can substitute or complement each other. Helpman (1984b) and Helpman and Krugman (1985) illustrate that the degree of specialisation is a positive function of relative factor endowments. If differences in factor endowments are not substantial, a capital-abundant country will produce capital-intensive differentiated goods at home and exchange them for the labour-intensive homogeneous good from a labour-abundant country. However, if there are substantial differences in factor endowments, the capital-abundant country tends to export headquarters services (such as R&D) into the labour-abundant country in exchange for finished varieties of differentiated goods and homogeneous goods rather than simply export the differentiated goods. Thus, FDI generates complementary trade flows from the labour-intensive country. In addition, parent firms may export intermediate inputs to their subsidiaries if vertical integration is involved. As noted by Markusen and Maskus (1999), the model developed by Helpman (1984b) captures the notion of vertically integrated firms, but does not allow FDI to occur between very similar countries.

Based on the assumption that countries are symmetric in terms of size, factor endowments and technologies, Brainard (1993), Markusen (1984) and Horstman and Markusen (1992) develop a model which distinguishes between plant- and firm-level scale economies and acknowledges the existence of trade barriers such as tariffs and transport costs. They argue that the choice between horizontal FDI and international trade at both firm and country levels depends on the trade-off between proximity and concentration. Proximity means that firms have an incentive to overcome various barriers to trade by launching FDI in a foreign market. Multi-plant economies of scale generated by high fixed costs of R&D and other headquarters activities also justify FDI. Concentration refers to increasing returns to scale at the plant level. If proximity advantages overweigh concentration advantages, there will be more FDI instead of trade. Therefore, there can be a substitution relationship between FDI and trade.

Given the fact that countries differ in relative endowments, Markusen and Venables (1995, 1996, 1998) and Markusen (1998) introduce countries' asymmetries in explaining the choice between international trade and FDI. For convenience, firms tend to be national and located in the advantaged countries. As the disadvantaged country develops in terms of local market size, factor endowments and technological efficiency, an increasing number of firms from the advantaged country will establish subsidiaries in the disadvantaged country. Thus, FDI and trade can exist simultaneously. Multinationals become more important relative to trade as countries become more similar in size, relative endowments, and as world income grows. Brainard (1997) also suggests that multinational activity is more likely the more similar are the home and foreign markets. This suggests that multinational production will substitute for trade when countries are similar.

While market size, relative endowments (or comparative advantage) and technical efficiency are identified as the further common influences on trade and FDI, it may not be easy to predict the relationship between trade and FDI when a host country expands its GDP rapidly and becomes similar to a home country in size. In this case, trade may increase in response to the increased market size. Although some amount of trade may be replaced by FDI, total trade may still be higher because of the larger market size. Thus it may be difficult to observe the substitution between trade and FDI at the national level.

As can be seen from the above, the linkages between FDI and trade are complex. It is very difficult, if not impossible, to predict whether FDI and trade are substitutes or complements. As a summary, Dunning (1998) suggests that the relationship between trade and FDI is conditional on the kind of trade and FDI being considered, and the conditions under which each takes place. Petri (1994) specifies that market-oriented investments are attracted by the site-specific advantages of a market that may derive from buyers' characteristics such as wealth, or from natural or policy barriers which protect local producers. Production-oriented investments are attracted to low-cost production sites. Trade-facilitating investments are motivated by the need to provide services (after-sale services, finance etc.) to exporting activities. It seems clear that market-oriented FDI tends to substitute for trade, while production-oriented and trade facilitating FDI tends to increase trade. Gray (1998) also indicates that market-seeking production affiliates can displace international trade and efficiency-seeking production affiliates will increase the volume of trade.

7.2.2 Empirical Evidence

Existing empirical studies use different data and estimation techniques, and it is not surprising that the results are mixed. Lipsey and Weiss (1981, 1984) estimate trade and affiliate productions using cross-sectional firm level data. Their trade equations include several other variables such as size of parent company and income of the involved area. They find a positive relationship between US firms' outputs in a foreign area and the firms' exports from the United States to that area. Using trade equations and US and Swedish firm-level data, Blomstrom et al. (1988) find that the relationship between FDI and export sales is complementary.

Pfaffermayr (1996) estimates a simultaneous equations system using time-series and cross-section industry-level data from Austrian manufacturing, and finds a significant complementary relationship between FDI and exports in the 1980s and early 1990s.

Using bilateral data for Japan and its 20 major trading partners for the period 1982-95, Bayoumi and Lipworth (1997) regress trade flows on the stock and flow of FDI from Japan, aggregate demand in foreign (home) market and relative prices between the export and import markets. They use the size and significance of the coefficient on the stock of FDI as a measure of the long-run impact of FDI on trade, and those on the flow of FDI as more temporary trade effects, and conclude that outward FDI from Japan has a temporary impact on exports but a permanent effect on imports.

Using an augmented export demand model and a panel data set at the economy level for 11 Organisation for Economic Co-operation and Development (OECD) countries for the period 1971-92, Pain and Wakelin (1998) find evidence of heterogeneity in the relationships between FDI and exports. In general, however, outward FDI has a negative impact on trade shares while inward FDI has a positive impact.

Based on panel data for 10 countries for the period 1982-94, Gopinath et al. (1999) use a four-equation system with foreign affiliate sales, exports, affiliate employment and FDI as endogenous variables to assess the relationship between FDI and trade in the US food industry. Their results indicate that foreign sales and exports are substitutes in the industry.

7.3 FOREIGN DIRECT INVESTMENT AND TRADE LINKAGES IN CHINA

In chapter 2 a relatively detailed description of the development trends, sources and types, and regional and sectoral distributions of FDI is presented. In addition, the impact of FDI on trade is very briefly evaluated by examining the share of foreign-invested enterprises (FIEs) in China's total foreign trade. It is found that although FIEs play an increasing role in China's foreign trade, their imports have been persistently larger than their exports. Although the net trade effect of FIEs seems to be negative, it is not clear whether the overall impact of FDI on China's *total* trade is negative. The machinery and equipment imported by FIEs may embody new technologies and help enhance their productivity. This may have demonstration and competition effects so that indigenous Chinese firms may adopt advanced technologies and raise their productivity and exports. Whether FDI has an overall positive impact on China's total foreign trade may be examined by relating FDI to total exports, imports and trade. Using a table and three scatter diagrams this section describes the connections between FDI and trade in China.

As indicated earlier, China's foreign trade and inward FDI have expanded rapidly since its adoption of the policy of opening up to the outside world. Table 7.1 demonstrates that the top ten investors for both 1997 and 1998 were from the same countries/regions. Furthermore, nine of the top ten investors were among the top ten trading partners for 1997 and these top ten investors were just the top ten trading partners for 1998. This suggests that the intensive foreign investors in China were also China's intensive trading partners. Table 7.1 also shows that the top ten investors were the top ten importers of China's goods and services, but not necessarily the top ten exporters to China.

Table 7.1 also presents the Spearman rank correlation coefficients between variables in 1997 and 1998. The results show that FDI is significantly correlated with trade, exports and imports at the 10% level in both 1997 and 1998.

Table 7.1 Top ten foreign investors and their trading ranks in China, 1997 and 1998

US$ million

PANEL A	FDI			Trade		
	Rank			Rank		
Country	1998	1997	1998	1998	1997	1998
Total			45463			323923
Hong Kong	1	1	18508	3	2	45412
United States	2	4	3898	2	3	54937
Singapore	3	5	3404	7	6	8154
Japan	4	2	3400	1	1	57899
Taiwan	5	3	2915	5	19	20499
South Korea	6	6	1803	4	4	21264
United Kingdom	7	7	1175	8	8	6584
Germany	8	8	737	6	5	14348
Netherlands	9	10	719	10	10	5995
France	10	9	715	9	9	6027
	Export			Import		
	Rank			Rank		
Country	1998	1997	1998	1998	1997	1998
Total			183757			140166
Hong Kong	1	1	38753	6	5	6658
United States	2	2	37976	2	3	16961
Singapore	8	7	3930	7	7	4224
Japan	3	3	29692	1	1	28207
Taiwan	9	9	3870	3	2	16630
South Korea	5	4	6269	4	4	14995
United Kingdom	7	8	4632	17	16	1952
Germany	4	5	7354	5	6	6994
Netherlands	6	6	5162	22	20	834
France	10	10	2823	9	10	3205

Table 7.1 Continued

PANEL B - Spearman's Rank Correlation Coefficient

	FDI	Trade	Export	Import
FDI	-	0.5775**	0.5394*	0.7818***
Trade	0.7576***	-	0.8571***	0.5228*
Export	0.5879**	0.7091**	-	0.4424*
Import	0.5394*	0.9030***	0.4424*	-

Notes:

1. *, ** and *** denote significance at the 10%, 5% and 1% level, respectively (one-tail test).
2. The lower part of Panel B in the table displays the Spearman's rank correlation coefficients in 1998, and coefficients in 1997 are shown above the diagonal.

Source: SSB, China Statistical Yearbook 1999 and authors' own calculations.

An econometric investigation of whether FDI positively contributes to China's trade and vice versa will be conducted in the next section using such variables as the trade and investment intensity (gravity) indexes. In the remainder of this section these indexes are described and a visual examination of the relationship between trade and FDI intensities is provided.

A general form of the intensity index is defined as the ratio of the share of partner *b* in the investment of country *a* (or trade with country *a*) to the share of *b* in all world investment (or trade), excluding country *a* (see Petri, 1994). Algebraically,

$$q_{ab} = (Y_{ab} / Y_{a*}) / [Y_{*b} / (Y_{**} - Y_{*a})] \tag{7.1}$$

where q_{ab} = intensity of *a*'s investment in, or trade with *b*, Y_{ab} = investment by *a* (home) in partner *b* (host), or trade between *a* and *b*, $*$ = summation across all partners (world).

In this study the trade, export, import and FDI intensity indexes are calculated using the data as described in the next section. It should be noted that the export intensity here is defined as the ratio of the share of the partner's exports to China in the partner's total exports to the share of China's total imports in all world exports excluding the partner country/region. Similarly, the import intensity is defined as the ratio of the share of China's exports to the partner in China's total exports to the share of the partner's total imports from China in all world exports excluding China's total exports. The trade and FDI intensities are defined in the normal way.

Foreign Direct Investment in China

Figures 7.1-7.3 contain three scatter diagrams. Figure 7.1 shows the relationship between the average trade intensity and FDI intensity over the period 1984-98. The rhombic dots form a pattern which shows the positive relationship between FDI and trade intensity on average. Figures 7.2 and 7.3 also tend to reveal a positive relationship between the export and FDI intensity and that between the import and FDI intensity. The very high values for Hong Kong and Thailand constitute two extremes and are excluded from the diagrams.

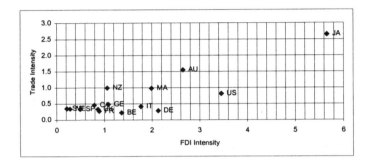

Notes:
SW = Sweden; NE = Netherlands; SP = Spain; CA = Canada; UK = United Kingdom; FR = France; NZ = New Zealand; GE = Germany; BE = Belgium; IT = Italy; MA = Malaysia; DE = Denmark; AU = Australia; US = United States; JA = Japan.

Figure 7.1 FDI and trade intensity

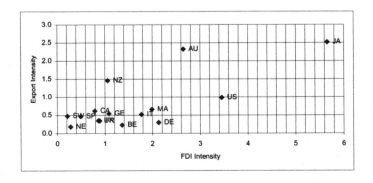

Notes: As Figure 7.1

Figure 7.2 FDI and export intensity

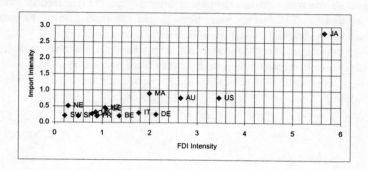

Notes: As Figure 7.1

Figure 7.3 FDI and import intensity

7.4 EMPIRICAL MODEL, DATA AND METHODOLOGY

While showing the positive relationships between FDI and trade, Figures 7.1-7.3 could not reveal whether the two variables are inter-determined. As indicated in section 7.2 however, recent literature tends to argue that FDI and trade can be a two-way flow of influence because they may substitute for or complement each other. In addition, the two variables may have a number of common determinants such as comparative advantage or factor endowments, market size or income levels and international transaction costs. Thus, an empirical model may start with a multiple equation model taking into consideration possible interactions between FDI and trade. In this study, the following two models are estimated:

$$TI_{it} = \alpha_1 + \alpha_2 PR_{it} + \alpha_3 GR_{it} + \alpha_4 GEOD_i + \alpha_5 GEOD2_i + \alpha_6 FI_{it} + \varepsilon1_{it} \quad (7.2.1)$$

$$FI_{it} = \alpha_7 + \alpha_8 PR_{it} + \alpha_9 GR_{it} + \alpha_{10} GEOD_i + \alpha_{11} GEOD2_i + \alpha_{12} TCD$$
$$+ \alpha_{13} TI_{it} + \varepsilon2_{it} \quad (7.2.2)$$

$$i = 1, 2, ..., 18; \, t = 1984, 1985, ..., 1998.$$

where i and t denote country/region and time respectively. $\varepsilon1$ and $\varepsilon2$ represent the error terms of the two equations of the system. TI and FI are the trade intensity index and the FDI intensity index, respectively. PR is the ratio of Chinese population to the partner's population, and GR is the ratio of China's GDP to the partner's GDP. GEOD is the geographic distance between China and the partner, GEOD2 is the squared geographic distance to capture the possible non-linear relationship between the geographic distance and the trade and FDI intensities. Finally, TCD is total cultural differences between China and the partner.

To examine the relationships between the FDI, export and import intensities a three-equation system is constructed:

$$II_{it} = \beta_1 + \beta_2 PR_{it} + \beta_3 GR_{it} + \beta_4 GEOD_i + \beta_5 GEOD2_i + \beta_6 FI_{it} + \delta 1_{it} \quad (7.3.1)$$

$$EI_{it} = \beta_7 + \beta_8 PR_{it} + \beta_9 GR_{it} + \beta_{10} GEOD_i + \beta_{11} GEOD2_i + \beta_{12} FI + \delta 2_{it} \quad (7.3.2)$$

$$FI_{it} = \beta_{13} + \beta_{14} PR_{it} + \beta_{15} GR_{it} + \beta_{16} GEOD_i + \beta_{17} GEOD2_i + \beta_{18} TCD$$
$$+ \beta_{19} II_{it} + \beta_{20} EI_{it} + \delta 3_{it} \quad (7.3.3)$$

$$i = 1, 2, ..., 18; t = 1984, 1985, ..., 1998.$$

where II and EI are the import and export intensity indexes respectively, and all other variables are the same as in (7.2.1) and (7.2.2).

As can be seen from the above equations, the common determinants of trade and FDI are the population ratio, GDP ratio and geographic distance. The population ratio is used to measure the relative change in the Chinese market size. The GDP ratio can be seen as an additional proxy for the market size or, as in the case of Nachum et al. (2000), a rough proxy for the relative economic structure of the Chinese economy. The signs on these two proxies are expected to be positive since the bigger the Chinese market (or the higher the Chinese economic activities), the more trade and inward FDI China would experience.

Geographic distance may not just measure transportation costs only. Following Linneman (1966) geographic distance is also employed as a proxy for international transaction costs. As a matter of fact, transportation costs are only marginally affected by distance and are small compared with international cost differentials. Given its strong explanatory power for bilateral trade patterns in the literature, Petri (1994) argues that geographic distance is 'at least partly a proxy for the information costs of doing business abroad, including knowledge of the partner's culture and economy'. Thus, the negative relationship between trade and FDI intensities and geographic distance is expected.

In addition to geographic distance, another proxy for international transaction costs in the equations is total cultural difference. This variable is adopted as an exogenous determinant of FDI. The greater the cultural difference between the partners, the higher the international transaction costs. Thus, similar to geographic distance, the negative relationship between FDI and cultural distance is expected. The measure of international transaction costs in this way is consistent with Kogut and Singh (1988).

As discussed in section 7.2, comparative advantage is another possible common determinant of trade and FDI. In the empirical literature however, export share is often used as a proxy for comparative advantage (see, for example, Nachum et al., 2000). By definition, the trade, export or import intensity index not only directly measures the relative position of trading activities between the partners, but also at least partly and indirectly captures the relative comparative advantage of both partners. A high trade intensity may reflect a high complementary comparative advantage of both partners relative to the rest of the world. A high export (import) intensity may indicate a high comparative advantage of the partner (China) relative to China (the partner). In this sense, the trade, export or import intensity can also be employed as a crude proxy for comparative advantage in the FDI equation.

The data on population, GDP, total exports, imports and trade for each country are from *International Financial Statistical Yearbook*; those on geographic distance, total cultural difference and China's exports, imports and trade with its partner are from the same sources as described in the Appendix to chapter 3; those on FDI stock are from *The International Direct Investment Statistics Yearbook*, *World Investment Report* and *World Investment Directory*. A more detailed description of the data sources is provided in the Appendix to this chapter.

As in the empirical studies in chapters 3, 4 and 6 of this book, the IPS unit root tests are first conducted to check the data properties of the variables PR, GR, TCD, FI, TI, II and EI. Given the stationarity of the data, a long-run relationship among variables may possibly exist. Then, systems (7.2) and (7.3) are estimated and the Lagrange multiplier tests - λ_{LM2} and λ_{LM3} are conducted to select the best statistical model from the OLS, WLS and SUR estimation results. When two systems are estimated in this way, we are most interested in the relationship between FDI and trade. If FDI and trade are found to be inter-determined, the next step is to estimate the systems using the generalised method of moments (GMM) so that the endogeneity issue can be dealt with. The detailed description of different estimation techniques and statistical tests is provided in section 5.3 of chapter 5.

7.5 EMPIRICAL RESULTS

Table 7.2 provides the descriptive statistics and IPS panel data unit root test results for each variable. The coefficients on all variables are statistically significant at the 1% level. This suggests that all variables are stationary and there exits some kind of long-run relationship among these variables. This result may not be a surprise given that all the variables are measured in terms of ratios.

Table 7.2 Descriptive statistics and unit root test results

Variable	Maximum	Minimum	Mean	Std. Dev.	t-bar Test
PR	433.0196	4.4629	98.8762	111.4855	-14.1685***
GR	13.3910	0.0015	2.7462	3.2484	-13.9603***
FI	330.6256	0.0445	11.9223	33.2766	-12.5201***
TI	26.8231	0.1601	1.3015	2.6438	-11.4338***
EI	37.1759	0.0823	1.3941	3.4855	-11.6431***
II	16.4195	0.1115	1.2043	1.9915	-12.1662***
TCD	172.0000	25.0000	106.1111	35.8589	
GEOD	42.8000	5.4000	23.8611	10.2376	
GEOD2	1831.8400	29.1600	673.7761	512.4806	

Notes:
1. PR = the ratio of Chinese population to the partner's population; GR = the ratio of China's GDP to the partner's GDP; FI = FDI intensity; TI = trade intensity; EI = export intensity; II = import intensity; TCD = total cultural differences between China and the partner; GEOD = the geographic distance between China and the partner; GEOD2 = the squared geographic distance.
2. There are 270 observations for all variables except for TCD, GEOD and GEOD2.
3. Std. Dev. represents the standard deviation.
4. *** denotes significance at the level of 1% with the critical value of -2.57.

The OLS, WLS and SUR regression results for the system of (7.2.1) and (7.2.2) are presented in Table 7.3. All the coefficients in the OLS/WLS regressions are statistically significant at the 1% level, which suggests that China's relative market size and relative level of general economic activities positively affect the trade and FDI intensities and that international transaction costs negatively influence these intensities. The significant negative sign on the GEOD variable and the significant positive sign on the GEOD2 variable jointly indicate that the influence of geographic distance on trade and FDI is non-linear. The total cultural difference variable as the additional proxy for international transaction costs has a negative impact on the FDI intensity. Furthermore, the trade and FDI intensities are inter-determined. This apparently lends support to the theoretical linkage between trade and FDI. The positive sign of the coefficients suggests a complementary connection between trade and FDI intensities.

Table 7.3 OLS, WLS and SUR results for trade and FDI intensities

	OLS/WLS		SUR	
	Trade Intensity	FDI Intensity	Trade Intensity	FDI Intensity
C	4.2860***	53.3951***	2.5990***	25.6666***
	(0.6001) [a]	(7.9384)	(0.5810)	(7.5552)
	(0.5934) [b]	(7.8348)		
PR	0.0034***	0.0472***	0.0022**	0.0234**
	(0.0010)	(0.0130)	(0.0010)	(0.0126)
	(0.0010)	(0.0128)		
GR	0.0970***	2.0637***	0.0420	1.2831***
	(0.0359)	(0.4404)	(0.0353)	(0.4303)
	(0.0355)	(0.4347)		
GEOD	-0.3190***	-2.3207***	-0.1947***	-0.7089
	(0.4816)	(6.1318)	(0.4678)	(5.9116)
	(0.4762)	(6.0518)		
GEOD2	0.00537***	0.03490***	0.00349***	0.00784
	(0.0906)	(1.1444)	(0.0886)	(1.1104
	(0.0896)	(1.1294)		
TCD		-0.2506***		-0.1811***
		(0.0433)		(0.0392)
		(0.0427)		
FI	0.0343***		0.0557***	
	(0.0043)		(0.0040)	
	(0.0043)			
TI		5.0987***		8.6628***
		(0.6737)		(0.6139)
		(0.6649)		
R^2	0.5492	0.5868	0.5074	0.5415
Tests	*OLS vs. WLS*: 262.6646***		*OLS vs. SUR*: 46.0488***	

Notes:

1. [a] Standard errors are in parentheses when groupwise heteroscedasticity is not taken into account; [b] Standard errors are in parentheses when groupwise heteroscedasticity is taken into account.
2. *** and ** denote significance at the level of 1% and 5%, respectively.

Although the results from OLS and WLS look impressive in terms of the significance levels of all variables, the λ_{LM3} statistic of 46.05 shows that there exists heteroscedasticity and contemporaneous correlation. Therefore, SUR is a better statistical model in Table 7.3. In the SUR regressions, the level of significance of the coefficients on PR reduces to 5%. The GR variable is no longer statistically significant in the trade intensity equation. Furthermore, the GEOD and GEOD2 variables are statistically insignificant in the FDI intensity equation. The coefficient on TCD is still highly significant. Finally, both the trade intensity and FDI intensity are as highly significant as in the case of the OLS and WLS regressions.

Turning to Table 7.4, the OLS and WLS results for the system of (7.3.1) to (7.3.3) show that the PR, GR, GEOD and GEOD2 are the common determinants of the import, export and FDI intensities. In common with its impact on the trade intensity, the FDI intensity positively affects both import and export intensities. The TCD variable is again highly significant in explaining FDI. Finally, the import intensity is not a significant determinant of the FDI intensity while the export intensity is positively associated with the FDI intensity. It should also be noted that PR and GR are only statistically significant at the 10% and 5% levels, respectively, in the export intensity equation.

Similar to the result in Table 7.3, the Lagrange multiplier test statistic (λ_{LM3}) of 262.14 indicates that the SUR model is the statistically preferred one in Table 7.4. In terms of the levels of significance of all the variables the results from the SUR regressions are again not as good as those from the OLS and WLS regressions. Both PR and GR are statistically insignificant in the export intensity equation, as are GEOD and GEOD2 in the FDI intensity equation.

Although there is some inconsistency between the OLS/WLS and SUR results, the central message from these regressions is that FDI and trade are closely related. In either of the OLS/WLS and SUR models the FDI, trade and export intensities are inter-determined. Although the import intensity has no significant impact on the FDI intensity, the reverse relationship holds. All this indicates a two-way flow of influence between FDI and international trade. Thus, there is a need for the treatment of endogeneity between these variables.

One sensible way of tackling the endogeneity problem is the adoption of GMM estimation techniques. However, as widely discussed in the literature, the fundamental problem with any instrumental variable technique is the difficulty of finding good instruments. Nevertheless, we try to control for the endogeneity problem by using such instruments as fixed effects dummy variables, exogenous variables of PR and GR, and the lagged endogenous variables including FI, EI, II and TI. The GMM regression results are presented in Table 7.5. The reported results are qualitatively similar to those obtained by OLS/WLS estimation. Since the GMM model is more appropriate than any other models for the current investigation, the results from the GMM regressions form the basis of our economic interpretation.

Table 7.4 OLS, WLS and SUR results for import, export and FDI intensities

	OLS/WLS		
	Import Intensity	Export Intensity	FDI Intensity
C	5.5301***	2.9915***	51.2051***
	(0.8358)[a]	(0.4297)	(7.8257)
	(0.8264)[b]	(0.4249)	(7.7089)
PR	0.0050***	0.0012*	0.0550***
	(0.0014)	(0.0007)	(0.0128)
	(0.0014)	(0.0007)	(0.0126)
GR	0.1487***	0.0499**	2.1460***
	(0.0501)	(0.0257)	(0.4338)
	(0.0495)	(0.0254)	(0.4274)
GEOD	-0.4279***	-0.2112***	-2.2274***
	(0.6706)	(0.3448)	(6.0388)
	(0.6631)	(0.3409)	(5.9487)
GEOD2	0.0070***	0.0039***	0.0310***
	(0.1262)	(0.0649)	(1.1341)
	(0.1247)	(0.0641)	(1.1172)
TCD			-0.2546***
			(0.0426)
			(0.0419)
FI	0.0415***	0.0263***	
	(0.0060)	(0.0031)	
	(0.0060)	(0.0031)	
II			-0.2475
			(0.8990)
			(0.8856)
EI			7.9358***
			(1.6821)
			(1.6570)
R^2	0.5204	0.5150	0.6013

Table 7.4 Continued

	SUR		
	Import Intensity	Export Intensity	FDI Intensity
C	3.5794***	1.7586***	23.1641***
	(0.8141)	(0.4153)	(7.4059)
PR	0.0036***	0.0003	0.0360***
	(0.0014)	(0.0007)	(0.0124)
GR	0.0851*	0.0097	1.4292***
	(0.0493)	(0.0253)	(0.4224)
GEOD	-0.2841***	-0.1204***	-0.6913
	(0.6548)	(0.3344)	(5.7976)
GEOD2	0.0048***	0.0025***	0.0036
	(0.1237)	(0.0634)	(1.0959)
TCD			-0.1781***
			(0.0381)
FI	0.0663***	0.0419***	
	(0.0057)	(0.0028)	
II			-0.1480
			(0.7978)
EI			12.6877***
			(1.5015)
R^2	0.4898	0.4681	0.5549
Tests:	λ_{LM2} : 265.4240***		λ_{LM3} : 262.1443***

Notes:

1. ^{a} Standard errors are in parentheses when groupwise heteroscedasticity is not taken into account; ^{b} Standard errors are in parentheses when groupwise heteroscedasticity is taken into account.

2. *** and ** denote significance at the level of 1% and 5%, respectively.

The most noticeable feature of the GMM results is that all explanatory variables are statistically significant at the 1% level. Put another way, GMM provides the best results in terms of the significance levels of all variables. The regression results from (7.2.1) and (7.2.2) are provided in columns (2) and (3), respectively. As can be seen, geographic distance variables (GEOD and GEOD2) are an important common determinant of both trade and FDI intensity. The positive sign on GEOD2 again shows that the relationship between geographic distance and trade and FDI is non-linear. The negative sign on GEOD indicates that both trade and FDI are negatively affected by international transaction costs. In addition, as in the OLS/WLS and SUR regressions, the negative impact of total cultural differences as a further proxy for international transaction costs on the FDI intensity is as substantial as geographic distance in terms of the significance. GR and PR are the other two common determinants of the trade and FDI intensities. They show the positive and significant relationships between the relative levels of general economic activities and market size on the one hand, and trade and FDI on the other.

Table 7.5 GMM results for trade, FDI, import and export intensities

	(I)		(II)		
	Trade Intensity	FDI Intensity	Import Intensity	Export Intensity	FDI Intensity
C	2.6930***	31.5083***	3.2482***	2.0855***	35.7586***
	(0.1277)	(3.8505)	(0.1014)	(0.1369)	(3.2301)
PR	0.0020***	0.0354***	0.0027***	0.0006***	0.0413***
	(0.0002)	(0.0030)	(0.0001)	(0.0001)	(0.0025)
GR	0.0554***	1.4368***	0.0823***	0.0334***	1.5356***
	(0.0032)	(0.1131)	(0.0029)	(0.0028)	(0.0908)
GEOD	-0.1986***	-0.9890***	-0.2538***	-0.1447***	-1.2329***
	(0.0870)	(2.3097)	(0.0756)	(0.0922)	(1.9753)
GEOD2	0.0035***	0.0132***	0.0043***	0.0028***	0.0169***
	(0.0141)	(0.3596)	(0.0125)	(0.0147)	(0.3011)
TCD		-0.2174***			-0.2255***
		(0.0116)			(0.0090)
FI	0.0446***		0.0580***	0.0309***	
	(0.0032)		(0.0027)	(0.0021)	
TI		8.8808***			
		(0.2993)			
II					4.0961***
					(0.2747)
EI					4.2329***
					(0.3832)
R^2	0.5927	0.6263	0.5766	0.5763	0.6222

Notes:
1. GMM estimation was carried out on two systems of equations for the periods 1984-98, using as instruments: fixed effects dummy variables, PR, GR, the lagged values of EX, IM, TI and FI.
2. *** denotes significance at the level of 1%.
3. White-heteroscedasticity corrected standard errors are in parentheses.

As in the OLS, WLS and SUR regressions, trade and FDI are found to be inter-determined in the GMM regression results in columns (2) and (3) of Table 7.5. However, it is interesting to note that the interactive relationship between the trade and FDI intensities is far from symmetric. While a 1 unit increase in FDI intensity raises the trade intensity by only 0.04 units, a 1 unit rise in the trade intensity leads to as high as an 8.88 unit increase in the FDI intensity. This suggests that the impact of trade intensity on FDI intensity is much greater than that of FDI intensity on trade intensity.

Columns (4), (5) and (6) of Table 7.5 show the GMM regression results from (7.3.1) to (7.3.3). PR, GR and GEOD are the significant common determinants of the import, export and FDI intensities. TCD is again a negative and significant determinant of the FDI intensity. In the economic sense it is perfectly sound to suggest that export, import and FDI intensities are negatively influenced by international transaction costs proxied by geographic distance. It can also be argued that they are positively affected by China's relative market size and relative level of general economic activities.

However, it may appear puzzling that the import intensity is also positively connected with China's relative market size and relative level of general economic activities. One possible explanation is that while China's relatively higher level of general activities implies a sufficiently higher level of products which are able to meet the increased demand from both domestic and foreign markets, China's relatively larger market size proxied by the relatively higher population ratio may happen to coincide with China's relative level of economic activities.

Given the theme of this chapter, we are more interested in the relationships between FDI intensity on the one hand, and export and import intensities on the other. Columns (4) and (5) of Table 7.5 shows that when the FDI intensity increases by 1 unit, the import intensity will increase by 0.058 units, holding other things constant. Moreover, a 1 unit rise in the FDI intensity will lead to about a 0.031 unit rise in the export intensity, holding other things constant. The Wald tests reject the hypothesis that the coefficient on FDI in the import intensity equation is statistically equal to that in the export intensity equation, and accept the hypothesis that the difference between the two coefficients is 0.027. This indicates that the positive impact of the FDI intensity on the import intensity is almost twice as high as that on the export intensity in terms of the magnitude.

From column (6), it can be seen that both the import and export intensities have a significant and positive impact on the FDI intensity. This indicates that both the export and import intensities are complementary with the FDI intensity. Therefore, an intensive trade partner of China, either intensive exporter, or intensive importer or both, is an intensive foreign investor in China. While the reverse relations are also valid, the impact of the import and export intensities on the FDI intensity is much more powerful than the reverse impact. Moreover the magnitudes of the coefficients on the import and export intensities are very close. In fact, the Wald test for the equality of these two coefficients can not be rejected (with the probability of 82%), which suggests that they are not statistically different from each other.

7.6 CONCLUSIONS AND POLICY IMPLICATIONS

This chapter has examined the relationships between FDI and trade intensities and those between FDI, export and import intensities. To construct multiple regression equations, the following three common determinants of FDI, trade, imports and exports are incorporated: the population ratio as a proxy for the relative market size, the GDP ratio for the relative level of general economic activities, and geographic distance for international transaction costs. Total cultural differences are also employed as an additional proxy for international transaction costs in the FDI equations.

The analysis starts with estimations of OLS/WLS and SUR models to see if there are any possible interactive relationships between FDI and trade. Given a two-way flow of influence between these two variables, the more appropriate GMM models are employed to estimate the coefficients from the equation systems. The results confirm that international transaction costs measured by geographic distance, the relative level of general economic activities and relative market size are the common determinants of the FDI, import, export and trade intensities. International transaction costs proxied by total cultural distance are also a significant determinant of the FDI intensity.

The FDI intensity reinforces the trade, import and export intensities. However, the flows of influence between FDI and trade are not symmetric. The positive impact of the trade (as well as import and export) intensity on the FDI intensity is much stronger than the reverse impact. It is interesting to note that the positive effect of the FDI intensity on the import intensity is almost twice as large as that on the export intensity in terms of the magnitude. This suggests that the FDI intensity could make more substantial contributions to the relative level of China's exports than that of China's imports.

As defined, the export intensity to some extent reflects the comparative advantage in the partner country while the import intensity reveals the comparative advantage in China. Given that both the export and import intensities positively and significantly affect the FDI intensities, the Chinese evidence fails to support the hypothesis that outward FDI takes place in the home country, which is comparatively disadvantageous. However, as discussed in section 7.2, different types of FDI are motivated differently and the impact of factor endowments on efficiency or strategic asset-seeking investment is very limited. The current study uses the data at the national level and is not able to differentiate the varieties of FDI.

At the highly aggregate level of the data the current study tends to conclude that FDI and trade are directly connected. More specifically, the positive signs on the FDI, trade, import and export intensity variables suggest complementary relationships between them.

An important policy implication emerges from the empirical results of this study. Given the positive linkages between FDI and trade, the Chinese government needs to co-ordinate its FDI and trade policies to maximise their synergies for economic growth and development. To prepare for entry into the WTO, China needs to further reduce trade and non-trade barriers. As a result, more trade is expected. This will in turn bring about more inward FDI. Thus, there can be a virtuous circle of international integration through trade and FDI. Since FDI is found to have a positive impact on productivity and both FDI and trade are found to have a positive impact on per capita income as indicated in chapters 5 and 6, the trade-FDI virtuous circle can be extended to incorporate economic growth.

APPENDIX 7A DATA DESCRIPTION AND SOURCES

Population, GDP and total trade, exports and imports for each country/region are from IMF: *International Financial Statistical Yearbook* 1999.

Geographic distance, total cultural differences and China's trade, exports and imports with its partners are defined in the same ways and from the same sources as specified in the Appendix to Chapter 3.

The main sources for outward FDI stock data are as follows:

1. OECD: *The International Direct Investment Statistics Yearbook* (1993-98), (hereafter IDISY)
2. UNCTD: *World Investment Report* (1992-99) (hereafter WIR)
3. UNCTD: *World Investment Directory*, Volume 1, Asia and the Pacific, 1992 (hereafter WID)

United States, Canada, Australia, Japan, Germany, Italy, Spain and United Kingdom ~
> stock data for 1984-96 from IDISY; data for 1997-98 from WIR.

New Zealand ~
> stock data for 1985, 1990 and 1992-98 from WIR; data for 1984, 1986-89 and 1991 derived by interpolation using outflow data in IDISY.

Belgium ~
> stock data for 1984-89 from IDISY; 1990 and 1992-98 from WIR; data for 1991 derived by interpolation using outflow data in IDISY.

Denmark ~
> stock data for 1985, 1990 and 1992-98 from WIR; data for 1984, 1986-89 and 1991 derived by interpolation using outflow data in IDISY.

Finland ~
> stock data for 1984-96 from stock data for 1985, 1990 and 1992-98 from WIR; data for 1984, 1986-89 and 1991 derived by interpolation using outflow data in IDISY; data for 1997-98 from WIR.

France ~
> stock data for 1989-96 from IDISY; data for 1984-88 derived by interpolation using outflow data in IDISY; data for 1997-98 from WIR.

Netherlands ~
> stock data for 1984-95 from IDISY; data for 1996-98 from WIR.

Sweden ~
> stock data for 1986-96 from IDISY; data for 1997-98 from WIR.

Switzerland ~
    stock data for 1985-96 from IDISY; data for 1997-98 from WIR.

China ~
    stock data for 1984-89 from WID converted from Chinese yuan to US dollars using annual average exchange rates in IMF: *International Financial Statistics Yearbook 1999*; data for 1990 and 1992-98 from WIR: data for 1991 derived by interpolation using outflow data in WIR.

Hong Kong ~
    stock data for 1984-87 from WID converted from Hong Kong dollars to US dollars using annual average exchange rates in IMF: *International Financial Statistics Yearbook 1999*; data for 1990 and 1992-98 from WIR: data for 1988, 1989 and 1991 derived by interpolation.

South Korea ~
    stock data for 1985-96 from IDISY; data for 1997-98 from WIR.

Malaysia ~
    stock data for 1984-88 from WID converted from ringgit to US dollars using annual average exchange rates in IMF: *International Financial Statistics Yearbook 1999*; data for 1990, and 1992-98 from WIR; data for 1989 and 1991 derived by interpolation.

Singapore ~
    stock data for 1985, 1990 and 1992-98 from WIR; data for 1984, 1986-89 and 1991 derived by interpolation using outflow data in WIR. .

Thailand ~
    stock data for 1984-88 from WID converted from baht to US dollars using annual average exchange rates in IMF: *International Financial Statistics Yearbook 1999*; data for 1990, and 1992-98 from WIR; data for 1989 and 1991 derived by interpolation using outflow data in WIR.

World ~
    stock data for 1985, 1990 and 1992-98 from WIR, and the data for the remaining years were derived from IDISY.

8.   Conclusions

8.1 INTRODUCTION

This book analyses the determinants and impact of foreign direct investment (FDI) in China. Compared with the existing books in this area, the main features of the current volume include the adoption of a panel data approach and the introduction of such new topics as productivity spillovers from FDI and the linkage between international trade and FDI. Chapter 1 provides a very brief preview of FDI in China and introduces the empirical research topics to be covered by the book. Chapter 2 extends the preview by providing a more detailed description of the development trends and impact of FDI in China. Chapters 3-7 provide five empirical studies. More specifically, chapters 3 and 4 deal with the determinants of FDI at the national and regional levels respectively. Chapter 5 examines the effect of FDI on labour productivity in China's electronics industry. Chapter 6 investigates the impact of FDI on economic growth and regional income convergence in China. Next, chapter 7 discusses the relationship between FDI and international trade intensities. This concluding chapter summarises the main findings of the book and discusses policy implications.

The remainder of this chapter is organised as follows. Section 8.2 provides an overall summary of the empirical results of the book. Section 8.3 discusses the policy implications for attracting further FDI inflows, while section 8.4 discusses those for enhancing the positive impact of FDI on economic growth. Finally, section 8.5 discusses the contributions and limitations of the current study and suggests future topics for research.

8.2 OVERALL SUMMARY

At the national level, FDI inflows are positively influenced by China's relative market size and economic integration represented by real exports and imports, and negatively determined by China's relative real wage rates, country risk, cultural differences and borrowing costs. At the regional level, the positive and significant determinants of FDI include GDP growth, the level of international trade, R&D manpower, infrastructure, and the availability of information and investment incentives. Effective wage rates are negatively associated with FDI inflows into Chinese regions. The common determinants at the national and regional levels are market size or growth, international trade and wage rates. Since a host country and a special location within that country are often chosen simultaneously, it may not be surprising that these explanatory variables are statistically significant at both national and regional levels.

The evidence on the determinants of FDI in China is generally consistent with received theory. Given that home-country firms possess ownership advantages and wish to reduce information or transaction costs and improve competitive or strategic advantage, the locational advantages provided by China have attracted substantial FDI inflows. Following Dunning's (1993) analysis of types of international production, FDI in China has been motivated by several factors. First, foreign investors may be interested in the Chinese market. This is confirmed by the significant coefficient on the relative GDP size and GDP growth at the national and regional level. Second, foreign investors would like to seek efficiency of production, especially of production processes. The significant coefficients on the labour cost and the availability of information and investment incentives suggest that this is the case. The significant R&D manpower variable also suggests that what foreign investors need is not just cheap labour but also scientific and technical personnel. The significant coefficients on the country risk, infrastructure and R&D manpower variables support industrial location theory and endogenous growth theory.

However, FDI in China has its own features. A great deal of FDI in China has been made by overseas Chinese. The significant and negative relationship between cultural differences and inward FDI indicates the importance of Chinese culture as a determinant. This culture advocates affection for the home of origin and commitment to the family. The significant and positive relationship between relative borrowing costs and inward FDI in China reflects the fact that the dominant type of FDI takes the form of joint ventures where Chinese partners also need to make financial contributions. This challenges the conventional wisdom that predicts a positive relationship between FDI and host country borrowing costs.

FDI has played a positive role in China's economic development. The evidence from China's electronics industry indicates that FDI is positively associated with labour productivity in the Chinese electronics industry. The empirical study on regional economic growth suggests that investment in physical and human capital, R&D, FDI and international trade all enhance economic growth. Population growth, however, has a negative effect. If these regional characteristics were not controlled for, there would be persistent divergence in regional per capita income. Put another way, FDI, together with other explanatory variables, helps promote regional convergence in per capita income.

It should be noted that the direct impact of FDI on labour productivity in China's electronics industry and on regional economic growth is limited given the relatively small magnitude of the coefficient on the FDI variable. Domestic investment in physical and human capital, R&D expenditure and firm size have made more important contributions than FDI to productivity or economic growth. Although the importance of FDI has been rising, the share of FDI in China's fixed capital formation remains relatively low. This may partly explain the limited role of FDI but may also suggest great potential for FDI in economic development in China.

Endogenous growth theory emphasises the role of R&D, human capital accumulation and externalities in the rate of economic growth. It also suggests that international trade and FDI facilitate technological diffusion and imitation and provide positive spillover effects or externalities for trading partners and host countries. The Chinese evidence provides strong support for endogenous growth theory because investment in physical and human capital, R&D, trade and FDI are found to be the significant determinants of economic growth.

The positive role of FDI also includes its interaction with international trade. The empirical results suggest that intense FDI partners are also intense trading partners of China. FDI helps trade expansion and *vice versa*. International trade and inward FDI in China reinforce one another. In addition to its direct impact, FDI indirectly promotes technological progress and economic growth by directly bringing about trade.

8.3 POLICY IMPLICATIONS FOR ATTRACTING FOREIGN DIRECT INVESTMENT IN CHINA

The findings from this book have important policy implications for future expansion of inward FDI in China. First, since economic growth and inward FDI are closely related, the Chinese government's efforts to promote economic growth help to increase the relative market size and attract more market-seeking FDI. Given the positive impact of FDI on economic growth, there can be a virtuous circle from which China can benefit.

Second, relatively lower labour costs still attract efficiency-seeking FDI. While China can still make use of this locational advantage for a certain period, there is increasing competition for FDI from countries with even lower labour costs. Since FDI provides developing countries with important benefits, China's neighbouring countries such as Vietnam, Laos, and India have already adopted various preferential policies to attract FDI (Jiao, 1998).

All these countries are endowed with a cheap labour force. Faced by competition China needs to move to attract other types of FDI. Dunning and Robson (1988) observe that different production stages require completely different types of manpower. Lower labour cost locations only attract routine production stages. While there remains a need for China to continue absorbing routine production based on cheap labour costs, China may adopt a new strategy to expand FDI at other production stages. To achieve this, investment in human capital should be strengthened.

Clegg and Scott-Green (1999) suggest that higher value-added production requires skilled labour at medium labour cost. Furthermore, if administrative and R&D stages of production are pursued, then professional and scientific manpower is needed which is associated with higher labour costs. The fact that R&D manpower is important in attracting FDI in Chinese regions demonstrates the evidence and development of the R&D stage of foreign production in China. It is sometimes suggested that countries with low levels of education and low rates of FDI grow much more slowly than countries with high education rates and high levels of FDI inflows (Borensztein et al., 1998). Countries with high educational levels but low FDI, or with low educational levels but high FDI, do little better than countries that score low on both measures. Sufficiently well-educated workers are needed to facilitate continuous transfer of technology (World Bank, 2000). Thus, the third policy implication of this book is that China needs to pay more attention to education and training in order to attract relatively higher-quality FDI.

Fourth, while the cultural similarity helps China to receive a good deal of investment from overseas Chinese, there is a need to attract more technology-intensive FDI. Capital intensity is an important criterion for assessing the technical level of the production process. Although several studies have stressed the role of overseas Chinese FDI in providing entrepreneurial, managerial and international marketing skills, and technical know-how, especially for mature products (Thoburn et al., 1990; Hobday, 1995; Weidenbaum and Hughes, 1996), Lemoine (2000) indicates that affiliates from Hong Kong, Macao and Taiwan are much less capital-intensive than others. Furthermore, the World Bank (1994) and Liu and Song (1997) suggest that much of FDI by overseas Chinese displaces the production of labour-intensive and low-value products from Hong Kong and Taiwan to the mainland, where wages are lower and the labour force is reasonably skilled. Hayter and Han (1998) contend that the largest Hong Kong firms have not been much involved in high-tech activities. This may be consistent with the empirical result from this book that the impact of FDI on economic growth is limited in China.

As summarised by Hayter and Han (1998) however, there can still be opportunities to obtain high-tech know-how from overseas Chinese FDI. For instance, the biggest Hong Kong firms have the massive financial and managerial resources to acquire the necessary know-how. In Taiwan and Singapore there is an increasing number of successful Chinese-controlled high-tech firms. The extent to which technologies can be transferred or diffused depends partly on indigenous firms' technological capabilities. If China's industrial and technological capability rises, a large number of Chinese firms will be able to benefit more from the presence of high-tech companies. Thus, the Chinese government may further encourage high-tech FDI by appropriate policies.

FDI from developed countries is generally more capital- and technology-intensive. So far, such investment remains very limited compared with that from overseas Chinese although China is a major host in the world. China received only 3.8, 1.3, 1.1 and 1.0 per cent of total outward FDI stocks from Japan, Zealand, Australia and the United States respectively. The percentages from other developed countries are even smaller than 0.6. As shown in chapter 2, small FDI from developed countries is closely associated with the limited market size in China. The Tenth Five-Year Plan (2001-2005) indicates that China wants to maintain a relatively high growth rate for the national economy. In addition, China aims to adjust the structure of its economy and enhance the quality and efficiency of economic growth. The target of economic development is to double China's 2000 GDP by the year 2010. It follows that the Chinese economy will experience continuous fast growth, and so will the relative size of the Chinese market. This suggests a great potential for further growth of inward FDI from developed countries.

Fifth, further expansion of international trade is needed to facilitate more FDI inflows. Given that FDI and trade are closely related, an increase of trade/FDI will lead to an increase in FDI/Trade. de Mello (1997) argues that FDI has a more profound impact on growth in countries that pursue policies promoting exports than it does in countries that follow import substitution. The World Bank (1999) recommends the liberalisation of trade regimes. This is partly because multinational corporations aiming for global competitiveness and international markets have a greater incentive to bring in technology and training - with the accompanying spillover benefits. Furthermore, a liberal trade regime is an important determinant of FDI inflows. Following the formation of the North American Free Trade Agreement (NAFTA) for instance, there were substantial FDI inflows into Mexico, which was regarded as a production base for the US market. China is now the ninth-largest trading country in the world. Being in the process of entering the WTO, China has been relaxing its control of both imports and exports, and is expected to become an even more important trading country.

Sixth, FDI needs to be encouraged to the central and western areas. Despite the impressive overall achievement in attracting an increasing amount of FDI at the national level, regional distribution remains extremely uneven. If the central and western areas followed a similar pattern of absorbing FDI to that of the coastal areas, then total FDI in China would be greatly increased. The central and western areas have their own advantages of relatively lower labour costs and easy access to national resources, but have the disadvantages of relatively poor infrastructure, lower R&D manpower and lack of information. The Tenth Five-Year Plan calls for the development of the western areas. Accordingly, the central government has decided to invest more in infrastructure, education, environment protection, natural resource exploitation and special high-tech projects in the western areas and encourage close co-operation between the coastal and western areas. In addition, special policy incentives are offered to foreign businesses to invest in the western areas, as shown in chapter 4. All this helps to enhance the attractiveness of inland areas as the regional hosts for FDI.

Seventh, certain investment incentives may still be needed at the moment and should be phased out very carefully in the near future. As indicated in the empirical results from this book, the concentration of FDI in the coastal areas (especially in the SEZs and ETDZs) is partly influenced by the favourable fiscal and financial policies offered by the central and local government authorities. The availability of investment incentives does play a positive role in attracting FDI in China. Zhang (1998) argues that, because many developing countries adopt preferential policies to attract FDI, it may be necessary for China to follow suit. Given that China is already in the process of transition from a planned economy into a market-oriented economy, much needs to be done to further improve the investment environment. During this process certain investment incentives may be desirable.

It is very important to keep relevant policies stable. During the 1990s China's average customs duty was gradually reduced and was as low as 17 per cent in 1995. Given this fact, on 28 December 1995 the State Council decided to gradually provide foreign investors with national treatment and remove the tax exemption on capital goods imported by foreign-invested firms. This policy change had a negative impact on foreign investors and discouraged reinvestment by some existing foreign-invested firms (Zhang, 1998). As a response, in 1997 the State Council announced that an FDI project belonging to the category encouraged by the Chinese government would receive an indefinite extension of the exemption from tariffs and VAT on imported capital goods. This was actually an easing of this controversial revocation of preferential policies (McDaniels 1998). This indicates the importance of the relative stability of FDI policy.

The World Bank (2000) suggests the avoidance of inducements for foreign investors because policies such as subsidies and tax holidays may encourage investment, but for society as a whole losses too often outweigh the gains. In the case of China, Broadman (1995) estimates that the 'better-than-national-treatment' concessions had an opportunity cost (of foregone tax revenue) of 1.2 per cent of China's GDP, but few real incentives were yielded. With continuous improvement of the investment climate the current investment incentives for foreign investors may be carefully phased out. When China's FDI policy regime and general investment environment reach international standards, financial inducements may no longer be necessary.

8.4 POLICY IMPLICATIONS FOR ECONOMIC GROWTH

The empirical results from this book have important policy implications for economic growth. The determinants of economic growth identified in the book include capital intensity, human capital, R&D expenditure, trade, FDI and population growth. In this section we address the policy issues for national and regional economic development based on our empirical findings.

The ultimate purpose of China's economic reform and opening up to the outside world is to stimulate economic development and improve living standards. Considering that the central and western areas were poorer than the coastal areas, the central government regarded the reduction of regional disparities as an important task under the Ninth Five-Year Plan (1996-2000). In the Tenth Five-Year Plan (2001-05) the central government requires that regional development should be co-ordinated and that the coastal areas should by all means support the development of the central and western areas. As mentioned earlier, the central government is also increasing its investment in the western areas. The empirical evidence from this book suggests that all positive determinants of economic growth also help reduce regional disparities. Government policy that stimulates economic growth in an individual region will simultaneously promote regional convergence in per capita income and improve overall living standards.

Investment in physical capital often implies an enhancement in capital intensity and embodied technology. To upgrade technological capabilities the Chinese government needs to encourage firms to introduce new 'hard' technologies and improve efficiency. In line with the concept of demonstration effects from endogenous growth theory, if some firms adopt new machinery and equipment to produce goods or services more efficiently, other firms will follow suit and upgrade their technologies. This will enhance overall productivity in the whole industry.

As confirmed by the Chinese data, human capital is extremely important in economic growth. The World Bank (1999) indicates that it is the gaps in know-how that separate poor countries from rich and poor people from non-poor. Narrowing the gap can increase economic growth in developing countries, raise income, reduce environmental degradation, and generally improve the quality of life. Human capital is a key element for building a knowledge base as it is required to conduct domestic innovation and absorb global knowledge. Education and on-the-job training are two key means to accumulate human capital stock.

As suggested by Liu and Song (1997), given the limited public resources in China, private schools and universities should be encouraged. The World Bank (1999) argues that an effective education system is crucial to creating people's ability to absorb knowledge. For transition economies like China, governments have a role in improving the content, delivery, and funding of education to respond to market demands and tight budgets. China also needs to strengthen job training. While a large number of workers have been released from traditional industries such as textiles, there is a lack of a skilled labour force in new industries such as information technology and services. China has been establishing job training centres to help workers move from traditional to new industries. But on-the-job training provided by firms in new industries should be encouraged.

Coe and Helpman (1995) argue that a country's productivity depends on its own R&D as well as on the R&D efforts of its trade partners. Own R&D produces goods and services that encourage more effective use of existing resources and therefore raise a country's productivity level. Furthermore, own R&D enhances a country's benefits from foreign technical advances. The Chinese government has paid special attention to R&D activities. It has its own long- and medium-term science and technology development strategies. In 1986, the Chinese government announced a High Technology Development Plan (called 863 after the year and month in which it was initiated). Under this plan, seven high-technology areas (biotechnology, space technology, lasers, energy, automation, information technology and raw materials) were identified for support. A follow-up scheme, known as the Torch Plan, initiated in 1988, was designed to support the commercialisation of advanced technologies. The government's direct support for R&D includes the establishment and continuous finance of universities, government research institutes and science parks. However, the Chinese government can also provide indirect support for R&D by offering incentives for private R&D. As suggested by the World Bank (1999), the incentives include preferential finance, tax concessions and matching funding.

International trade and FDI are the two important vehicles for knowledge dissemination and have been regarded as the essential sources for economic growth in developing countries. It is argued that one of the main reasons the

East Asian economies were able to grow so fast for so long was their ability to build strong links with world markets and to draw upon the technology flowing through these markets (World Bank, 1999). However, as discussed earlier, the Chinese data show that the positive impact of FDI on economic growth is very limited, probably due to its relatively small share in total investment in China, and the replication of may industrial projects with low technology intensity. The positive impact of FDI may be enhanced by targeting different foreign investors for different purposes and by providing guidelines for investment directions. As for the first aspect, Zhuang (1999) divides foreign investors in China into three groups. The first comprises American and European multinational corporations whose projects have high-tech contents and are often the leaders in the corresponding industries. The second comprises East Asian multinational corporations represented by Japanese firms whose projects are relatively mature and can have quick returns. The final group are the overseas Chinese who share a similar culture and are very responsive to China's modernisation drive, but many of their projects have low-tech contents and are not very competitive in international markets. While low-tech and labour-intensive FDI projects are still welcomed as China is endowed with a large and cheap labour force, special attention should be paid to the introduction of high technology projects especially from North America, Europe and Japan.

With regard to investment directions, China started to encourage high-tech FDI projects as early as 1986 when the State Council formulated the 'Provisions of the State Council of the People's Republic of China for the Encouragement of Foreign Investment' (also known as the 'Twenty Two Articles'). Under these provisions special tax preferences were granted to technologically advanced as well as export-oriented foreign enterprises in order to 'better introduce advanced technology, improve product quality, expand exports to generate foreign exchange and develop the national economy'. In 1997 China released a new Guiding Catalogue for Foreign Investment in Industry, effective from 1 January 1998. The new catalogue classified investments in industries as 'encouraged', 'restricted', or 'prohibited'. Investments labelled 'encourage' may take advantage of preferential policies and include those utilising high technology. Investments labelled 'restricted' require approval by either the central or provincial government. By doing so, the Chinese authorities aim to avoid unnecessary replication of industrial projects with low technology and enhance the positive impact of FDI on productivity and economic growth in China.

Finally the control of population growth is still needed. China started its policy of 'one family, one child' as early as the 1970s. Although it has been controversial politically, the adoption of this policy has substantially reduced the growth rate of the Chinese population. As the empirical results show that population growth has a significantly negative impact on per capita income growth, it is necessary to control population in China if the improvement in living standards of Chinese people is aimed at. Other things being equal, with a low rate of population growth, relatively more resources can be devoted to education and training, health, housing and environment protection. All this helps the improvement of population quality and the accumulation of human capital, and promotes economic growth.

8.5 LIMITATIONS, CONTRIBUTIONS AND FUTURE RESEARCH

An important limitation of the current study is its use of secondary data which may sometimes be problematic. First, as noted in chapter 1, China's reported FDI inflows were thought to be overestimated because of over-valuation of capital equipment contributed by foreign investors to joint ventures and 'round-tripping' investment by indigenous Chinese firms to receive benefits provided by the Chinese government. Thus, the positive impact of FDI, already limited compared with domestic investment, can be exaggerated.

Second, because of data limitation we can not compare the contributions of FDI by different investors to productivity or economic growth in China. As mentioned earlier, FDI from different groups of countries contains different levels of technology and would have different impacts on economic development. However, the existing data are very aggregate and it is impossible to find out the information on the origin of foreign investors and their corresponding activities at the regional or industrial level. Thus, we have to examine the effects of foreign-invested firms as a whole, whether they come from the United States, Europe, Japan or other countries or regions.

Third, since the study is carried out at the national, regional and industrial level respectively, the policy implications provided are mainly confined to these levels. Although the result that capital intensity, human capital, firm size and R&D are important in productivity or economic growth can also be very useful for enterprise managers, it is impossible for the current study to offer detailed suggestions for organisational or managerial changes at the firm level.

Despite its limitations the current study is believed to contribute to the literature in several aspects. The appropriate panel data approach has been adopted for all empirical work and some case analyses have been incorporated in the economic interpretations to provide more insights. Such new topics as the trade-FDI linkages and the spillover effect from FDI have been introduced for China. A number of interesting empirical results have been obtained and their policy implications discussed. The study is thought to be useful for China, other developing countries and transition economies to adjust their policy regimes so that more FDI can be attracted and a more positive impact of FDI expected.

Future research can be carried out at the firm level. If data from official sources are not available, surveys can be conducted. Corresponding to the topics studied in this book, the following issues can be examined at the firm level: why did a foreign investor choose to invest in China and a particular location within China? Did different groups of foreign investors have different motivations for investment? How did foreign investors transfer their technologies? What were the mechanisms by which spillover effects occurred? Did FDI substitute or complement trade? How did foreign investors help improve productivity? Research at the firm level would certainly provide more insights into the behaviour of foreign-invested firms.

References

Agarwal, J., 1980. 'Determinants of Foreign Direct Investment: A Survey', *Weltwirtschaftliches Archiv*, **116**, 739-73.

Aitken, B., Hanson, G. H. and Harrison, A. E., 1997. 'Spillovers, Foreign Investment, and Export Behaviour', *Journal of International Economics*, **43(1-2)**, 103-32.

Aitken, B. J. and Harrison, A. E., 1999. 'Do Domestic Firms Benefit from Direct Foreign Investment? Evidence from Venezuela', *American Economic Review*, **89(3)**, 605-18.

Ajami, R. A. and BarNiv, R., 1984., 'Utilising Economic Indicators in Explaining Foreign Investment in the US', *Management International Review*, **24(4)**, 16-26.

Aliber, R. Z., 1970. 'A Theory of Foreign Direct Investment', in Kindleberger, C. (ed.), *The International Corporation*, Cambridge, MA: MIT Press.

Amponsah, W., Colyer, D. and Jolly, C., 1999. 'Global Trade Integration and Economic Convergence of Developing Countries', *American Journal of Agricultural Economics*, **81(5)**, 1142-48.

Andres, J., Domenech, R. and Molinas, C., 1996. 'Macroeconomic Performance and Convergence in OECD Countries', *European Economic Review*, **40**, 1683-1704.

Aristotelous, K. and Fountas, S., 1996. 'An Empirical Analysis of Inward Foreign Direct Investment Flows in the EU with Emphasis on the Market Enlargement Hypothesis', *Journal of Common Market Studies*, **34(4)**, 571-83.

Bajo-Rubio, O. and Sosvilla-Rivero, S., 1994. 'An Econometric Analysis of Foreign Direct Investment in Spain, 1964-1989', *Southern Economic Journal*, **61(1)**, 104-20.

Balasubramanyam, V. N., Salisu, M. and Sapsford, D., 1996. 'Foreign Direct Investment and Growth in EP and IS Countries', *Economic Journal*, **106**, 92-105.

Balasubramanyam, V. N., Salisu, M. and Sapsford, D., 1999. 'Foreign Direct Investment as an Engine of Growth', *Journal of International Trade and Economic Development*, **8(1)**, 27-40.

Baltagi, B. H., 1995. *Econometric Analysis of Panel Data*, New York: Wiley.

Banerji, K. and Sambharya, R. B., 1996. 'Vertical Keiretsu and International Market Entry: the Case of the Japanese Automobile Ancillary Industry', *Journal of International Business Studies*, **27(1)**, 89-113.

Barrell, R. and Pain, N., 1996. 'An Econometric Analysis of US Foreign Direct Investment', *Review of Economics and Statistics*, **78(2)**, 200-07.

Barrell, R. and Pain, N., 1997a. 'The Growth of FDI in Europe', *National Institute Economic Review*, **160**, 63-75.

Barrell, R. and Pain, N., 1997b. 'Foreign Direct Investment, Technological Change and Economic Growth within Europe', *Economic Journal*, **107**, 1770-86.

Barrell, R. and Pain, N., 1999. 'Trade Restraints and Japanese Direct Investment Flows', *European Economic Review*, **43**, 29-45.

Barro, R. J. and Sala-i-Martin, X., 1991. 'Convergence across States and Regions', *Brookings Papers on Economic Activity*, **2**, 107-58.

Barro, R. J. and Sala-i-Martin, X., 1992a. 'Convergence', *Journal of Political Economy*, **100**, 223-51.

Barro, R. J. and Sala-i-Martin, X., 1992b. 'Regional Growth and Migration: A US and Japan Comparison', *Journal of the Japanese and International Economies*, **6(4)**, 312-46.

Barro, R. J. and Sala-i-Martin, X., 1995. *Economic Growth*, New York: McGraw Hill.

Bartik, T. J., 1985. 'Business Location Decisions in the United States: Estimates of the Effects of Unionisation, Taxes and Other Characteristics of States', *Journal of Business and Economic Statistics*, **3**, 14-22.

Bayoumi, T., Coe, D. T. and Helpman, E., 1999. 'R&D Spillovers and Global Growth', *Journal of International Economics*, **47**, 339-428.

Bayoumi, T. and Lipworth, G., 1997. 'Japanese Foreign Direct Investment and Regional Trade', *IMF Working Paper*, **WP/97/103**. IMF.

Belderbos, R. and Sleuwaegen, L., 1996. 'Japanese Firms and the Decision to Invest Abroad: Business Groups and Regional Core Networks', *Review of Economics and Statistics*, **78(2)**, 214-20.

Benito, G. R. G. and Gripsrud, G., 1992. 'The Expansion of Foreign Direct Investments: Discrete Rational Location Choices or a Cultural Learning Process?', *Journal of International Business Studies*, **23(3)**, 461-76.

Blomstrom, M., 1989. *Foreign Investment and Spillovers: A Study of Technology Transfer to Mexico*, London: Routledge.

Blomstrom, M. and Lipsey, R. E., 1989. 'The Export Performance of US and Swedish Multinationals', *Review of Income and Wealth*, **35**, 245-64.

Blomstrom, M., Lipsey, R. E. and Kulchycky, K., 1988. 'US and Swedish Direct Investment and Exports', in Baldwin, R. E. (ed.) *Trade Policy Issues and Empirical Analysis*, Chicago: University of Chicago Press.

Blomstrom, M. and Persson, H., 1983. 'Foreign Investment and Spillover Efficiency in an Underdeveloped Economy: Evidence from the Mexican Manufacturing Industry', *World Development*, **11**, 493-501.

Blomstrom, M. and Kokko, A., 1998. 'Multinational Corporations and Spillovers', *Journal of Economic Surveys*, **12(2)**, 1-31.

Blomstrom, M. and Wolff, E., 1994. 'Multinational Corporations and Productivity Convergence in Mexico', in Baumol, W., Nelson, R., and Wolff, E. (eds.), *Convergence of Productivity: Cross-National Studies and Historical Evidence*, Oxford: Oxford University Press.

Borensztein, E., de Gregorio, J. and Lee J-W., 1998. 'How does Foreign Direct Investment Affect Economic Growth?', *Journal of International Economics*, **45**, 115-35.

Brainard, S. L., 1993. 'A Simple Theory of Multinational Corporations and Trade with a Trade-off between Proximity and Concentration', *NBER Working Paper* **No. 4269**.

Brainard, S. L., 1997. 'An Empirical Assessment of the Proximity-Concentration Trade-off Between Multinational Sales and Trade', *American Economic Review*, **87(4)**, 520-44.

Braunerhjelm, P. and Svensson, R., 1996. 'Host Country Characteristics and Agglomeration in Foreign Direct Investment', *Applied Economics*, **28**, 833-40.

Breslin, S., 1996. 'China in East Asia: the Process and Implications of Regionalization', *Pacific Review*, **9(4)**, 463-87.

Breusch, T. and Pagan, A., 1980. 'The LM Test and its Applications to Model Specification in Econometrics', *Review of Economics Studies*, **47**, 239-54.

Broadman, H. G., 1995. 'China: Tax Policy toward Foreign Direct Investment', *Economic Policy Note*, World Bank, **August**.

Broadman, H. G. and Sun, X., 1997. 'The Distribution of Foreign Investment in China', *World Economy*, **20**, 339-61.

Buckley, P. J. and Casson, M., 1976. *The Future of the Multinational Enterprise*, London: Macmillan.

Buckley, P. J. and Casson, M. C., 1981. 'The Optimal Timing of a Foreign Direct Investment', *Economic Journal*, **91**, 75-87.

Cantwell, J., 1991. 'A Survey of Theories of International Production', in Pitelis, C. and Sugden, R. (eds.), *The Nature of the Transnational Firm*. 16-63, London: Routledge.

Casson, M., 1994a. 'Why are Firms Hierarchical?', *Journal of the Economics of Business*, **1**, 47-76.

Casson M., 1994b. 'Information Costs: Their Influence on Organisational Structure and the Boundaries of the Firm', *Proceedings of EMOT Workshop*, Como, Italy.

Caves R. E., 1971. 'Industrial Corporations: the Industrial Economics of Foreign Investment', *Economica*, **38**, 1-27.

Caves, R. E., 1974. 'Multinational Firms, Competition and Productivity in Host-Country Markets', *Economica*, **41**, 176-93.

Cellini, R., 1997. 'Growth Empirics: Evidence from a Panel of Annual Data', *Applied Economic Letters*, **4**, 347-51.

Chen, C., 1999. 'The Impact of FDI and Trade', in Wu, Y. (eds.), *Foreign Direct Investment and Economic Growth in China*, Aldershot, UK and Brookfield, US: Edward Elgar.

Chen, C., 1997. 'Provincial Characteristics and Foreign Direct Investment Location Decision within China', *Chinese Economy Research Unit Working Paper* **No. 97/16**, University of Adelaide.

Chen, J. and Fleisher, B. M., 1996. 'Regional Income Inequality and Economic Growth in China', *Journal of Comparative Economics*, **22**, 141-64.

Cheng, L. K. and Kwan, Y. K., 2000. 'What are the Determinants of the Location of Foreign Direct Investment? The Chinese Experience', *Journal of International Economics*, **51**, 379-400.

Choi, H. and Li, H., 2000. 'Economic Development and Growth Convergence in China', *Journal of International Trade and Economic Development*, **19(1)**, 37-54.

Chu, B., 1987. *Foreign Investment in China: a Question-and-Answer Guide*, Hong Kong: University Publisher and Printer.

Chuang, Y. C. and Lin, C. E., 1999. 'Foreign Direct Investment, R&D and Spillover Efficiency: Evidence from Taiwan's Manufacturing Firms', *Journal of Development Studies*, **35(4)**, 117-37.

Clegg, J. and Scott-Green, S., 1999. 'The Determinants of New FDI Capital Flows into the EC: A Statistical Comparison of the USA and Japan', *Journal of Common Market Studies*, **37(4)**, 597-616.

Coakley, J. and Kulasi, F., 1997. 'Cointegration of Long Span Saving and Investment', *Economics Letters*, **54**, 1-6.

Coe, D. T. and Helpman, E., 1995. 'International R&D Spillovers', *European Economic Review*, **39**, 859-87.

Coe, D. T., Helpman, E. and Hoffmaister, A. W., 1997. 'North-South R&D Spillovers', *Economic Journal*, **107**, 134-49.

Coughlin, C. C., Terza, J. V. and Arromdee, V., 1991. 'State Characteristics and the Location of Foreign Direct Investment within the United States', *Review of Economics and Statistics*, **73**, 675-83.

Coughlin, C. C. and Segev, E., 2000. 'Foreign Direct Investment in China: A Spatial Econometric Study', *World Economy*, **23(1)**, 1-23.

Crafts, N., 1996. 'Post-Neoclassical Endogenous Growth Theory: What are its Policy Implications?' *Oxford Review of Economic Policy*, **12**, 30-47.

Cui, M. X. and Kong, Y. T., 1998. 'An Analysis of Changes in the Development and Distribution of Foreign Direct Investment in China', *Journal of Shanxi Finance and Economics University*, **3**, 4-7.

Culem, C., 1988. 'The Locational Determinants of Direct Investments among Industrialised Countries', *European Economic Review*, **32**, 885-904.

Cushman, D., 1985. 'Real Exchange Rate Risk, Expectations, and the Level of Direct Investment', *Review of Economics and Statistics*, **67**, 297-308.

Cushman, D., 1987. 'The Effects of Real Wages and Labour Productivity on Foreign Direct Investment', *Southern Economic Journal*, **54**, 174-85.

Das, S., 1987. 'Externalities and Technology Transfer through Multinational Corporations: a Theoretical Analysis', *Journal of International Economics*, **22**, 171-82.

Davidson, W. H., 1980. 'The Location of Foreign Direct Investment Activity: Country Characteristics and Experience Effects', *Journal of International Business Studies*, **12**, 9-22.

de Mello, L. R., 1997. 'Foreign Direct Investment in Developing Countries and Growth: A Selective Survey', *Journal of Development Studies*, **34(1)**, 1-34.

de Mello, L. R., 1999. 'Foreign Direct Investment-led Growth: Evidence from Time Series and Panel Data', *Oxford Economic Papers*, **51**, 133-51.

Dees, S., 1998. 'Foreign Direct Investment in China: Determinants and Effects', *Economics of Planning*, **31(2-3)**, 175-94.

Dewenter, K. L., 1995. 'Do Exchange Rate Changes Drive Foreign Direct Investment?', *Journal of Business*, **68(3)**, 405-33.

Dougherty, S., 1997. *The Impact of Technology Transfer on Industry Productivity in China: 1980-95*, MIT Science and Technology Working Paper: Beijing: American Embassy.

Driffield, N. and Munday, M., 2000. 'Industrial Performance, Agglomeration, and Foreign Manufacturing Investment in the UK', *Journal of International Business Studies*, **31(1)**, 21-38.

Dunning, J. H., 1977. 'Trade, Location of Economic Activities and the MNE: A Search for an Eclectic Approach', in Ohlin, B., Hesselborn, P. O. and Wijkman, P. M. (eds.), *Proceedings of a Nobel Symposium in Stockholm*, London: Macmillan.

Dunning, J. H., 1979. 'Explaining Changing Patterns of International Production: In Defence of the Eclectic Theory', *Oxford Bulletin of Economics and Statistics*, **November**, 34-48.

Dunning, J. H., 1980. 'Toward an Eclectic Theory of International Production: Some Empirical Tests', *Journal of International Business Studies*, **11**, 9-31.

Dunning, J. H., 1981. *International Production and the Multinational Enterprise*. London: Allen and Unwin.

Dunning, J. H., 1988. *Explaining International Production*. London: Unwin Hyman.

Dunning, J. H., 1993. *Multinational Enterprises and the Global Economy*, Wokingham, Berks: Addison-Wesley.

Dunning, J. H., 1998. 'The European Internal Market Program and Inbound Foreign Direct Investment', in Dunning, J. H. (ed.) *Globalisation, Trade and Foreign Direct Investment*, Oxford: Elsevier.

Dunning, J. H. and Robson, P., 1988. 'Multinational Corporate Integration and Regional Economic Integration', in Dunning, J. H. and Robson, P. (eds.) *Multinationals and the European Community*, Oxford: Blackwell, 1-23.

Eicher, T. S., 1996. 'Interaction between Endogenous Human Capital and Technological Change', *Review of Economic Studies*, **63**, 127-44.

Findlay, R., 1978. 'Relative Backwardness, Direct Foreign Investment and the Transfer of Technology: a Simple Dynamic Model', *Quarterly Journal of Economics,* **92(1)**, 1-16.

Fleisher, B. M. and Chen, J., 1997. 'The Coast-noncoast Income Gap, Productivity and Regional Economic Policy in China', *Journal of Comparative Economics*, **25(2)**, 220-36.

Frobel, F., Heinrichs, J. and Kreye, O., 1980. *The New International Division of Labour*, Cambridge: Cambridge University Press.

Froot, K. and Stein, J., 1991. 'Exchange Rates and Foreign Direct Investment: an Imperfect Capital Markets Approach', *Quarterly Journal of Economics*, **106**, 1191-217.

Globerman, S., 1979. 'Foreign Direct Investment and Spillover Efficiency Benefits in Canadian Manufacturing Industries', *Canadian Journal of Economics*, **12**, 42-56.

Gold, T. B., 1991. 'Can Pudong Deliver?', *China Business Review*, **November-December**, 22-9.

Gong, H., 1995. 'Spatial Patterns of Foreign Investment in China's Cities, 1980-1989', *Urban Geography*, **16**, 198-209.

Gopinath, M., Pick, D. and Vasavada, U., 1999. 'The Economics of Foreign Direct Investment and Trade with an Application to the US Food Processing Industry', *American Journal of Agricultural Economics*, **81(2)**, 442-52.

Gray, H. P., 1998. 'International Trade and Foreign Direct Investment: The Interface', in Dunning, J. H. (ed.) *Globalisation, Trade and Foreign Direct Investment*, Oxford: Elsevier.

Greene, W., 2000. *Econometric Analysis*, 3rd, NJ: Prentice Hall.

Grether, J. M., 1999. 'Determinants of Technological Diffusion in Mexican Manufacturing: A Plant-Level Analysis', *World Development*, **27(7)**, 1287-98.

Griliches, Z., 1979. 'Issues in assessing the contribution of research and development to productivity growth', *Bell Journal of Economics*, **10**, 92-116.

Grossman, G. M. and Helpman, E., 1991. *Innovation and Growth in the Global Economy*, Cambridge, MA and London: MIT Press.

Grosse, R. and Goldberg, L. G., 1991. 'Foreign Bank Activity in the United States: An Analysis by Country of Origin', *Journal of Banking and Finance*, **15**, 1093-112.

Grosse, R. and Trevino, L. J., 1996. 'Foreign Direct Investment in the United States: An Analysis by Country of Origin', *Journal of International Business Studies*, **27(1)**, 139-55.

Haddad, M. and Harrison, A., 1993. 'Are There Positive Spillovers from Direct Foreign Investment? Evidence from Panel Data for Morocco'. *Journal of Development Economics*, **42**, 51-74.

Han, S. S. and Wong, S. T., 1994. 'The Influence of Chinese Reform and Pre-reform Policies on Urban Growth in the 1980s'. *Urban Geography*, **15**, 537-64.

Harrold, P. and Lall, R., 1993. 'China's Reform and Development in 1992-1993', *World Bank Discussion Paper*, **215**, Washington D.C.

Hayter, R. and Han, S. S., 1998. 'Reflections on China's Open Policy towards Foreign Direct Investment', *Regional Studies*, **32(1)**, 1-16.

Head, K. and Ries, J., 1996. 'Inter-city Competition for Foreign Investment: Static and Dynamic Effects of China's Incentive Areas', *Journal of Urban Economics*, **40**, 38-60.

Helpman, E., 1981. 'International Trade in the Presence of Product Differentiation, Economies of Scale and Monopolistic Competition: A Chamerlin-Heckscher-Ohlin Approach', *Journal of International Economics*, **11(3)**, 305-40.

Helpman, E., 1984a. 'Increasing Returns, Imperfect Markets, and Trade Theory', in Jones, R. W. and Kenen, P. B. (eds.) *Handbook of International Economics, Vol. 1, International Trade*, Amsterdam, North-Holland, 325-65.

Helpman, E., 1984b. 'A Simple Theory of International Trade with Multinational Corporations', *Journal of Political Economy*, **92(3)**, 451-71.

Helpman, E. and Krugman, P. R., 1985. *Market Structure and Foreign Trade*, Cambridge: MIT Press.

Henley, J., Kirkpatrick, C. and Wilde, G., 1999. 'Foreign Direct Investment in China: Recent Trends and Current Policy Issues', *World Economy*, **22(2)**, 223-43.

Herz, B. and Roger, W., 1995. 'Economic Growth and Convergence in Germany', *Weltwirtschaftliches Archiv*, **131(1)**, 132-43.

Hobday, M., 1995. *Innovation in East Asia: The Challenge to Japan*, Cheltenham: Edward Elgar.

Hofer, H. and Worgotter, A., 1995. 'Regional Per Capita Income Convergence in Austria', *Regional Studies*, **31**, 1-12.

Hofstede, G. H., 1980. *Culture's Consequences: International Differences in Work-Related Values*. Calif: Sage Publication.

Hong Kong Monetary Authority, 1995. *Monthly Statistical Bulletin*, Hong Kong.

Hong Kong Government Information Services, *Hong Kong (Annual Review)*. The Government Printing Department. Various Issues.

Horst, T., 1972. 'The Industrial Composition of US Exports and Subsidiary Sales to the Canadian Market'. *American Economic Review*. **62**, 37-45.

Horstman, I. and Markusen, J. R., 1992. 'Endogenous Market Structures in International Trade', *Journal of International Economics*, **20**, 225-47.

Hsiao, C., 1986. *Analysis of Panel Data*. Cambridge: Cambridge University Press.

Hu, Z., 1989. *China's Open Policy*, Chengdu, China: Chengdu University of Science and Technology Publishing Press.

Hymer S., 1960. *International Operations of National Firms: A Study of Foreign Direct Investment*. Cambridge: MIT Press, 1976.

Im, K. S., Pesaran, M. H. and Shin, Y., 1997. 'Testing for Unit Roots in Dynamic Heterogenous Panels', *mimeo*, Department of Applied Economics, University of Cambridge.

Imamura, H., 1999. 'Challenges Faced by Multinational Corporations in China', *International Economic Co-operation*, **3**, 29-33.

International Monetary Fund, *International Financial Statistics Yearbook*, Washington, D.C. Various Issues.

International Labour Office, *Yearbook of Labour Statistics*. Geneva. Various Issues.

Islam, N., 1995. 'Growth Empirics: a Panel Data Approach', *Quarterly Journal of Economics*, **110**, 1127-70.

Jeon, Y. D., 1992. 'The Determinants of Korean Foreign Direct Investment in Manufacturing Industries'. *Weltwirtschaftliches Archiv*. **128**, 527-41.

Jian, T., Sachs, J. D. and Warner, A. M., 1996. 'Trends in Regional Inequality in China', *China Economic Review*, **7**, 1-21.

Jiao, H. F., 1998. 'Study on the Regional Structure of Capital Market of Foreign Direct Investment in Mainland China', *Scientia Geographica Sinica*, **18(2)**, 106-12.

Judge, G. G., Griffiths, W. E., Hill, R. C., Lutkepohl, H., Lee, T. C., 1985. *The Theory and Practice of Econometrics*, 2nd, New York: John Wiley and Sons.

Jun, K. W. and Singh, H., 1996. 'The Determinants of Foreign Direct Investment in Developing Countries', *Transnational Corporations*, **5(2)**, 67-104.

Kindleberger, C. P., 1969. *American Business Abroad: Six Lectures on Direct Investment*. New Haven CT: Yale University Press.

Klein, M. W. and Rosengren, E., 1994. 'The Real Exchange Rate and Foreign Direct Investment in the United States'. *Journal of International Economics*. **36**: 373-89.

Knight, M., Loayza, N. and Villanueva, D., 1993. 'Testing the Neoclassical Theory of Economic Growth - a panel data approach', *International Monetary Fund Staff Papers*, **40**, 512-41.

Kobrin, S. J., 1979. 'Political Risk: A Review and Reconsideration'. *Journal of International Studies*. **10(1)**: 67-80.

Kogut, B. and Chang, S. J., 1996. 'Platform Investments and Volatile Exchange Rates: Direct Investment in the US by Japanese Electronic Companies', *Review of Economics and Statistics*, **78(2)**, 221-31.

Kogut, B. and Singh, H., 1988. 'The Effect of National Culture on the Choice of Entry Mode'. *Journal of International Business Studies*. **19(3)**, 411-32.

Kogut, B. and Zander, U., 1993. 'Knowledge of the Firm and the Evolutionary Theory of the Multinational Corporation'. *Journal of international Business Studies*. **24(4)**, 625-45.

Kokko, A., 1994. 'Technology, Market Characteristics, and Spillovers'. *Journal of Development Economics*, **43**, 279-93.

Kokko, A., Tansini, R. and Zejan, M., 1996. 'Local Technological Capabilities and Productivity Spillovers from FDI in the Uruguayan Manufacturing Sector'. *Journal of Development Studies*, **32**, 602-11.

Krugman, P., 1980. 'Scale Economies, Product Differentiation, and the Pattern of Trade', *American Economic Review*, **December**, 950-59.

Krugman P., 1991a. 'Increasing Returns and Economic Geography', *Journal of Political Economy*, **99**, 483-500.

Krugman P., 1991b. *Geography and Trade*. Cambridge, MA: MIT Press.

Kueh, Y. Y., 1992. 'Foreign Investment and Economic Change in China', *China Quarterly*, 637-90.

Kumar, N., 1994. 'Determinants of Export Orientation of Foreign Production by US Multinationals: an Inter-Country Analysis', *Journal of International Business Studies*, **25(1)**, 141-56.

Lall S., 1980. 'Monopolistic Advantages and Foreign Involvement by US Manufacturing Industry', *Oxford Economic Papers*, **32**, 102-22.

Lancaster, K., 1980. 'Intra-Industry Trade Under Perfect Monopolistic Competition', *Journal of International Economics*, **10**, 151-75.

Lardy, N., 1995. 'The Role of Foreign Trade and Investment in China's Economic Transformation', *China Quarterly*, **144**, 1065-82.

Lee, C., 1997. 'Foreign Direct Investment in China: Do State Policies Matter?', *Issues and Studies*, **33(7)**, 40-61.

Lee, J. Y. and Mansfield, E., 1996. 'Intellectual Property Protection and US Foreign Direct Investment', *Review of Economics and Statistics*, **78(2)**, 181-86.

Lee, D. W. and Lee, T. H., 1995. 'Human Capital and Economic Growth: Tests Based on the International Evaluation of Educational Achievement'. *Economic Letters*, **47**, 219-25.

Lee, K. Pesaran, M. H. and Smith, R., 1997. 'Growth and Convergence in a Multi-Country Empirical Stochastic Solow Model', *Journal of Applied Econometrics*, **12**, 357-92.

Leibenstein, H., 1966. 'Allocative Efficiency versus X-efficiency', *American Economic Review*, **June**, 392-415.

Lemoine, F., 2000. 'FDI and the Opening up of China's Economy', *CEPII Working Paper*, **No. 00-11**, June.

Levin, A. and Lin, C. F., 1992. 'Unit Root Test in Panel Data: Asymptotic and Finite Sample Properties', University of California at San Diego, *Discussion Paper* **No. 92-93**.

Levin, A. and Lin, C. F., 1993. 'Unit Root Test in Panel Data: New Results', University of California at San Diego, *Discussion Paper* **No. 93-56**.

Lichtenberg, F. R., 1994. 'Testing the Convergence Hypothesis', *Review of Economics and Statistics*, **76**, 576-79.

Lim, D., 1983. 'Fiscal Incentives and Direct Foreign Investment in Less Developed Countries', *Journal of Development Studies*, **19**, 207-12.

Lin, S. A. Y., 1996. 'Causes of Japanese Firms' Direct Investments in US Manufacturing Industries', *Applied Economics*, **28(9)**, 1143-51.

Linneman, H., 1966. *An Econometric Study of International Trade Flows*, Amsterdam: North Holland.

Lipsey, R. E. and Weiss, M. Y., 1981. 'Foreign Production and Exports in Manufacturing Industries', *Review of Economics and Statistics*, **63**, 488-94.

Lipsey, R. E. and Weiss, M. Y., 1984. 'Foreign Production and Exports in Manufacturing Industries', *Review of Economics and Statistics*, **66**, 304-8.

Liu, X. D., 1983. *General Situations of China's Utilising Foreign Funds*, Beijing, China: People's Publishing House.

Liu, X. M., 1993. *Foreign Direct Investment in the People's Republic of China*. Unpublished PhD Thesis, Strathclyde University.

Liu X. M. and Song H. Y., 1997. 'China and the Multinationals ~ A Winning Combination', *Long Range Planning*, **30**, 74-83.

Liu, X. M., Song, H. Y., Wei, Y. Q. and Romilly, P., 1997. 'Country Characteristics and Foreign Direct Investment in China: A Panel Data Analysis', *Weltwirtschaftliches Archiv*, **133(2)**, 313-29.

Liu, X. M., Siler, P., Wang, C. Q. and Wei, Y. Q., 2000. 'Productivity Spillovers from Foreign Direct Investment: Evidence from UK Industry Level Panel Data', *Journal of International Business Studies*, **31(3)**, 407-25.

Loree, D. W. and Guisinger, S. E., 1995. 'Policy and Non-policy Determinants of US Equity Foreign Direct Investment', *Journal of International Business Studies*, **26(2)**, 281-300.

Mankiw, N. G., Romer, D. and Weil, D. N., 1992. 'A Contribution to the Empirics of Economic Growth', *Quarterly Journal of Economics*, **107**, 407-37.

Mansfield, E. and Romeo, A., 1980. 'Technology Transfer to Overseas Subsidiaries by US-based Firms', *Quarterly Journal of Economics*, **95**, 737-50.

Mariotti, S. and Piscitello, L., 1995. 'Information Costs and Location of FDI within the Host Country: Empirical Evidence From Italy', *Journal of International Business Studies*, **26**, 815-40.

Markusen, J. R., 1984. 'Multinational, Multi-plant Economies, and the Gains from Trade', *Journal of International Economics*, **16**, 205-66.

Markusen, J. R., 1998. 'Multinational Firms, Location and Trade', *World Economy*, **21(6)**, 733-56.

Markusen, J. R. and Maskus, K. E., 1999. 'Multinational Firms: Reconciling Theory and Evidence', *NBER Working Paper* **7163**.

Markusen, J. R. and Venables, A. J., 1995. 'Multinational Firms and the New Trade Theory', *NBER Working Paper* **5036**.

Markusen, J. R. and Venables, A. J., 1996. 'The Increased Importance of Direct Investment in North Atlantic Economic Relationships: A Convergence Hypothesis', in Canzoneri, M. W., Ethier, W. J. and Grilli, V. (eds.) *The New Transatlantic Economy*, London: Cambridge University Press.

Markusen, J. R. and Venables, A. J., 1998. 'Multinational Firms and the New Trade Theory', *Journal of International Economics*, **46**, 183-203.

Markusen, J. R. and Venables, A.J., 1999. 'Foreign Direct Investment as a Catalyst for Industrial Development', *European Economic Review*, **43**, 335-56.

Maskus, K. E. and Webster, A., 1995. 'Comparative Advantage and the Location of Inward Foreign Direct Investment – Evidence from the UK and South Korea', *World Economy*, **18(2)**, 315-28.

Matyas, L. and Korosi, G., 1996. 'The Determinants of Foreign Direct Investment in Transforming Economies: A Comment'. *Weltwirtschaftliches Archiv.* **132(2)**, 391-3.

McAleese, D., 1985. 'American Investment in Ireland', in Drudy, P. J. (ed.) *The Irish in America: Emigration Assimilation and Import*, Cambridge: Cambridge University Press.

McCoskey, S. K. and Selden, T. M., 1998. 'Health Care Expenditures and GDP: Panel Data Unit Root Test Results', *Journal of Health Economics*, **17**, 369-76.

McDaniels, I., 1998. 'Beijing Rethinks Investment Policies', *China Business Review*, **March-April**, 4.

Mee-kau, N., 1993. 'Direct Foreign Investment in China: Trends, Performance, Policies and Prospects', in Yu-shek, J. C. and Brosseau, M. (eds.) *China Review*, Hong Kong: The Chinese University of Hong Kong, 16.2-16.38.

Meyer, K. E., 1995. 'Direct Foreign Investment in Eastern Europe: The Role of Labour Costs', *Comparative Economic Studies*, **37(4)**, 69-88.

Miller, S. M., 1996. 'A Note on Cross-country Growth Regressions', *Applied Economics*, **28**, 1019-26.

Milner, C. and Pentecost, E., 1996. 'Locational Advantage and US Foreign Direct Investment in UK Manufacturing', *Applied Economics*, **28(5)**, 605-15.

Ministry of China Information Industry, *Yearbook of China's Electronics Industry, 1997, 1998 and 1999*. Beijing, China: Electronics Industry Press.

MOFERT (Ministry of Foreign Economic Relations and Trade of the People's Republic of China). *Almanac of Foreign Economic Relations and Trade of China,* Beijing, China: Social Press, Various Issues.

MOFTEC (Ministry of Foreign Trade and Economic Co-operation of the People's Republic of China), 1999. 'A Summary of China's Absorption of Foreign Investment', *Foreign Investment in China*, **9**, 8-15.

Moore, M. O., 1993. 'Determinants of German Manufacturing Direct Investment: 1980-1988'. *Weltwirtschaftliches Archiv*. **129**, 120-37.

Mody, A. and Wang, F. Y., 1997. 'Explaining Industrial Growth in Coastal China: Economic Reforms ... and What Else?', *World Bank Economic Review*, **11**, 293-325.

Murthy, N. R. V. and Chien, I. S., 1997. 'The Empirics of Economic Growth for OECD Countries: Some New Findings', *Economics Letters*, **55**, 425-29.

Murthy, N. R. V. and Ukpolo, V., 1999. 'A Test of the Conditional Convergence Hypothesis: Econometric Evidence from African Countries', *Economics Letters*, **65**, 249-53.

Nachum, L., 1999. *The Origin of the International Competitiveness of Firms: The Impact of Location and Ownership in Professional Service Industries*, Aldershot and Brookfield: Edward Elgar.

Nachum, L., Dunning, J. H. and Jones, G. G., 2000. 'UK FDI and the Comparative Advantage of the UK', *World Economy*, **23(5)**, 701-20.

Nagaraj, R., Varoudakis, A., and Véganzonès, M. A., 2000. 'Long-run Growth Trends and Convergence across Indian States', *Journal of International Development*, **12(1)**, 45-70.

Nigh, D., 1985. 'The Effect of Political Events on United States Direct Foreign Investment: a Pooled Time-Series Cross-Sectional Analysis', *Journal of International Business Studies*, **16(1)**, 1-17.

Okamoto, Y., 1999. 'Multinationals, Production Efficiency, and Spillover Effects: The Case of the US Auto Parts Industry', *Weltwirtschaftliches Archiv*, **135(2)**, 241-60.

Pain, N., 1993. 'An Econometric Analysis of Foreign Direct Investment in the United Kingdom', *Scottish Journal of Political Economy*, **40(1)**, 1-23.

Pain, N., 1997. 'Continental Drift: European Integration and the Location of UK Foreign Direct Investment', *Manchester School Supplement*, **65**, 94-117.

Pain, N. and Lansbury, M., 1997. 'Regional Economic Integration and Foreign Direct Investment: the case of German Investment in Europe', *National Institute Economic Review*, **No. 160**, 87-99.

Pain, N. and Wakelin, K., 1998. 'Export Performance and the Role of Foreign Direct Investment', *Manchester School*, **66**, 62-88.

Pan, Y., 1996. 'Influences on Foreign Equity Ownership Level in Joint Ventures in China', *Journal of International Business Studies*, **27(1)**, 1-26.

Pearce, R. D. and Singh, S., 1992. 'Internationalisation of R&D among the world's leading enterprises', in Grandstrand, O., Sjolander, S. and Hakanson, L. (eds.) *Internationalisation of R&D and Technology*, Wiley, Chichester, UK

Peck, F. W., 1996. 'Regional Development and the Production of Space: the Role of Infrastructure in the Attraction of New Inward Investment', *Environment and Planning A*, **28**, 327-39.

Persson, J., 1997. 'Convergence across the Swedish Counties', *European Economic Review*, **41**, 1835-52.

Petri, P. A., 1994. 'The Regional Clustering of Foreign Direct Investment and Trade', *Transnational Corporations*, **3(3)**, 1-25.

Pfaffermayr, M., 1996. 'Foreign Outward Direct Investment and Exports in Austrian Manufacturing: Substitutes or Complements?', *Weltwirtschaftliches Archiv*, **132(3)**, 501-52.

Pitelis, C., 1996. 'Effective Demand, Outward Investment and the (Theory of the) Transnational Corporation: An Empirical Investigation', *Scottish Journal of Political Economy*, **43(2)**: 192-206.

Pomfret, R., 1997. 'Growth and Transition: Why Has China's Performance Been So Different?', *Journal of Comparative Economics*, **25**, 422-40.

Porter, M., 1990. *The Competitive Advantage of Nations*, London: Macmillan.

Quah, D., 1992. 'International Paterns of Growth: I. Persistence in Cross-Country Disparities', unpublished manuscript, London School of Economics.

Quah, D., 1994. 'Exploiting Cross-Section Variation for Unit Root Inference in Dynamic Data', *Economics Letters*, **44**, 9-19.

Radner, R., 1992. 'Hierarchy: the Economics of Managing', *Journal of Economics Literature*, **30**, 1382-1415.

Ray, E. J., 1989. 'The Determinants of Foreign Direct Investment in the United States: 1979-1985', in Freestra, R. (ed.) *Trade Policies for International Competitiveness*, Chicago: University of Chicago Press.

Romer, P. M., 1986. 'Increasing Returns to Scale and Long-Run Growth', *Journal of Political Economy*, **94**, 1002-37.

Romer, P. M., 1993. 'Idea Gaps and Object Gaps in Economic Development.' *Journal of Monetary Economics*, **32**, 543-73.

Rugman, A. M., 1981. *Inside the Multinationals*. Croom Helm, London.

Sachs, J. D. and Warner, A. M., 1995. 'Economic Convergence and Economic Policies', *NBER Working Paper* **No. 5093**. Cambridge, MA: National Bureau of Economic Research.

Sala-i-Martin, X. X., 1990. 'Lecture Notes on Economic Growth', *NBER Working Paper* **No. 3563**, Cambridge.

Sala-i-Martin, X. X., 1994. 'Economic Growth ~ Cross-sectional Regressions and the Empirics of Economic Growth', *European Economic Review*, **38(3-4)**, 739-47.

Sala-i-Martin, X. X., 1996. 'Regional Cohesion: Evidence and Theories of Regional Growth and Convergence', *European Economic Review*, **40**, 1325-52.

Salvatore, D., 1995. *International Economics*, New Jersey: Prentice-Hall.

Shi, Y., 1998. *Chinese Firms and Technology in the Reform Era*, London: Routledge.

Sicular, T., 1998. 'Capital Flight and Foreign Investment: Two Tales from China and Russia', *World Economy*, **21(5)**, 589-602.

Solocha, A. and Soskin, M. D., 1990. 'Determinants of Foreign Direct Investment: a Case of Canadian Direct Investment in the United States', *Management International Review*, **30**, 371-86.

Solocha, A. and Soskin, M. D., 1994. 'Canadian Direct Investment, Mode of Entry, and Border Location', *Management International Review*, **34**, 79-95.

SSB (State Statistical Bureau of the People's Republic of China). *China Statistical Yearbook*, Beijing, China: China Statistical Publishing House, Various Issues.

SSB (State Statistical Bureau of the People's Republic of China). *China Foreign Economic Statistical Yearbook*, Beijing, China: China Statistical Publishing House, Various Issues.

Sun, H., 1999. 'FDI, Trade and Transfer Pricing', in Wu, Y. (eds.), *Foreign Direct Investment and Economic Growth in China*, Aldershot, UK and Brookfield, US: Edward Elgar.

Swedenborg, B., 1979. *The Multinational Operations of Swedish Firms: an Analysis of Determinants and Effects*, Stockholm: Industriens Utrednings-institut.

Tallman, S. B., 1988. 'Home Country Political Risk and Foreign Direct Investment in the United States', *Journal of International Business Studies*, **19(2)**: 219-34.

Thoburn, J. T., Leung, H. M., Chau, E. and Tang, S. H., 1990. *Foreign Investment in China under the Open Policy*. Avebury, Aldershot.

Tsionas, E. G., 2000. 'Regional Growth and Convergence: Evidence from the United States', *Regional Studies*, **34(3)**, 231-38.

Tu, J. H. and Schive, C., 1995. 'Determinants of Foreign Direct Investment in Taiwan Province of China: a New Approach and Findings', *Transactional Corporations*, 4(2), 93-103.

UNCTC (United Nations Centre on Transnational Corporations), 1982. *Transnational Corporations in World Development, Third Survey*, United Nations, New York.

UNCTC, 1985. *Trends and Issues in Foreign Direct Investment and Related Flows*, United Nations, New York.

UNCTC, 1988. *Foreign Direct Investment in the People's Republic of China*, United Nations, New York.

UNCTD (United Nations Conference on Trade and Development). *World Investment Report*, New York and Geneva: United Nations, Various issues.

UNCTD, 1994. *China, Foreign Trade Reform*, New York and Geneva: United Nations.

UNCTD, 1995. *Trade and Investment Report*. New York and Geneva: United Nations.

UNTCD, 1996. *Trade and Development Report*. New York and Geneva: United Nations.

Venables, A., 1993. 'Equilibrium Location of Vertically Linked Industries', *CPER Discussion Paper* **82**, London School of Economics, London.

Vernon, R., 1966. 'International Investment and International Trade in the Product Cycle', *Quarterly Journal of Economics*, **80**, 190-207.

Veugelers, R., 1991. 'Locational Determinants and Ranking of Host Countries: an Empirical Assessment', *KYKLOS - International Review for Social Science*, **44**, 363-82

Wakasugi, R., 1994. 'Is Japanese Foreign Direct Investment a Substitute for International Trade?', *Japan and the World Economy*, **6(1)**, 45-52.

Walz, U., 1997. 'Innovation, Foreign Direct Investment and Growth', *Economica,* **4**, 65-79.

Wang, L., 1997. *Report on Foreign Direct Investment in China: Industrial Distribution of Foreign Direct Investment*, Beijing, China: Economic Management Press.

Wang, X., 1998. 'Analysis of Canadian Direct Investment in China'. *International Economic Co-operation*, **3**, 49-53.

Wang, Y., 1990. 'Situations, Policies and Prospects of China's Absorbing Foreign Direct Investment', *Intertrade Monthly*, Beijing, **No. 102**, June.

Wang, Z., 1994. *Successful Co-operation, Broad Prospects: Direct Investment by German Corporations in China,* Beijing, China: China Social Sciences Press.

Wang, Z., 1996. *Korean Corporations' Investment in China*, Beijing, China: China Economic Press.

Wang, Z., 1998. *Japanese Corporations' Investment in China*, Beijing, China: China Economic Press.

Wang, Z., 1999. *American Corporations' Investment in China*, Beijing, China: China Economic Press.

Wang, Z. Q. and Swain, N. J., 1995. 'The Determinants of Foreign Direct Investment in Transforming Economies: Empirical Evidence from Hungary and China', *Weltwirtschaftliches Archiv*, **131(2)**, 359-82.

Wei, S. J., 1995. 'Attracting Foreign Direct Investment: Has China Reached Its Potential?', *China Economic Review*, **6(2)**, 187-99.

Wei, Y. Q., Liu, X. M., Parker, D. and Vaidya, K., 1999. 'The Regional Distribution of Foreign Direct Investment in China', *Regional Studies*, **33(9)**, 857-67.

Wei, Y. Q., Liu, X. M., Song, H. Y. and Romilly, P., 2001, 'Endogenous Growth Theory and Regional Income Convergence in China', *Journal of International Development*, forthcoming.

Weidenbaum, M. and Hughes, S., 1996. *The Bamboo Network: How Chinese Entrepreneurs Are Creating a New Economic Superpower in Asia*. New York: Martin Kessler.

Wheeler, D. and Mody, A., 1992. 'International Investment Locational Decisions ~ the Case of US Firms', *Journal of International Economics*, **33**, 57-76.

Woodward, D. P. and Rolfe, R. J., 1993. 'The Location of Export-Oriented Foreign Direct Investment in the Caribbean Basin', *Journal of International Business Studies*, **24(1)**, 121-44.

World Bank, 1994. *China, Foreign Trade Reform*, World Bank.

World Bank, 1999. *World Development Report, 1998/1999*. World Bank.

World Bank, 2000. *World Development Report, 1999/2000*. World Bank.

World Bank. *World Tables*, The Johns Hopkins University Press. Various Issues.

Yamawaki, H., 1991. 'Locational Decisions of Japanese Multinational Firms in European Manufacturing Industries', *Proceedings of the XVIII EARIE Conference*, Ferrara, Italy.

Yin, Z. M., 1997. 'Characteristics, Roles and Problems of the Direct Investment by Well-Known Transnational Corporations in China', Paper presented at the *China World Economy Association Annual Conference*, China.

Zhang, D. X., 1998. 'On the New Situation and Corresponding Strategy of China's Utilisation of Foreign Direct Investment', *Henan Social Sciences*, **No. 2**, 34-7.

Zhang, K. H., 2000. 'Why Is US Direct Investment in China So Small?', *Contemporary Economic Policy*, **18(1),** 82-94.

Zhang L. Y., 1994. 'Location-specific Advantages and Manufacturing Direct Investment in South China', *World Development,* **22**, 45-53.

Zhu, R. J., 2000. 'The Explanations of the Formulation of the Tenth Five-Year Plan for National Economic and Social Development', *People's Daily, Overseas Edition*, 9 October.

Zhuang, J., 1999. 'The Group Effects of Inward Investment by Multinational Corporations in China and Strategy Issues', *Foreign Capital in China*, **11**, 10-3.

Author Index

Subject Index